OXFORD HISTORICAL MONOGRAPHS

MUSIC
FOR THE
PEOPLE

Popular Music and Dance
in Interwar Britain

JAMES J. NOTT

OXFORD
UNIVERSITY PRESS

OXFORD
UNIVERSITY PRESS

Great Clarendon Street, Oxford OX2 6DP

Oxford University Press is a department of the University of Oxford.
It furthers the University's objective of excellence in research, scholarship,
and education by publishing worldwide in

Oxford New York

Auckland Bangkok Buenos Aires Cape Town Chennai
Dar es Salaam Delhi Hong Kong Istanbul Karachi Kolkata
Kuala Lumpur Madrid Melbourne Mexico City Mumbai Nairobi
São Paulo Shanghai Singapore Taipei Tokyo Toronto

and an associated company in Berlin

Oxford is a registered trade mark of Oxford University Press
in the UK and in certain other countries

Published in the United States
by Oxford University Press Inc., New York

British Library Cataloguing in Publication Data
Data available

Library of Congress Cataloging in Publication Data
Data available

ISBN 0–19–925407–9

1 3 5 7 9 10 8 6 4 2

Typeset in Plantin
by Graphicraft Limited, Hong Kong
Printed in Great Britain
on acid-free paper by
Biddles Ltd, Guildford and King's Lynn

For my parents,
BARBARA *and* TERENCE NOTT,
with love.

ACKNOWLEDGEMENTS

I am indebted to many friends and colleagues for supplying information, advice, and assistance of various kinds and owe particular thanks to Ross McKibbin, whom I could always rely on both for the necessary advice, warnings, and criticism, as well as enthusiastic encouragement. Thanks also to Cyril Ehrlich, who offered invaluable advice on the conversion of my material to book form. To the various libraries and archives that I have used I also owe considerable debt, not only for the right to use material but also for the friendly atmosphere in which to work. The staff at the Upper Reading Room, Bodleian Library were always helpful. I must also give particular thanks to Ray Luker at the Performing Right Society Archive and James Codd at the BBC Written Archive Centre in Caversham. Lastly, and by no means least, I must give my heartfelt love and thanks to my family, especially my parents, Barbara and Terence, to whom this book is dedicated.

I would like to thank the following for permission to reproduce material: Extracts from Mass-Observation reproduced with permission of Curtis Brown Group Ltd, on behalf of Mass-Observation Archive Copyright Trustees of the Mass-Observation Archive.

Song lyrics are reproduced by permission as follows: 'I've Gone and Lost My little yo-yo' by Kemp and Shuff, © 1932 Campbell, Connelly and Co. Ltd. Used by permission of Music Sales Ltd. All Rights Reserved. International Copyright Secured. 'My Ukulele' by J. Cottrell, © 1933 Campbell, Connelly and Co. Ltd. Used by permission of Music Sales Ltd. All Rights Reserved. International Copyright Secured 'She was only a Postmasters daughter' by Jevon, Dolphe, Wolfe and Gordon. Published by Sylvester Music Co Ltd 1932 copyright all countries of the world. 'Masculine Women, Feminine Men' Words and Music by Edgar Leslie and James Monaco, © 1925, Clarke & Leslie Songs Inc, USA. All Rights Reserved—Used by Permission—50% Redwood Music Ltd (Carlin) London NW1 8BD on behalf of the Estate of James V Monaco. Remaining 50%—Reproduced by permission of EMI Music Publishing Ltd, London WC2H 0QY.

I would like to thank the following for permission to use photographs and other illustrative material: EMI Records Ltd for Plates 1, 4, 5, 6, 7, 8, 9 and 18; Hulton-Getty Images for Plates 19 and 20; National Museums of Scotland (Scottish Life Archive) for Figures Plates 2, 3, 14 and 15; Oxfordshire County Council Photographic Archive for Figures Plates 16 and 17. Plates 10–13 come from a private collection.

CONTENTS

PART TWO

The 'Live' Popular Music Industry

PART THREE

Popular Music and Popular Music Artists

LIST OF ILLUSTRATIONS

(between pp. 146–147)

LIST OF TABLES

ABBREVIATIONS

BB	*Ballroom and Band*
GR	*Gramophone Review*
GTMN	*Gramophone and Talking Machine News*
MM	*The Melody Maker (and British Metronome)*
MNDB	*Musical News and Dance Band*
PMDW	*Popular Music and Dancing Weekly*
PRG	*The Performing Right Gazette*
RP	*Radio Pictorial*
TMN	*Talking Machine News*
TT	*Tune Times*

BBC WAC	BBC Written Archive Centre
M-O A	Mass-Observation Archive (MDJ = Music, Dancing, and Jazz)
PRS A	Performing Right Society Archive

EMI	Electrical and Music Industries
HMV	His Master's Voice
IBC	International Broadcasting Company
ISBA	Incoporated Society of British Advertisers Limited

Note: Unless otherwise stated, place of publication is London.

INTRODUCTION

The enjoyment of music and music making has been a constant theme in history but during the interwar period it reached new levels of popularity, becoming available to a wider audience than at any time hitherto. Music was more popular than ever before. As one music critic noted in 1935:

Never probably in the whole course of the world's history has music played so important a part in the life of the community as it plays today. It may truly be said that for the majority of civilised mankind, music has ceased to be a luxury: it is no longer the monopoly of a rich and privileged few, but has been brought within the reach of all sorts and conditions of men. In the home, in the theatre, in the street, in (and on) the air, music now figures so prominently as a means of entertainment that it would be impossible to contemplate a world in which it no longer provided such a constant source of popular enjoyment.[1]

The sales of certain products of the popular music industry give testament to this popularity. In 1919, for example, the song 'That Old Fashioned Mother of Mine' sold more sheet music copies than there were members of the Churches of England, Wales, and Scotland combined.[2] Similarly, the value of the musical instruments trade in 1924 was equivalent to one-third of government expenditure on the Royal Air Force.[3] In 1930 there were over three times as many gramophones sold as the number of houses built that year[4] and there was more than one record sold for every single person in Britain.[5] Popular music was thus a powerful

---

[1] Anon., *Radio and the Composer: The Economics of Modern Music* (1935), 1.

[2] Sheet music sales of the song were over 3 million (see Chapter 4 below). Combined membership of these Churches in 1919 was 2,455,000 (see R. Currie, A. Gilbert, and L. Horsely, *Churches and Churchgoers* (1977), 134–5).

[3] The value of the musical instruments trade in 1924 was £5 million (see Chapter 4 below). Expenditure on the RAF in 1924/5 was £14 million (see Board of Trade, *Statistical Abstract for the United Kingdom*, 70 (1927), 110–11).

[4] In 1930, 778,492 gramophones were sold in Britain (see Table 1). From 1928 to 1932, the annual average number of houses built was 200,900 (see B. R. Mitchell, *British Historical Statistics* (1988), 390, 394).

[5] In 1930 nearly 60 million records were sold (see Table 3). The population of Britain in 1929 was 45,685,000 (see *Statistical Abstract*, 80 (1937), 4–5).

and persistent influence in the daily life of millions in interwar Britain. Unfortunately, the extent to which popular music and the popular music industry did play a role in people's lives has so far remained a matter for speculation because these crucial years in the development of the industry have rarely been the subject of detailed investigation. Whilst the study of other popular entertainments of the interwar period, such as cinema and radio, has been widespread, historians have failed to look exclusively at popular music and the industry which provided it.

This is an important omission and one which provides a fascinating challenge. The purpose of this book is to examine the changes to popular music and the popular music industry and their impact on British society and culture from 1918 to 1939. The book will establish how popular music became a habitual part of life for millions of people. It will explore the reasons for the popularity of such entertainment and examine the audience reactions to it.

The period 1918 to 1939 was crucial in the development of popular music and the popular music industry for a number of reasons: the audience for popular music grew to an unprecedented extent, the provision of popular music was commercialized to a greater degree than ever before, and the use of technologies enabled the rapid diffusion of popular music to every corner of the nation from every corner of the globe. All three phenomena were interlinked and these complex relationships had major consequences for the nature of the music, the way it was produced, and the impact it had on listeners.

The increased enjoyment of popular music was a reflection of increasing living standards for large numbers of people in interwar Britain. One of the most important developments of the period was the rapid expansion in the provision and consumption of leisure products and facilities of all kinds. The extent to which those companies within the 'leisure industry' experienced growth is hard to determine because of a lack of detailed data. However, estimates of annual spending on entertainment put the figure for the 1920s and 1930s at around £200 to £250 million.[6]

There were numerous reasons for this increased expenditure on leisure and increased enjoyment of it. A shorter working week, holidays with pay, and increases in real income for large sections of the population were among the most important. Between 1914 and 1938 the average working week fell from 54 to 48 hours. Average weekly money wages rose from

---

[6] R. Stone and D. A. Rowe, *The Measurement of Consumers' Expenditure and Behaviour in the United Kingdom, 1920–1938*, vol. ii (Cambridge, 1966).

£1 12s. 0d. in 1913 to £3 10s. 0d. in 1938, by which time nearly 42 per cent of workers received paid holidays. These changes meant that a wide range of leisure activities fell within the reach of working-class pockets. Traditional activities, such as the theatre, music hall and the pub were good value, with seats at 6d. or lower and beer at 3d. to 6d. per pint. Sports matches were also available from only 6d. Joining these, were the cinema and dance hall with entrance from 3d. to 6d. Budget records were also available at Marks and Spencers and Woolworths from only 6d.[7]

Another major feature of popular music during this period was the extent to which its provision attracted the interest of entrepreneurs. It was not alone in this respect nor was it without precedent. Commercialisation of leisure was well underway by the end of the nineteenth century, as industrialisation created large markets in the towns and cities. Entertainment itself also became industrialised with the application of technology. However, some leisure activities were more 'entrepreneurial' than others and there remained large regional variations both in character and in the availability of provision. During the 1920s and 1930s, commercialization of leisure both accelerated and expanded in scope. Big business was able to infiltrate nearly all aspects of the leisure industry and the scale of its interest was reflected in the emergence of large national companies.

The interwar period was also the first period when the necessary technological advances became dynamic and self-sustaining. For the first time the cinema, the radio, and the gramophone were helping to bring about a 'mass audience'. This recreational and entertainment revolution transformed the way in which the popular music industry worked.

Any study of popular music and the popular music industry has to come to terms with the problems of definition. What is 'popular music'? What constitutes the 'popular music industry'? The term 'popular' is one that is particularly problematic. Most commonly it has positive class-oriented connotations associated with those things specifically produced by and for the 'lower classes'. In relation to music, 'popular music' has been regarded as that music which comes from 'the people'. Such a definition has several problems. It raises the question of who constitutes 'the people', or , moreover, who does not constitute 'the people'. During the interwar period 'popular music' was not exclusive to the working class, though predominantly aimed at them, in terms of both its production and enjoyment. This makes the terms of reference too narrow.

---

[7] S. G. Jones, *Workers at Play: A Social and Economic History of Leisure 1918–1939* (1986), 15–20.

'Music of the people' or traditional folk songs were an unwritten, oral tradition. In passing from person to person, individuals adapted them according to their local circumstances, adding important nuances and creating differing interpretations. Passing from generation to generation they were also similarly altered. One common or shared story, therefore, could provide the basis for many songs. For the period under investigation, such an anthropological or 'folk' definition of 'the popular' is nonsensical. The majority of 'people' did not produce their own music if, indeed, they ever had. The folk tradition of creating and recreating music had largely gone. The 'music of the people' was most likely to be that which was produced and sold by music publishers, record companies, and other sectors of the industry.

However, 'popular' has also been used as a legitimizing term, associated with the term 'well favoured' in the late eighteenth century, or 'well liked' or judged to be good in the nineteenth century. Such definitions take account of the notion of 'popularity' and are more useful when considering interwar popular music. In the twentieth century and beyond a market-led or commercial definition of 'popular music' is more appropriate than a 'folk' definition. This recognizes that cultural practices and forms have become increasingly commercialized and subject to business interests, products of the so-called 'culture industries'. In this definition things are said to be popular because masses of people listen to them, buy them, consume them, and seem to be enjoying them. It focuses on the quantitative dimension of 'popular music', looking at those items which are the most widely disseminated items in the mass media. It forms the basis of the definition used in this book. The measurement of this dimension is not, of course, always easy. Surviving sales figures for the interwar period are difficult to find and 'hit charts' did not exist before 1948. These figures themselves are, anyway, subject to pressures from the music industry. The choice of output by record companies and radio stations determines, to some extent, what sells and thus becomes 'popular'. These influences must be taken into account. Furthermore, 'hit chart' popularity is not the only measure. This measurement of which music is the most 'popular' tends to stress the importance of the 'moment of exchange' (sales) rather than the 'moment of use'—that is, dissemination through radio listening, background music, and live performance. It is necessary therefore to look beyond headline crazes and also take into account the huge provision of other genres such as light music and military and brass band music, older forms which survived and remained popular with the great mass of the British public during this time and which were played on the radio, in the theatre, and elsewhere. The measurement of sales also tends to standardize diachronically when in fact different musical styles may sell at different rates over different time spans. This also discounts those who could not afford sheet music, the piano, or the gramophone. The audience for these older forms of music must be examined as well. Thus, the purely commercial or market definition of the term 'popular' measures sales and not necessarily long-lasting popularity. 'Popularity' is conceived purely in terms of 'how many'. However, with the qualifications and additions noted above, such a quantitative approach to defining 'popular music' is valid, especially as, during this period, popular music became increasingly dominated by businesses and directed by the criteria of 'sales', and sales, though not perfect, are undoubtedly one measure of popularity.

Having established a working definition of 'popular music' it is necessary to establish what areas actually constitute the 'popular music industry' and what will be studied. In examining popular music it is important to note that music making and the enjoyment of popular musical entertainment among the general public took place both at a personal and social level, in the home and also in the public sphere in various 'community' and 'commercial' arenas. At one level there was considerable activity in the public sphere, with various local music societies and choral groups continuing to thrive. The growth of adult education facilities also encouraged a considerable section of the working and lower middle classes to take up music as a hobby. Brass bands, considered to be the 'working man's orchestra', still occupied an important role in working-class musical culture, despite a declining interest from their peak in the nineteenth century. In addition, there were new phenomena like the brief popularity of 'community singing' in the late 1920s and the growth of accordion clubs.[8] Whilst recognizing the continued importance of such 'community' music making and enjoyment, the focus of this book will be the commercialized areas of the popular music provision. This is justified in particular by the fact that business interests assumed a dominant role in the provision and direction of popular music between 1918 and 1939.

In the period before 1918, the 'popular music industry' was made up of just a handful of main components—the sheet music publishers, certain

---

[8] For a full discussion of all of these traditional music-making arenas see B. S. Rowntree, *Poverty and Progress: A Second Social Survey of York* (1941), 374–5; D. C. Jones (ed.), *The Social Survey of Merseyside* (Liverpool, 1934), iii. 284–5; H. Llewellyn Smith, *The New Survey of London Life and Labour* (1935), ix. 62–3.

musical instrument manufacturers, and commercialized entertainments such as the music hall. This definition of the industry becomes too narrow, however, with the widespread application of technology in the supply and consumption of popular music and increasing commercialization of many other aspects after 1918. As the 'industry' was not a clearly distinctive one, in the way that publishing might be for example, and as it overlapped with many other industries, such as the communications industry, there is difficulty in knowing what to exclude. The music instrument trade for example, whilst clearly an important aspect in the provision of popular music, is not exclusively concerned with popular music—its products can be used for the production of all forms of music. Similarly, the record industry produced recordings of all varieties of music. However, as there is considerable evidence which suggests that a substantial, in some cases a majority, of the products sold by such firms were used for popular music then they are included in this definition. The area for investigation is, therefore, sufficiently wide as to encompass both traditional and newer forms of popular music businesses. This book will examine music publishers, gramophone and record producers, musical instrument makers, theatres, and film studios.

The difficulty in defining what constitutes the popular music industry and the lack of a centralized 'archive' is perhaps one reason why there has been no previous attempt to bring the disparate threads together. Although there is a significant contemporary literature—which is used widely here—the scholarly secondary literature is comparatively limited. There has been significant research on the period preceding 1918, especially in relation to music hall,[9] but the huge changes that occurred to music and the industry after this date have not been comprehensively investigated. Popular music has been studied tangentially in histories of the leisure industry and the mass communications industry. Thus, Stephen Jones's survey of interwar leisure examines aspects of the music industry.[10] Jones argues that the period witnessed a massive increase in demand for musical and other entertainment brought about by rising living standards and the onset of a more consumer-oriented society. Similarly, David Le Mahieu's study of interwar mass communications includes examination of the gramophone industry and popular

---

[9] See P. Bailey, *Music Hall: The Business of Pleasure* (Milton Keynes, 1986); D. Cheshire, *Music Hall in Britain* (1974); E. Lee, *Folk Song and Music Hall* (1982); and R. Poole, *Popular Leisure and the Music Hall in Nineteenth Century Bolton* (Lancaster, 1982).

[10] See Jones, *Workers at Play*, 14, 34–8, 44–5, 50–5, 107, 196.

music.[11] Le Mahieu highlights the extent to which the mass media widened access to music and information of all sorts, although he emphasizes its effects on the educated. Those studies which have looked specifically at aspects of the interwar popular music industry have isolated single components and individual firms or institutions. Popular music has also been studied tangentially in the histories of the great entertainment institutions of the period, radio and the cinema. Thus Asa Briggs and Paddy Scannell and David Cardiff discuss the music policies of the BBC and outline the provision of various types of popular music up to 1939, and beyond.[12] Briggs, Scannell, and Cardiff all point to the huge impact of the BBC on popular music—bringing about an unprecedented supply, transforming its content, and dominating the employment of musicians involved in popular music. Jeffrey Richards, Stephen Shafer, and Charles Barr have also looked at interwar popular music on the screen via the careers of artists such as Gracie Fields, George Formby, and Jessie Matthews.[13] They point to the great popularity of such film stars who were steeped in a musical tradition and to the enduring popularity of 'musical' films throughout this time. Studies by Simon Frith, Mark Hustwitt, and Cyril Ehrlich isolate single components or themes, such as the record industry, dance music, or professional musicians.[14] Both Frith and Hustwitt argue that the interwar years were a boom period for the gramophone industry and highlight the success of leading companies such as Columbia and HMV. Ehrlich's excellent work illustrates how the music profession was altered dramatically by these developments in mechanized musical media which dominated this period. Peter Martland provides a good history of the EMI group,[15] and the emergence

---

[11] See D. Le Mahieu, *A Culture for Democracy: Mass Communications and the Cultivated Mind in Britain between the Wars* (Oxford, 1988).

[12] See A. Briggs, *The History of Broadcasting in the United Kingdom* (5 vols., new edn., Oxford, 1995) and P. Scannell and D. Cardiff (ed.), *A Social History of Broadcasting*, i (1991).

[13] See J. Richards, *The Age of the Dream Palace: Cinema and Society in Britain 1930–1939* (1984); S. C. Shafer, *British Popular Films 1929–1939* (1997); Charles Barr (ed.), *All Our Yesterdays: 90 Years of British Cinema* (1996).

[14] See S. Frith, 'Playing with Real Feeling: Jazz and Suburbia', in S. Frith, *Music for Pleasure: Essays in the Sociology of Pop* (Cambridge, 1988), 45–63 and id., 'The Making of the British Record Industry 1920–64', in J. Curran, A. Smith, and P. Wingate (ed.), *Impacts and Influences: Essays on Media and Power in the Twentieth Century* (1987), 278–90. See also M. Hustwitt, 'Caught in a Whirlpool Sound: The Production of Dance Music in Britain in the 1920s', *Popular Music*, 3 (1983), 7–31 and C. Ehrlich, *Harmonious Alliance: A History of the Performing Right Society* (Oxford, 1989) and id., *The Music Profession since the Eighteenth Century: A Social History* (Oxford, 1988).

[15] See P. Martland, *Since Records Began: EMI the First 100 years* (1997).

of jazz in Britain is also described by Jim Godbolt.[16] They lay the founda-
tions for the basis of further research.

Although scholarly literature on the music industry as a whole is relatively scarce, there are numerous antiquarian works on various aspects of
the interwar popular music industry. Despite their obvious limitations
such works also provide a valuable introduction to the subject. Ronald
Pearsall, who attempts general histories of popular music during the
1920s and before, is often illuminating.[17] Most antiquarian studies, however, are concerned with individual sectors of the popular music industry.
P. J. S. Richardson's history of English ballroom dancing, for example,
provides an interesting account of the development of dancing styles and
dancers.[18] Aspects of the record industry are documented in great detail
by the discographer Brian Rust.[19] These studies, in common with the
scholarly literature, also tend to focus on the musicians and individual
institutions themselves.

The obvious corollary to this approach is to attempt a complete study
of the various components of the industry, bringing them altogether
and including the audience as well as the musicians and other production
professionals. This book attempts a comprehensive examination of all
aspects of the industry, not only the development of institutions but
also the growth of the audience and the impact of these developments on
individuals on a day-to-day basis. The popular music industry will be
examined as a part of the leisure industry and, where appropriate, as a
part of the new mass communications industries. Some sectors of the
popular music industry—the gramophone, radio, and cinema—were
part of these so-called 'new industries'. This book thus makes a contribution to the 'Two Britains' debate concerning the interwar period,
where mass unemployment and industrial decline are seen alongside the
expansion of more modern industries and economic growth.[20] Dancing
and the wider enjoyment of popular music reflected improved living

[16] J. Godbolt, *A History of Jazz in Britain 1919–50* (1984) and id., *All this and 10 per cent* (1976).

[17] See R. Pearsall, *Popular Music of the Twenties* (Newton Abbot, 1976) and id., *Edwardian Popular Music* (Newton Abbot, 1975).

[18] See P. J. S. Richardson, *A History of English Ballroom Dancing 1910–1945: The Story of the Development of the Modern English Style* (1945).

[19] See B. Rust, *British Music Hall on Record* (Harrow, 1979); id., *British Musical Shows on Record 1897–1976* (Harrow, 1977) and B. Rust and S. Forbes, *British Dance Bands on Record 1911 to 1945 and Supplement* (Harrow, 1989).

[20] See J. Stevenson and C. Cook, *The Slump: Society and Politics during the Depression* (1977).

standards for many people and the part of the popular music industry in improving the lifestyles of the majority will be examined. To achieve a full understanding of twentieth-century British history, it is as necessary to examine the impact of the everyday cultural experiences of the 'majority', as it is to study specific political events.

The broad distribution and nature of the sources has led to a series of different approaches. As the popular music industry was made up of several separate sectors, there were no industry-wide surveys and sources are thus scattered. Each sector must be examined separately. For reasons of clarity this examination of the popular music industry is divided into two. The first investigates the 'mechanized' popular music industry and includes investigation of the gramophone industry, radio, and the cinema. The second section investigates the 'live' popular music industry (including dance bands and dance halls, the theatre, music hall, and sheet music publishers). The commercial histories of each sector of the industry and individual companies are documented. Several sectors of the popular music industry were the subject of official investigation and census returns and 'Statement of Trade' figures are available. Archives remain which detail the history of other related sectors and businesses. The Performing Right Society Archive is used to establish the economic fortunes of the sheet music publishers, the BBC archives are used for discussion of both the BBC and the commercial radio stations it monitored, and the Mass-Observation archive is used for details of the dance hall industry. The historian is also well served by a large and well-written trade press. Journals such as the *Gramophone*, *Talking Machine News*, *Gramophone Review*, and *Melody Maker* are analysed to establish the salient themes in the economic development of different sectors of the industry and individual companies.

The question of audiences also requires several approaches. Unlike the audience for radio and cinema there were no comprehensive surveys of the audience for popular music because it was so widely distributed. Establishing the size of the audience is not merely a case of examining the number of radio licences issued or compiling the number of admissions to cinemas. For this reason, the audience of each sector of the industry is examined in turn, via consumption and production patterns which help to build a fairly reliable impression of the emerging market. The audience for commercial radio stations, for example, was the subject of exhaustive research by advertising agencies and market research companies. But establishing the age, class, gender, and regional distribution of the various audiences for popular music is more complicated. Mass-Observation carried out detailed surveys of the audiences for dancing, jazz, and dance music but its results need to be considered with caution. Some of the reports obtained were highly subjective and it was often the atypical or unusual that caught the attention. Nor are Mass-Observation's samples wholly reliable. However, as long as we bear these precautions in mind, the material from these Mass-Observation investigations is still extremely valuable. The large number of contemporary social surveys is another rich source, together with a wide range of contemporary literature on leisure and recreation.

The impact of these developments on audiences, music, and society is then considered. The trade press provides a useful source for the social history of certain aspects of the popular music industry. There are analyses of readers' letters, articles on technological concerns, and cultural debates on recording artists and music policies. In addition, analysis of the catalogues and other advertising material of the major recording and publishing companies throughout the period is used to demonstrate the changing nature of popular music. Mass-Observation is particularly useful for recreating the experience of dancing and its impact on society and individuals.

Finally, there are several fundamental questions about the music itself. What were people listening to? What were their preferences? How did the music change? What did the music say? I have tried to answer these questions by detailing a 'hit parade' of the most popular songs. This, too, can be problematic. As has been noted, 'hit parade' statistics were not collated before 1948 in Britain. Nonetheless, it is possible to get a fairly accurate indication of the most popular songs from a variety of other sources. The output of radio stations, sales from record catalogues, and frequency of the mention in trade press are all used to build up such a picture. The songs themselves are then analysed in terms of their lyrics and song content. This has been done using recordings from the National Sound Archive and private collections and from sheet music copies of the music. Lastly, some factors involved in the shaping of popular tastes are examined by using BBC archives, and various other contemporary publications, of which the most important were *Melody Maker*, *Tune Times*, *Ballroom and Band*, *Musical News and Dance Band*, and *Popular Music and Dancing Weekly*.

Part One

THE 'MECHANIZED' POPULAR MUSIC INDUSTRY

I

THE RISE OF THE GRAMOPHONE AND THE DEVELOPMENT OF THE BRITISH GRAMOPHONE INDUSTRY

Introduction

The gramophone and gramophone records were one of the most popular forms of entertainment for an increasing number of people during the interwar period. Though less popular than the cinema and radio, the gramophone was historically the first element in the explosion of mass media based entertainment. All three industries were closely linked through technological production processes or by cultural bridges. Film and record 'tie-ups', and record 'plugging' on the radio meant that the radio, cinema, and gramophone were inextricably connected, especially in the dissemination of popular music and in promoting popular music stars.

Unlike the radio and cinema, which were two public forms of entertainment (the former a licence fee financed 'public service' and the latter a 'social habit'), the gramophone was largely private and domestic. For this very reason it has remained hidden. There were no great statistical surveys of the gramophone and record industries, nor was it subject to governmental concern, unlike the wireless and cinema. Where historians have touched on the history of the gramophone, they have looked only briefly at the extent of its popularity. This study will provide firm evidence of just how popular the gramophone and gramophone records were. This will be done in two ways. First, the production patterns for the industry are examined. These statistics will give tangible evidence where there was previously only suggestion. Secondly, the development of the British gramophone industry will be mapped; particular attention is paid to the largest firms involved in gramophone and record production. Thus, by looking at the consumers and their consumption patterns, the potential influence of this new form of entertainment as a disseminator of popular music will be established.

1.1 Production patterns of the British gramophone industry, 1907–1939

First, it is necessary to look at both domestic and foreign provision of gramophone goods for the United Kingdom. The domestically produced product was by far the most popular but imports were available and, conversely, a considerable amount of domestic production was also exported.

Production of gramophones, parts, and records vastly increased during the first four decades of the twentieth century, particularly in the interwar period. In 1907, the gross output of the gramophone industry was valued at £74,000, rising to £2,285,000 in 1924, peaking at £7,824,000 in 1930, and falling back to £3,423,000 in 1935.[1] Not only are these significant figures in themselves, but the increasing influence of the gramophone and records is clearly shown by the importance they assumed as a part of the 'musical instruments industry' with which they were classified for census purposes. By 1930 the gramophone industry was the largest sector in the musical instrument trade, accounting for 68 per cent of its output value, and it was the single biggest source of musical entertainment (with the possible exception of the radio, which was the most popular multi-purpose entertainer). In terms of the number of people employed, the industry also occupied an important position. By 1930 nearly 60 per cent of the total number of persons employed in the musical instruments industry were employed in the gramophone industry.[2] Whilst the depression and a gradual fall in the relative growth of demand meant a drop in output, the gramophone industry remained the largest single sector in the music industry throughout the rest of the period.

[1] Calculated from *Final Report on the First Census of Production of the United Kingdom 1907* (1912), *Final Report on the Third Census of Production of the United Kingdom 1924* (1931), Part IV, *Final Report on the Fourth Census of Production 1930* (1935), Part IV, *Final Report on the Fifth Census of Production 1935* (1940), Part IV.
[2] *Final Report on the Fourth Census of Production 1930* (1935), 545.

TABLE I. *Home production of gramophones, 1924–1937*

Date	Acoustic gramophones		Electric gramophones		Total	
	Number	Value (£)	Number	Value (£)	Number	Value (£)
1924	279,500	907,000	—	—	279,500	907,000
1930	769,995	2,280,000	8,497	321,000	778,492	2,601,000
1934	112,667	340,000	125,800	2,167,000	238,467	2,507,000
1935	93,570	278,000	149,900	1,766,000	243,470	2,044,000
1937	107,600	313,000	120,000	1,954,000	227,600	2,267,000

Notes: In 'current' money value. Tables are not standardized but this does not affect the overall tendency of the figures. 'Electric gramophones' includes radio gramophones, electric pick-ups, but not electrically powered acoustic machines.

Source: *Census of Production*, 1924, 1930, 1935, 1948.

When the figures are disaggregated, it can be seen that the production of gramophones and records over the period was extremely large. Table 1 shows that British domestic production of gramophones from 1924 to 1937 was high, peaking at 778,492 in 1930. There were two main types of gramophone available; those which used only acoustic technology and later those with electrical reproduction. Taking acoustic technology first, acoustic gramophones were the most popular, remaining popular, in part because of their cheapness, even after the introduction of electrical recording and reproduction in 1925. The arrival of electrical *recording* had a huge impact but electrical *reproduction* took longer to establish itself. A transitional phase between acoustic and electric technology allowed record companies to gradually replace their existing catalogues of acoustic recordings. Similarly, the acoustic gramophone was still able to play the new records perfectly well. The older, less efficient acoustic machines had their lives extended by a series of new soundboxes or needles designed to get the best from electrical recordings. With numerous attachable components by which gramophones could be updated, owners did not just consist of those who bought new machines. This older technology was particularly popular at the bottom end of the market with the availability of cheap, mass-produced portable gramophones. It was through the portable acoustic gramophone that the gramophone record first became a mass media form. Long before the 'wireless' became the symbol of the period's mass media, the portable

TABLE 2. *Acoustic gramophones available for the home market, 1924–1937*

Date	Domestic production	Retained imports	Total exports	% exported	Total available for home market	% of home market held by British goods
1924	279,500	64,573	87,515	31.3	256,522	78.84
1930	769,995	41,218	307,550	39.94	503,663	91.82
1934	112,667	3,802	83,988	74.55	32,481	88.29
1935	93,570	2,562	71,698	76.62	24,434	89.51
1937	107,600	4,000	71,000	65.99	40,600	90.15

Source: Calculated from *Census of Production* 1924, 1930, 1935, 1948; *Annual Statement of Trade of the UK with Other Countries* 1938, 1939.

acoustic gramophone had found an extremely large audience throughout Britain (see Table 2).

Having adjusted for exports and imports, it can be seen that the number of acoustic gramophones available for the home market nearly doubled in just six years from 256,522 in 1924 to 503,663 in 1930. The recession and electrical reproduction drastically cut back these sales to 24,434 in 1935. The reflationary effects of the government's rearmament programme, and rises in real income and wages, encouraged greater consumption, however, and production began to recover at the end of the period, with 40,600 acoustic gramophones being available for the home market in 1937.

Despite the slow take-up of the new technology, the successful commercial application of electrical reproduction in 1925 did provide the gramophone industry with new markets. The new recording process attracted the attention of those who had previously ignored the gramophone and the industry entered a boom that was curtailed only by the worldwide depression. However, the depression in Britain was brief compared with that in the USA. For a while there were enough enthusiasts to provide customers for both the acoustic and electrical machines. In the mid-1930s the availability of electric pick-ups that could be added to acoustic machines and plug-in record players that played through the radio expanded both markets. However, by the end of the 1930s fully electrical machines did begin to oust their older rivals. The rapid increase in the production of electric gramophones is shown in Table 1. This increase was despite the continued effects of the depression and relatively high prices.

Taken as a whole domestic production of all types of gramophones peaked in 1930. The depression clearly affected sales but recovery was also delayed by the impact of radio. To some extent the market for the gramophone had approached saturation point by 1930, although the effect of this was partly overcome by the export trade, whose proportionate decline was much less (see Table 2).

Imports of gramophones were never high in the interwar period, primarily because the industry was protected by a tariff of 33.3 per cent.[3] In addition, British technology was among the best in the world, at least in the latter half of the period, and the need to look elsewhere for high-quality machines was thus small. Imports tended to be cheap or took the form of novelties, such as the pocket watch sized gramophone (the 'Mikiphone') from Switzerland. With hardly any competition from abroad, the proportion of the home market held by British goods was extremely high. Even at its lowest in 1924, nearly 80 per cent of acoustic gramophones sold in Britain were manufactured in Britain. From 1930 to 1937, the figure was sustained at around 90 per cent. This was a considerable change from the pre-First World War position when foreign competitors overshadowed the British gramophone industry.

The gramophone industry was also involved in the production of gramophone records. Although a few companies made only records, the majority of companies produced both gramophones and records. Initially the record was of secondary importance to the gramophone. The gramophone was owned as an interesting piece of technology and records were merely something to play on them. Improvements in the quality of records, an increased variety of recordings, and reduced prices made the record more desirable in itself. Increasingly, people bought gramophones to play records.

If the figures for the production of gramophones appear impressive, then those for gramophone records are doubly so. Table 3 shows the production of gramophone records for the period 1924 to 1935. From a high starting point of over 22 million records produced in 1924, there was a more than threefold increase in production to 71,652,000 in 1930. The effects first of the depression and then the rapid growth of radio ownership meant that record sales followed the same pattern as gramophone sales and there was an enormous fall between 1930 and 1934. The industry responded to this by uniting and launching a series of inter-company promotional campaigns to increase record sales. The 'record player', an

---

[3] See below.

TABLE 3. *Records available for the home market, 1924–1935*

Date	Domestic production	Retained imports	Total exports	% exported	Total number available for home market	% of home market held by British goods
1924	22,368,000	72,000	6,924,000	30.95	15, 516,000	99.54
1930	71,652,000	324,000	12,732,000	17.7	59, 244,000	99.94
1934	29,700,000	58,248	5,364,000	18.06	24, 394,248	99.76
1935	25,068,000	74,364	5,169,576	20.62	19, 972,788	99.63

Sources: Calculated from *Census of Production* 1924, 1930, 1935, 1948 and *Annual Statement of Trade of the UK with Other Countries* 1938, 1939.

electric gramophone which attached to a radio set, was sold at a relatively low price to encourage people to buy more records. Even allowing for the effects of the depression and the radio over 25 million records were produced in Britain in 1935.

For this market, as with gramophones, imports were not large and the proportion of the home market for records held by British goods stayed at over 99 per cent for the whole of the period 1924 to 1935. Thereafter the pattern of imports goes against the trend for domestic sales, rising steadily from 1934 to 1937. The majority of imports, however, were for niche markets, such as enthusiasts of American jazz, a predominantly middle-class group, whose demand was fairly inelastic despite changing economic circumstances.[4] Exports of records always much exceeded imports. Nearly 7 million were exported in 1924, over 12 million in 1930, and over 5 million in 1935.

It was the record which eventually provided the gramophone industry with most of its profits. As Edward Lewis, the managing director of Decca, one of the largest manufacturers, said, 'a company manufacturing gramophones but not records was rather like one making razors but not the consumable blades'.[5] It follows then, that there was a large increase in the number of households with access to both gramophones and records. The evidence of sales and anecdotal evidence also suggests that, although predominantly a middle-class instrument, the gramophone was finding new audiences amongst lower social groups.[6] Even

---

[4] See Chapter 8 below.   [5] E. R. Lewis, *No C. I. C.* (1956), 10.
[6] See Chapter 2 below.

those who did not own a gramophone would be likely to have access to one, either at social institutions, clubs, or among friends—in short, it was difficult to escape from the gramophone and its records.

1.2 The development of the gramophone and record industries

The growth of the gramophone companies and the industry in general was part of a wider move within the British economy towards the production of 'consumer durables' and away from the traditional heavy industries.[7] The gramophone industry was an important symbol of this change and its leading companies were part of a growing internationalization of business, especially with America. In addition, the gramophone companies were among the first British companies to adopt aggressive 'American' marketing techniques, which was significant both economically and culturally. The development of the British industry, the key companies involved, and changes to the structure of the industry will now be discussed.

The British gramophone and gramophone record industry emerged, tentatively, at the end of the nineteenth century in the face of considerable foreign competition. Before 1914 the manufacture of records and gramophones was dominated by German companies who controlled a high proportion of the British market. There were also many German manufacturers located in Britain who produced a variety of gramophones and accessories such as the 'Favourite' and 'Beka' records, two of the most popular products on the market. Even those gramophones manufactured in England were, predominantly, either assembled 'kits' or else contained mostly foreign components, especially motors. The First World War brought about a dramatic change in this position. Home producers benefited as 'alien' gramophone businesses were closed down or confiscated by the government. More importantly, the war was to cripple the German gramophone industry and post-war anti-German feeling meant that Germany never regained its position in the British market.

Furthermore, in 1915 the Chancellor of the Exchequer imposed, as a wartime measure, high taxes on the imports of automobiles, films, and other luxuries, in an attempt to save space on ships for more vital imports

---

[7] The development of the record industry is also discussed by S. Frith, 'The Making of the British Record Industry 1920–64', in J. Curran, A. Smith and P. Wingate (ed.), *Impacts and Influences* (1987), 278–90.

and also to raise revenue. Included in these 'luxuries' were whole gramophones, their component parts, and gramophone records. The so-called
'McKenna duties' put a tariff of 33.3 per cent on imported gramophones.
Although intended as a wartime measure, the duties were retained until
the mid-1920s.

The effects of the war and the McKenna duties on the British
gramophone industry were substantial. With less competition from well-
established rivals, fledgling British companies were able to develop at
their own, increasingly rapid, pace. Before 1914, Britain imported 90 per
cent of the motors and other metal parts of gramophones. By 1923, 75 per
cent of the total output of these products was British made.[8] The Swiss,
however, still remained keen competitors in producing spring motors, a
large number of which were used in English gramophones, particularly
the portable models. The production of steel gramophone needles also
benefited from the McKenna duties. In 1920, the quantity of needles
turned out by the Gramophone Company at Hayes, Middlesex, reached
one and a half million per day. By contrast, in 1913 half the total of all
needles used in Britain had been foreign.[9] British gramophones were also
produced in much higher quantities than before the war. In 1913 the
Columbia Graphophone Company alone imported gramophones worth
£100,000. In 1923 their imports were worth less than £200 whilst their
trade was more than double the pre-war figures and included growing
export markets.[10]

It was not only the imposition of the McKenna duties that helped protect British industry; anti-German sentiment meant that many were
determined to keep German products off the British market, at least in
the immediate post-war period. In 1920 a large German firm planned to
flood the British market with cheap gramophone records. These records
would have sold, even after the McKenna tax was added, at one shilling
for a ten-inch disc, compared with similar British records then selling at
three to four shillings each. Another form of 'protection' was then introduced. Under the 1911 Copyright Act, British copyright owners had the
power to prohibit the import of any reproduction of their works. Francis,
Day, and Hunter, the music publishing firm, therefore organized other
London publishers and agreed a policy of disallowing the import of any
recorded works for which these firms held the copyright.[11] The policy
worked and was used repeatedly throughout the period.

[8] *GTMN*, Dec. 1923, p. 436.   [9] Ibid. 436.
[10] Ibid.   [11] *GTMN*, Jan. 1924, p. 10.

The McKenna duties were abolished in 1924 but after uproar from employers and employees in the gramophone industry the larger part of the duties was reinstated for the musical instruments industry. The gramophone industry, therefore, remained protected throughout the interwar period.

Despite the growing strength and independence of the British gramophone industry, 'British' firms remained reliant on American capital and ingenuity. The two biggest firms, the Columbia Graphophone Company and the Gramophone Company ('His Master's Voice'), retained close links with the United States. This was important both for production repertoire and production methods.

The Gramophone Company began its life in America when, in 1897, the National Gramophone Company of New York bought the English patent rights to Emile Berliner's invention, the gramophone.[12] In the same year this concern transferred its business to a company called the Gramophone Company, Limited, which was set up to manufacture and sell gramophones and phonographs. This company was still based in America but after a buyout by the Gramophone and Typewriter Company, a branch was established in London, with rights to sell Berliner's invention in Europe. In 1898 it made its first British gramophone recordings. The use of domestic talent recording domestic works considerably increased British interest in discs. By 1902 business proved so good that a new company was established in Britain with a share capital of £600,000; this was the Gramophone Company. A factory was opened in Hayes, Middlesex, in 1907. Although the Gramophone Company was financed from British capital, in the early years gramophones were assembled from parts imported from America. Once a British factory had been established, the Gramophone Company was able to reduce its dependence on American technology and production but continued to sell American gramophones until 1918. By the mid-1920s, however, the company had established its own research and development laboratories at Hayes which increased the British company's creative capacity. Supported by the McKenna duties, the Gramophone Company soon began to dominate the British market. It also became an increasingly multinational concern. Expansion into Europe had begun in 1899, with new branches in France, Italy, and Central Europe. Factories in Spain, France,

---

[12] Information in this section from O. Mitchell, *The Talking Machine Industry* (1922), 72–5. For a full discussion of the development of the Gramophone Company, Columbia, and EMI see P. Martland, *Since Records Began: EMI the First 100 Years* (1997).

Russia, and India soon followed. The company also scored a minor coup when it gained a majority interest in one of Europe's best record companies, Deutsche Grammophon of Germany.

The links with America continued, however. The control of financial decisions was carried out by an American dominated management board and Alfred Clarke, the company's managing director from 1908 to 1930 and chairman until 1946, was also American. Furthermore, the company built close alliances with its American counterparts. Two of the most important were the companies of Emile Berliner and Elridge Johnson. In 1901 these two businesses had merged to form the Victor Talking Machine Company. A series of reciprocal recording and trading arrangements were made between Victor and the Gramophone Company and in 1920 Victor bought a controlling interest in the company. British control was not regained until 1935. The Gramophone Company, therefore, despite promoting itself as a quintessentially British company, remained a multinational firm with strong American links.

The biggest rival to the Gramophone Company, the Columbia Graphophone Company, was also the product of American entreprise.[13] In 1887 the American Graphophone Company was established in order to put machines and cylinders on the market under licence from Bell and Tainter, who had improved on Thomas Edison's phonograph. Unable to cope with the extent of the business, the American Graphophone Company made arrangements with several firms to act as sales agencies. The Columbia Phonograph Company was thus established in 1899 as the sales agent for the District of Columbia, Delaware, and Maryland. The company proved so successful that it soon extended its business to the whole of the United States and then opened branches all over the world. A few years later the Columbia Phonograph Company bought up its parent company. The British branch of the company, established in 1897, soon became the controlling centre for Europe and a factory was built in Wandsworth, London, for the manufacture of gramophone discs. In 1901 it issued its first British recordings. Development of the British branch was rapid and in 1917 a British registered business, the Columbia Graphophone Company Limited, was created. Increasing profits and sales meant that in 1922 the British company bought out the parental controlling interest and became independent. The American 'Columbia Phonograph Company' ceased to have authority over the British 'Columbia Graphophone Company'. In 1925 the British company successfully bid for a controlling interest in its American former parent company. This dramatic reversal of fortune was seen as extremely important. As the *Talking Machine News* of 1925 noted:

England is now in fact 'top dog' throughout the world. . . . The tremendous developments of the interests of the Columbia Graphophone Company, Ltd. places that company in the position of the leading and most powerful gramophone company in the world, on account of the vast interests she has secured; interests on a scale which has not before been attained by any musical instrument company in England, Germany, America or any other country.[14]

Indeed, one the company's most important achievements was in helping to create a global record industry. A few months after the 1925 buyout, Columbia bought out the German company Carl Lindstrom AG of Berlin. Reflecting the increasingly multinational nature of the gramophone record, both economically and culturally, worldwide production, distribution and sales networks were created. In 1927 Columbia, already with seventeen factories around the world in Europe, North and South America, purchased the controlling interest in the Nipponophone Company, Japan's largest gramophone company and the key to lucrative Far Eastern markets.

Columbia was a remarkably successful company and yet, despite the apparent triumph of British industry, the Columbia Graphophone Company retained close links with America. This extended from the managing director, Louis Sterling, who was American, down to the many Americans who dominated the board of directors. As with the Gramophone Company, its relationship with America was a complex one.

Only one large company in the British gramophone industry, Decca, could claim to be truly British. It slowed the trend established by Columbia and HMV by establishing its own niche in the American record market. It was, however, still dependent on US business methods and US talent. The Decca company grew out of the London based musical instrument company Barnett-Samuels. Barnett-Samuels produced the first British portable gramophone in 1914. Despite difficult years following the First World War, by 1928 the now renamed 'Decca Gramophone Company' had seen big increases in its profits as records and gramophones became more popular.[15] The massive growth in the value of the shares of the two main record producers Columbia and the Gramophone Company, the result of a boom in record sales, had

[14] *GTMN*, Nov. 1925, p. 293.
[15] See Lewis, *No C. I. C.* for Lewis's own account of the development of Decca.

stimulated interest in gramophone and record production. Thus in 1928 a stock market flotation was arranged. Barnett-Samuels' accountants approached a young stockbroker named Edward Lewis, a product of Rugby School and Trinity College, Cambridge. Lewis brought about a successful flotation. By the end of 1928 Lewis set about realizing his aim of getting Decca into the lucrative business of record production. He found an ailing record company, the Duophone Company, bought it out and in February 1929 the Decca Record Company was launched. Lewis, keenly interested in the business opportunities available in the gramophone industry, rapidly manoeuvred with shareholders in order to become the managing director of Decca. Lewis was keen to exploit the possibilities of a flourishing new industry but, ironically, he was entering the business just as the bubble burst. For the gramophone industry, 1929 was a boom year, but such prolific success was short-lived.

The difficulties brought about by the world depression made these initial years traumatic and Decca lurched from one crisis to the next. Nevertheless, Lewis was a ruthless businessman and by launching a price war in the record industry in 1931 he was able to protect Decca against the threat of its large multinational competitors, Columbia and the Gramophone Company, which had merged that year to form the huge combine Electrical and Musical Industries (EMI). Lewis was particularly keen on adopting US marketing techniques. Within weeks of becoming the managing director, he was aggressively signing new artists like Gertrude Lawrence and he managed to catch the biggest dance bandleader of the time, Jack Hylton. Hylton asked for and received 40,000 ordinary shares in Decca as part of his new contract. The fact that Hylton's first record for Decca, 'Rhymes', sold 300,000 copies indicates the importance of this signing.[16] Indeed, the acquisition of Hylton established Decca as a serious competitor in the record industry.

In 1932 Lewis began to set his sights on the American market, aware that to be successful a British record company had to have access to American artists. The American popular music industry was huge. Britain had nothing that could compare with the size and influence of Hollywood and its music publishers dominated world markets. However, the effect of the depression on the US market was much more pronounced than in Britain. The old New York music publishers collapsed catastrophically, with dire consequences for other sections of the American popular music industry. Only Hollywood was robust enough

---

[16] Ibid. 30.

to survive relatively unscathed. Lewis thus tracked down another ailing record company, Brunswick. Hard hit by the depression, the American firm Warner Bros. had sold off the Brunswick radio and record business to the American Record Corporation. Brunswick had probably the best popular music catalogue in the USA and its artists included Bing Crosby, the Boswell Sisters, the Mills Brothers, and Louis Armstrong. In Britain, the Brunswick labels had first been distributed by the music publishing company Chappels and then by the record company British Brunswick but in 1932 Lewis secured a deal giving Decca the British rights to the label for £15,000. The deal gave Decca a considerable competitive edge in the popular music industry. It also gave Decca the skills of two American gramophone industry experts, H. F. Schwarz and H. G. Sarton, who were to contribute directly to marketing and promotion of stars and records for Decca. Lewis had even more ambitious plans, however, and was determined to expand directly into the United States record market on his own terms. In October 1934, he launched the US Decca Company. With the help of Jack Kapp, a chief figure in the American Brunswick labels whom Lewis 'poached', US Decca was then able to 'poach' Bing Crosby, Guy Lombardo, the Mills Brothers, and the Casa Loma Orchestra. It was not the best time to be launching a record business in America. Record sales there had slumped from a pre-depression total of 100 million records per annum to just 10 million. The collapse in record sales, as with the rest of the popular music industry, was much worse than in Britain, indeed many of the American stars sold more records in Britain than in the USA. In the USA sales of over 25,000 for any one record were rare but Bing Crosby's 'Please' sold over 60,000 records and his 'The Last Roundup' 80,000 copies in Britain.[17] Lewis was convinced of the potential demand for records in the USA and by 1946, largely as a result of Decca's success, US sales exceeded 330 million. The establishment of companies in both Britain and the USA allowed an interchange of musical talent that was to serve both markets well. Decca was, thus, a truly multinational company and had been the first major record company to develop in Britain and then move to America, rather than the other way round. Expansion at home continued as well. In 1937 Decca purchased the Crystallite Co., which owned the Rex, Vocalion, and Panachord record labels. The deal also included studios in Broadhurst Gardens, West Hampstead. In just sixteen years Edward Lewis had created one of the most successful and influential companies in the gramophone industry.

[17] Ibid. 44.

The 'British' gramophone industry thus developed into a world leader during the interwar period. By the mid-1920s, British products were regarded as amongst the best in the world. At the 1927 convention of the British Music Industries, for example, an 'authoritative report' suggested that gramophone records and machines manufactured in Britain 'were accepted as the standard of quality throughout the world'.[18] That same year HMV received the Gold Medal in the gramophone section of the International Music Exhibition at Geneva.[19] Discussing the importance of the export trade, the gramophone journal *Records* pointed as early as 1926 to the dominance of the British product in the world market:

No fewer than eighty-eight countries are now more or less dependent on Great Britain for these musical goods, and statistics show that such competitors as Italy, Austria and Germany, though they have factories of their own, are depending more and more on this country. It is an open secret in the trade that Great Britain exports more records to Italy than that country manufactures . . .[20]

In achieving this, however, the major companies had either been directly or indirectly influenced by America. This influence, in the case of Columbia, HMV, and, later, EMI (which only became independent from the Radio Corporation of America in 1935), came from management, capital, and production methods. At Decca it took the form of American marketing techniques. This was extremely important for the production and marketing of popular music.

No less important was the way in which the gramophone industry became concentrated into fewer and fewer hands. By 1918 there were about twenty independent record and gramophone companies in Britain, rising to just under fifty in the boom years of 1928 to 1929, together with a plethora of associated manufacturers. The industry was large and diverse, with firms of all sizes engaged in production. By 1937 just two huge enterprises remained in the British gramophone and record industry and virtually no independent manufacturers survived. This change had important effects.

The British gramophone and record industry expanded rapidly at the end of the First World War, and the industry developed a new, complex structure. The gramophone was sufficiently popular for large numbers of entrepreneurs to enter this new market and many small to medium size companies were established. Entry costs into the industry were relatively

---

[18] *Records,* June 1927, p. 374.   [19] *Records,* Oct.–Nov. 1927, p. 16.
[20] *Records,* Oct. 1926, p. 45.

low and the market for records and gramophones was also sufficiently diverse to allow a number of different manufacturers to survive. In effect, there were several different markets for gramophone products and this allowed a complex structure of small, medium, and large manufacturers to exist alongside one another.

At the lowest end of the market was that part of the industry concerned with the production of 'novelties' such as flexible discs, unbreakable discs, coloured discs, and picture discs containing advertisements. Indeed, before the advent of commercial radio, the 'advertising jingle' was pioneered on such picture discs. They were attractively produced with catchy tunes which made them desirable for gramophone owners, despite the advertising. The Durium company also held a substantial market for its flexible discs which were sent through the post on subscription from newsagents and provided two new 'hits' per week. Similarly many manufacturers specialized in producing novelty gramophones, such as the 'Peter Pan', which was compact enough to fold up into a case about the same size and design as a Box Brownie camera and was developed for walkers and cyclists. Closely associated with this section of the industry was a subsection which produced accessories. These ranged from attachments which provided scrolling pictures to accompany story discs for children, to dancing minstrels which were bolted on to the turntable of the gramophone. Next in the industry hierarchy were the many manufacturers who provided do-it-yourself kits and component parts for amateurs to construct their own gramophones. Such manufacturers operated mail order services advertised in the expanding popular press and provided very affordable instruments but of inferior quality.

One of the largest sections of the gramophone industry was that which provided 'budget-priced' records. Especially during the earlier part of the period, when the largest record companies sold records at relatively high prices, there was a big popular market for these low-priced discs. This enabled many small firms to produce budget labels catering specifically for popular music, engaging a large number of musicians who would never have been given the opportunity to record with the larger firms. However, there were also a considerable number of record manufacturers who were dealing with better artists and had high production values. Record companies such as Edison Bell, British Homophone, and Vocalion held a significant proportion of the record market during the 1920s and they offered some first-rate recordings. There were also several large manufacturers of gramophones such as Edison Bell and Aeolian, who were producing excellent machines for substantial markets. Many of these firms had previously been involved in the manufacture of musical instruments and thus had well-respected names. These mid-ranking firms were followed by the largest producers, Columbia, the Gramophone Company, and, later, Decca. These were giant companies with a large and diverse range of products. Above these, at the highest end of the industry, were a small number of specialist manufacturers catering for the enthusiast. The most successful of these was E. M. Ginn, whose 'EMG Handmade Gramophones' were extremely expensive but offered the best in acoustic reproduction.

The gramophone and record industry thus comprised a considerable number of different manufacturers and retailers. As the 1920s progressed, however, two firms began to dominate large sections of the British market. As indicated, the Gramophone and Columbia Graphophone Companies emerged as world-leading companies during this time. At home, they managed to dominate as no other companies could. In 1919, the Gramophone Company sold over 60,000 gramophones and 6 million records, more than any other single company. By 1929 nearly 12 million HMV and Zonophone records were sold in Britain and annual record production at Hayes reached 25 million.[21] Output of Columbia records increased during this decade from 6.7 million records in 1923 to 15.5 million in 1930.[22] Between them, Columbia and the Gramophone Company produced over half of Britain's records. Significantly, these large firms were involved in all aspects of production. They produced recording and reproduction equipment for the industry, they manufactured their own gramophones, their own records, their own needles, they established their own retail outlet networks, and, of course, they secured the best musicians for their records.

During the gramophone boom of 1925 to 1929, however, there was plenty of room for other companies apart from these two giants and the industry expanded in size and scope. The success of the gramophone and records was phenomenal. In November 1927, the gramophone journal *Records* reported, 'Gramophone factories are almost choked with orders, and the industry has never before had such phenomenal prosperity. The output of records has been trebled and quadrupled; profits and dividends are steadily rising.'[23] Indeed record after record was broken in the Stock Exchange as a result of the remarkable boom in gramophone shares. During 1927, the ordinary shares of the five best-known companies

---

[21] Martland, *Since Records Began*, 77, 86.   [22] Ibid. 117.
[23] *Records*, Oct.–Nov. 1927, p. 11.

increased in market value by a total of £8.5 million and the market value of the ordinary shares of these companies stood at nearly £15 million.[24] Of particular note was the success of the two leaders of the British gramophone industry, the Columbia Graphophone Co. Ltd. and the Gramophone Company Ltd. The shares of the Columbia Company saw an increase in market value of nearly £3.5 million in 1927–8, whilst those of the Gramophone Company increased in total market value by nearly £4 million.[25] Profits soared too. In the fifteen months to June 1928, Columbia's profits reached £491,305, over three times the 1926 figure of just over £150,000. The Gramophone Company's success was even more marked. Profits in 1925 were £266,087 but soared to £1,143,414 in 1928.[26] The shares of the smaller companies rose proportionately. The share price of the Vocalion Record Company rose from 5 shillings at the start of 1927 to 44s. 9d. by the end of the year, and those of Edison Bell rose to more than 30 shillings.[27] Such success encouraged speculative expansion in the industry. The year 1928 to 1929 was the high water mark for the gramophone industry before the Second World War. In 1928 alone, thirty new firms involved in the manufacture of records and gramophones were registered.[28] The estimated share capital, in aggregate, of these new British gramophone companies in 1928 was over £9 million.[29] New firms launched themselves with great confidence. Worldecho Records Ltd., for example, estimated that it would secure profits of £55,000 per annum for the first two years of operation on the basis of an output and sale of 15 million records per annum. Dominion Gramophone Records Ltd. estimated an annual profit of £60,000 on the basis of a production and distribution of 5 million records.[30] Others were more cautious. The trade journal *Talking Machine News*, for example, warned that the gramophone industry was in danger of overcrowding, with too many firms and too much capital being seen as a threat to sustainable success.[31]

The depression ensured that this success proved short-lived. Smaller companies such as Worldecho and Dominion were among the first to suffer. The larger companies were also hit hard. In 1930, the combined profits of the Gramophone Company and Columbia had been £1.42

[24] *Records*, Dec.–Jan. 1928, p. 93.   [25] Ibid. 93.
[26] Anon., *Gramophone Companies* (1929), 5 and 17.
[27] *Records*, Dec.–Jan. 1928, p. 93.   [28] Anon., *Gramophone Companies*, 1–26.
[29] *TMN*, Nov. 1928, p. 313.   [30] Anon., *Gramophone Companies*, 11 and 26.
[31] *TMN*, Nov. 1928, p. 313.

million; by 1931 they had fallen to just £160,000. Even the combined firm
EMI suffered, and from 1931 to 1934 it actually had a loss of over £1 million. Only in 1934 did it return its first profit of £500,000, and then
largely because the company had diversified into the production of radios
and other consumer durables, such as refrigerators. Sales of its records,
however, continued to plummet to a low of just under 5 million in 1937.[32]
Yet the sheer stature of EMI gave it a resilience which few others in the
gramophone industry had.

In the harsher conditions of the 1930s, the structure of the gramophone industry was dramatically transformed. There was little room for
manufacturers of novelty items as consumers became more careful about
how they spent their money and even the affordable do-it-yourself
machine manufacturers found it difficult to survive. Only the comparatively well-to-do were still able to buy new machines during the worst
period of the depression and they were not the section to which do-it-
yourself gramophones appealed. It was not only changes in consumer
demand that hit the structure of the industry, however. The emergence of
EMI and Decca as a duopoly from the 1920s altered the industry considerably. Entry into the market was now virtually impossible for smaller
firms. Both EMI and Decca had large, elaborate recording studios and
factories. Economic mass production of records and machines required
vast plants and both multinationals were thus well placed to take advantage of economies of scale. Similarly, using their huge economic muscle,
EMI and Decca were able to secure contracts for the best artists and
retain exclusive recording rights. Even if smaller companies did obtain
the services of popular music stars they lacked the resources to promote
them adequately. Perhaps hardest hit were the middle ranking record
producers whose products were neither cheap nor offered the very best
recording artists. Only the budget labels survived, although many of them
suffered too, as the larger record producers lowered their prices in order
to halt the decline in their sales. Ultimately, due to the huge resources
available to them, the largest companies were able to offer better artists at
comparable prices and they inevitably triumphed. Still, EMI had to work
hard to get rid of its budget rivals, as many held their own surprisingly
well.

Yet it was not only the economic downturn that affected the structure
of the industry; the gramophone and record industry suffered from the
increasing popularity of the radio, which offered an attractive alternative

[32] Martland, *Since Records Began*, 136.

source of musical entertainment. The gramophone had several advantages over the radio. It allowed a more personal choice of music; as one record industry slogan stated, it allowed one to 'Hear what you want, when you want.' In addition, records could be replayed. However, the radio was cheap. It provided all round entertainment with little additional cost above that of the initial outlay for the set and licence. The advent of hire purchase on a wide scale made it even more attractive. Thus, as the radio began to take off during the early 1930s, interest in gramophones and records as a whole began to suffer. This had two effects. First, as demand for gramophones and records declined, there was only room for a limited number of producers and unless they provided a distinctive and practical product, smaller manufacturers found it hard to compete with their larger rivals. Secondly, the technical advances that had brought about electrical recording and radio broadcasting (the two were inextricably linked) meant a radical restructuring of the industry. Increasingly the two industries began to merge, with radiograms being produced by both radio and gramophone manufacturers. In 1929, for example, the Gramophone Company had acquired the Marconiphone Co. and the Osram Valve Co. as a way into the new lucrative market. The new electrical technology meant that many older gramophone companies, which had developed from musical instrument companies and specialized in acoustic technology, were unable to survive the change. The smaller, independent producers were thus squeezed out of the market, as the costs of research and development, as well as production, increased.

In addition, the larger gramophone companies, chiefly Columbia and the Gramophone Company, actively squeezed their other competitors. As smaller companies felt the effects of the depression, the industry's giants, EMI and Decca, were able to swallow them up. Many independent British record labels disappeared in this way. EMI also consolidated its position in the rest of the world. The Gramophone Company bought labels and manufacturing plants throughout Europe; Columbia bought its various German, Italian, French, and Far Eastern labels. In Britain, by 1935, only three other rivals to EMI remained; Decca and the small independent firms Crystalate and British Homophone. By 1937 Decca had consumed Crystalate, and in the same year, together with EMI (a sign of the poor state of the market as whole), Decca also purchased the British Homophone Company. The two remaining firms also cooperated at an international level. Negotiations between Louis Sterling of EMI and Edward Lewis of Decca resulted in an agreement whereby EMI actually controlled Decca labels in South America, Australia, New Zealand and the Far East. Similarly, Decca controlled EMI's Parlophone and Odeon labels in North America. These two great rivals worked together, therefore, to overcome the economic downturn.

Thus the depression had a decisive effect on the structure of the gramophone industry by accelerating a process of integration and merger which had begun during the 1920s. As a result of the disappearance of smaller and independent record companies through buyout or failure, by the end of the interwar period there were only two major companies in the UK gramophone and record industry, Decca and EMI.

Conclusion

Not only did the gramophone industry become the most important element in the musical instruments industry, replacing pianos, but the large sales of gramophones and records gave unprecedented availability to recorded music in the interwar period. The gramophone was the first musical mass media form and it briefly pre-dated the radio, in the 1920s, as the most important technology based music medium. The gramophone and record industries were also among the most 'modern' of the growth industries and the most 'international'. British companies, as strong multinationals, were world leaders in both technology and production. One of the reasons for this British success was that popular music was so important to national culture. The British gramophone industry was created within, and benefited from, a long and deep popular music tradition. It was one of the few strong indigenous traditions outside the USA. Anglo-American interchange did not break this tradition completely. The concentration of the gramophone industry into just two large combines by the end of the period was a reflection of developments elsewhere in the entertainment industry and this cartelization was also Anglo-American in nature. Like similar developments in chemicals and publishing, it allowed British and American gramophone companies between them to carve up world markets for the gramophone and records with the British companies not necessarily taking on a junior role in this partnership.

2

THE ROLE OF THE GRAMOPHONE IN DAILY LIFE IN INTERWAR BRITAIN AND ITS EFFECT ON MUSICAL CULTURE

Introduction

The gramophone and gramophone record were important elements in the growth of both the popular music industry and the leisure industry as a whole. Both fast became part of daily life for millions in interwar Britain. One contemporary commentator wrote:

The gramophone is one of the greatest treasures of the modern home. The time is fast passing when the average man can profess to be beyond the spell of music . . . Music, in her various guises, can, through the gramophone, administer to the wants of all; and that is why none of us can afford to be without a gramophone.

A gramophone is as necessary to the tired mind as a rest in the field or in the sea is to the body. A Sunday morning outing, forty winks in the afternoon, and some Gramophone music in the evening, is a Day of Rest spent well indeed . . . In dealing with the gramophone, therefore, we are concerned with something that is both serious and delightful. Serious because it is fast becoming a necessity to every home and for the benefit of mental health, and delightful because it offers the whole range of the Joy of Music.[1]

In addition, the gramophone helped revolutionize both the supply and nature of popular music in Britain, bringing in new cultural influences and widening access to music to an unprecedented extent. This chapter examines the role of the gramophone in daily life, looking at the audience

---

[1] *GR*, May 1928, pp. 3–4.

or consumers themselves and how they used the gramophone. The music and marketing policies of the gramophone companies will be examined, particularly their attempts to be taken seriously by the music profession and for the gramophone to be seen as an 'instrument' not a 'gadget'. Lastly, the impact of the gramophone on musical culture will be discussed.

2.1 The gramophone in daily life

We have established the rapid growth in the production and sales of gramophones and records; it is now necessary to examine who the audience for this new form of entertainment was and how they used it, both at home and in public.

Due to the largely private and domestic role which the gramophone played in interwar life, determining the social status of the audiences for gramophones is difficult. Despite this, there are some indications of the sort of people who were exposed to its influence. In 1931 Compton Mackenzie, editor of the *Gramophone*, conducted a survey designed to establish the social make-up of the gramophone owners who were also readers of his journal.[2] At the outset it must be noted that the readership of the *Gramophone* tended to be middleclass. This was because the journal was read largely by those who wanted to enjoy classical music and its interpretation on records. McKenzie's survey of gramophone owners, though of doubtful reliability given its nature, nonetheless suggests that ownership was spreading among classes, even though it was predominantly a middle-class instrument. The occupations of the sample of 460 readers investigated were categorized as follows: nearly 23 per cent were of the 'scholastic class' (which also included music teachers, journalists, and clergymen); 16 per cent were independent and in business of their own of some kind; 16 per cent were on a weekly wage, many of them manual labourers; 14 per cent were clerks; 11 per cent were technicians such as engineers; 9 per cent were in law or medicine, and a further 9 per cent belonged to the civil service. Gramophone owners were thus occupied as anything from astronomer, botanist, psychologist, and pianoforte teacher to forester, sheep-farmer, and blacksmith. The income of these gramophone owners suggests a predominantly middle-class ownership.

In the early part of the period the gramophone was almost certainly a middle-class instrument, its prices necessarily excluding all but a few of

---

[2] *Gramophone*, Sept. 1931, pp. 110–11.

the working classes. The first gramophone enthusiasts were broadly of two types: those who bought the gramophone for technical interest and those who saw the possibilities of the gramophone as a musical educator. The technical enthusiast was well provided for; considerable space was devoted to technical matters in numerous trade journals. The *Talking Machine News*, *Gramophone*, *Gramophone Review*, and *Records*, all reviewed and discussed the latest technological developments. As a technology-based form of entertainment, the gramophone's early beginnings had an element of do-it-yourself amateurism. Many companies even offered cheap component parts to enable enthusiastic amateurs to construct their own machines. A whole sub-industry developed in order to satisfy the amateur's demands for constant improvement in gramophone technology. The whole tone of the gramophone industry's advertisements was geared to these enthusiasts, with developments given pseudo-scientific names and every advance hailed as the 'ultimate life-like reproduction of sound'. The enthusiasts soon became wary of such claims. In 1921, the *Musical Times* commented:

For many years there has been, and still is, far too much 'hot air' in connection with gramophone development. A mere piling-up of superlatives will no longer impress the serious critic, still less those of us who, time and again, have tested the 'revolutionary improvements' effected by the use of so-and-so's records, or sound box, or needles, or other patent appliances, only to find that such improvements, if evident at all, are evident on too slight a degree to merit very serious attention.[3]

The gramophone enthusiast too came under attack. Constant Lambert could write in 1934,

At one time a cautious glance round the room ensured one, through the absence of a piano, that there would at least be no music after dinner. But today the chances are that one's host is a Gramophone Bore, intent on exhibiting his 57 varieties of soundbox . . .[4]

Thus the gramophone became part of the 'hobby culture' of Britain, especially popular among the middle classes and in suburbia. It was also predominantly a male hobby. Unlike the piano, the gramophone industry aimed its technical advertising directly at men. It was a particularly British appropriation of an American invention and it was a private, individualistic enthusiasm. George Orwell talked about the

[3] *Musical Times*, July 1927, p. 477.
[4] C. Lambert, *Music Ho! A Study of Music in Decline* (1934), 236.

English characteristic which is so much a part of us that we barely notice it . . . the addiction to hobbies and spare-time occupations, the privateness of English life. We are a nation of flower-lovers, but also a nation of stamp-collectors, pigeon-fanciers, amateur carpenters, coupon-snippers, darts-players, crossword-puzzle fans.[5]

He could have added the record and gramophone enthusiast to his list.

Gramophone enthusiasts could also find a perfect means of expressing their love of the gramophone through the numerous gramophone societies which sprang up.[6] Such societies were formed with the intention of breaking down the prejudices against the gramophone and in order to give enthusiasts the opportunity to listen to the latest records and exchange information about inventions. Meetings were generally held once a month when all the most recent issues from the record manufacturers were listened to and their merits discussed. New soundboxes, needles, and other accessories were also tested. The advantage of such societies was that members could listen to a larger number and greater variety of recordings than was ordinarily possible, without having to worry about whether to buy them or not. Such societies could be found in most cities and large towns, even in villages. Membership was usually fairly small, from 5 to 100, but these were, nevertheless, a minority who had much influence over the gramophone companies, whose representatives often toured the societies demonstrating the latest products and developments. It was this band of enthusiasts who acted as a propaganda machine for the gramophone industry, imbuing it with a sense of respectability and seriousness at a time when some professional musicians and music critics remained hostile to the gramophone.

Several factors conspired to make the gramophone less exclusive as the period progressed. The purchasing power of individuals was an important element in the expansion of the gramophone's popularity. As we have seen, the average weekly money wage nearly trebled between 1913 and 1938.[7] This, combined with falling costs of living, increased the purchasing power of individuals. These changes meant that the gramophone and gramophone records increasingly fell within the reach of working-class pockets.

In addition, the advent of mass production and marketing methods brought widespread price deflation in the average price of entertainment and recreation in the period. During, the 1920s, the gramophone was still

---

[5] G. Orwell, *The Lion and the Unicorn: Socialism and the English Genius* (1982), 39.
[6] See *Gramophone*, Apr. 1934, p. 346.   [7] See Introduction, above.

a luxury item but by the 1930s prices had fallen dramatically as HMV, Decca, and others announced substantial price reductions across all of their gramophone range. By the mid-1930s there were gramophones to suit a wide range of incomes, ranging from the cheaper portables to the still fairly expensive radio gramophones. There was even greater 'value for money' due to technical improvements. The cheapest radiogram of 1939, for example, would incorporate a whole host of facilities that would not have been included on even the most expensive radiogram of 1930. Features such as automatic record changing, improved motors, and improved reproduction were an added incentive to consumers. Indeed, the commercial application of electrical recording and reproduction in 1925 was a major attraction to those who had previously ignored the gramophone.

The period also witnessed a dramatic reduction in the price of gramophone records. At the turn of the century records sold for as much as £1 each (nearly an average week's wage) and most ranged in price from ten shillings to two shillings and sixpence. However, as interest in the new forms of recorded music grew, prices fell. The most expensive records were, and remained, classical music records but records of popular music were more affordable. At the end of the First World War, the large record manufacturers introduced new labels specifically to cater for the popular market. The 'Zonophone' label by the Gramophone Company was joined by the budget 'Twin' and 'Cinch' labels, with records selling at two shillings and sixpence each. At Columbia, the 'Phoenix' and 'Regal' labels were launched at similar prices.

In addition to the labels from large record companies, the 1920s saw the emergence of a considerable number of companies wholly concerned with the low budget market. The 'Victory', 'Sterno', 'Eclipse', and 'Broadcast' labels were large sellers in this category. Such records, usually smaller in size than the standard ten-inch records, featured 'cover' versions of popular songs and tunes of the time, sometimes recorded by the best bands using pseudonyms. Much of the output, however, was of inferior quality to that offered by the larger labels. In the new high street chain stores these low-priced records were widely available. At Woolworths, the 'Crown' record was sold for sixpence. Marks and Spencer sold the 'Rex' label. The electrical retailer Currys had its own budget record label, although much of its output was identical to other budget records, often with its own label pasted over the top. This was radical retailing. Until the 1930s, gramophone records had been sold almost exclusively in music shops. Record companies maintained a monopoly over supply of their products with tied retail outlets and fixed prices. The HMV network of retail outlets, for example, was tightly controlled. Any retailer who tried to cut prices was denied supplies. Woolworths and the budget record companies were thus transforming the market.

Increasing competition from these smaller record companies, together with the arrival of the Decca label, sold at eighteen pence, saw prices fall even more during the 1930s. Price wars also helped. In 1935, in an attempt to make the gramophone more attractive in the face of ever increasing interest in the radio, EMI launched a price war in the record industry. In February 1935, therefore, Columbia, HMV, and Parlophone dance records were reduced to one shilling. Decca and its sister American company, Brunswick, responded by introducing various new labels at reduced prices. Although these price cuts were soon withdrawn, the budget sixpence records remained, and the cheaper records (at 1s. 6d.) increased the quality of their artists. As a result, the gramophone and gramophone records became an important element of both middle- and working-class culture in the 1920s and 1930s.

Despite its increasing ubiquity in daily life, the gramophone was nevertheless the source of much curiosity in interwar Britain, especially at the start of the period. The gramophone made a big impact in the home. It is difficult to re-create the experience of the gramophone in family life but it is not the case that the gramophone was just a 'background' supplier of music as it might be today. Like the wireless that followed it, it was a focal point in the room and a talking point which was proudly shown off when people visited. Indeed, in many homes the gramophone found itself assuming an almost sacred position in the 'front parlour' where adults retired after dinner to wind up the machine, place a new needle in the soundbox, and listen to the music of their choice (see Plate 1). Families listened together, with 'father' usually in control, an issue that was later to become central to teenage culture. Cabinet designs became increasingly elaborate and mock 'Chippendale', 'Regency', and 'Tudor' models were produced in an attempt to make the gramophone fit in with the architectural and decorative fashions of the time. In the early 1920s, the gramophone was popular as, among other things, a piece of technology and it required some technical knowledge in order to get the best from it. As the period progressed, however, the technology became more user-friendly and gramophone operation became a less demanding experience. It was considered by many to be the reserve of long dark cold winter and spring nights, providing amusement when it was difficult to get out of doors. H. Llewellyn Smith cites the example of a working-class railway worker from Lewisham, who had both a wireless and gramophone for relaxation indoors when the weather was bad.[8] Similar comments were made by an engine-driver from Willesden: 'We have a banjo and gramophone to amuse us if it's wet and we can't go out.'[9] Such comments can be substantiated by the large seasonal fluctuations in the sales of gramophones with the summer months being a low point, at least until the portable gramophone became popular.

The gramophone in the home was a musical companion and a source of relaxation. The effects of this relaxation often ran deep, especially for those alone. Jack Smith, a popular recording star of the 1920s, received the following fan letter from one such woman in 1927:

When I'm feeling blue and all alone I get one of your records out and play it softly until it seems that you are sitting right here with me understanding all the rotten things that make up my life. I don't know what you are like to look at; I don't very much care. I lost both my sons in the war, and there's a big ache left where there used to be a feeling of gladness. I'm writing to tell you . . . that you have done more towards soothing that ache than anybody else in the world.[10]

The gramophone served to offer a domestic alternative to the public forms of entertainment such as dance halls and cinema. For the middle classes too, the gramophone was thought to have speeded a rediscovery of home life after the hedonistic days of the immediate post-war period. As the *Gramophone Review* explained in 1928:

We are tired of spending money we can ill afford, the novelty of night life has worn somewhat thin, books and plays of 'high living and low morals' have lost their glamour for us, and these tendencies towards a home life are emphasised by a very potent factor . . . that is the gramophone.

Why, we ask ourselves, should we go out in cold and wet, into crowds, perhaps, to see some entertainment that we cannot be sure of enjoying, when we can have a comfortable chair and the fifteen new records of Rigoletto to entrance us? Or, why should we dance in a crowded restaurant among strangers when, in a few minutes, we can summon our especial friends and dance to Waring's Pennsylvanians? We can find no reasonable affirmatives to these questions and so . . . we stay at home.[11]

The popularity and use of the gramophone was also directly linked to the interwar craze for dancing.[12] To this public form of entertainment, the gramophone brought a domestic aspect. In an increasing number and

---

[8] H. Llewellyn Smith, *New Survey of London Life and Labour* (1935), ix. 303.
[9] Ibid. 496.   [10] *Gramophone*, July 1927, p. 417.
[11] *GR*, Nov. 1928, p. 8.   [12] See Chapters 6 and 7.

variety of locations throughout the country, dancing became one of the most popular national pastimes. In palais-de-danse, church and mission halls, club rooms, municipal halls, swimming baths, hotels, restaurants, and even cinemas, large numbers participated regularly in dancing. Such public settings were not the only location of dancing. The gramophone brought 'gramophone dances' into the home. With a selection of the latest dance band records and a gramophone, it was possible to hear the best in dance music at a fraction of the cost of going to see and hear them. Although dancing in the home was not new, certainly not for the middle classes, the gramophone made it possible for entertainment to be provided without musical knowledge or the means to hire musicians. The quality of entertainment was considered by many to be a great improvement on that of the amateur. As W. Somerset Maugham said, 'We all congratulate ourselves that the radio and gramophone have driven from our drawing-rooms the amateur pianist and the amateur singer.'[13] In the interwar period, especially before the rapid rise of the radio, the gramophone was used frequently for domestic parties and home entertainment. It was a cheap alternative to going out for the evening and was also regarded as a means of making such entertainment safe and respectable.

The gramophone then, was one of many technological changes (of which the radio was most important) that encouraged people to stay at home. Such changes, together with better housing, had some effect in strengthening interwar domesticity.

The gramophone was not, however, restricted wholly to a life indoors. Gramophone companies soon capitalized on its portability. From the earliest days of its history the gramophone was used in the summer months as an accessory to picnic parties, punting trips, and group outings. (See Plates 2 and 3) As early as 1910, Gramophone Concerts were held in London's parks, organized by London County Council, with over forty being held in that summer alone. The *East London Advertiser* stated: 'The Gramophone concerts are doing in the direction of musical education what the free libraries are accomplishing in literature, and the picture galleries in art.'[14] Public concerts were given in large towns all over the country. However, it was not until the widespread availability of cheap, lightweight portables in the 1920s that ordinary people could overcome the difficulties inherent in moving the heavy and cumbersome horn

[13] W. Somerset Maugham, 'The Summing up' (1938), quoted in British Library, *Revolutions in Sound* (1988), 7.
[14] *His Master's Voice and Gramophone News*, Oct. 1910, p. 10.

models of the pre-war era. The portable gramophone, first introduced in 1914, revolutionized gramophone usage. The portable was standardized, mass produced, and cheap. By the mid-1920s a range of portables was available for only £3 to £9. This made it possible for day trippers and holiday makers, of whom there were an ever increasing number, to take popular music with them wherever and whenever they wanted. The portable gramophone also helped to stem the seasonal drop in sales of gramophones and records and gave the gramophone a great advantage over its rival, the wireless. Where outdoor music had been previously provided by guitars, concertinas, and banjos, now the gramophone took over. It was a thoroughly modern instrument and was seen as such. The *Gramophone and Talking Machine News*, the oldest gramophone journal in Britain, declared in 1925:

The gramophone is ubiquitous. It can be heard anywhere, and—in its portable form—taken anywhere. Where no band, orchestra or singers are available, music can be had and all the suggestions that music makes can be indulged in. In the old days when gramophones were not, people on pleasure bent had not the opportunities afforded us to-day . . . In these days motor cars, charabancs or some other form of mechanical traction convey parties, large or small, to their destination in a fifth of the time formerly occupied and with far more comfort and means of enjoyment. One of the principal of these means is the portable gramophone. Probably two or three of these delightful instruments will be taken out by different members of a party, and they will give pleasure which nothing but music will give.[15]

Thus the gramophone had another role in interwar British life, as a social instrument for use out of doors, providing musical entertainment when people were on holiday, on works outings, or day tripping. It was difficult to get away from gramophones and gramophone records once the portable had become popular—a cause of annoyance to many. The use of the gramophone out of doors was important for two distinct reasons. First, it tended to kill the provision of music by individuals. Of course, live music making still persisted but, given the choice between a badly played accordion or a gramophone record, an increasing number of people chose the record. The gramophone was eroding personal music making and replacing 'active' musical entertainment with a more passive form. Secondly, the gramophone was making itself felt at a social level. Gramophone dances, in and out of doors, were another aspect of the increasing popularity of popular music in the interwar period. Gramophone records

[15] *GTMN*, July 1925, p. 246.

of the dance bands, public dance halls, and the wireless broadcasts of dance music all converged to create an unprecedented supply of popular music based cultural activity.

The gramophone made it possible to make music easily in a variety of community societies and associations, and people thought it both useful and beneficial. In London, Llewellyn Smith noted how the interest in dance music led to the development of numerous clubs where people, mostly young males, listened to gramophone records of their favourite bands and talked about their relative merits.[16] The unemployed were also involved. Rowntree noted that three York clubs organized a 'social' one evening a week which included a gramophone concert together with tea and soup. It is likely that similar facilities existed at the many unemployment clubs all over Britain. Other social centres also provided facilities for listening to gramophone records.[17] In 1935, Mrs Stanley Baldwin made an appeal for used gramophone records for a number of refuge and social clubs for women in the London area. The gramophone was even found afloat, providing competition for centuries of sea shanties and naval musical tradition. According to *Lloyd's List and Shipping Gazette* in 1927, 'It is a poor ship that has not its own gramophone nowadays, and sailormen are even keener than the average to make the best of one of their few means of recreation.'[18]

The gramophone also moved into other public spheres. Experiments were conducted with amplified radiograms in dance halls, serving as an early precursor to the 'discothèque'. The cost of a radiogram to the dance hall was considerably less than that of engaging musicians and so during the depression they became an attractive proposition. By 1930, for example, Provincial Cinematograph Theatres were employing radiograms in their Tottenham Palais dance hall and Astoria Ballroom, in place of dance orchestras.[19] Others followed but, despite the economic advantages, the idea never really caught on with the dancing public. The *Melody Maker* criticized the development, describing the dancers at the Tottenham Palais as 'miserable soulless automatons'.[20] Brass and military bands also found the gramophone challenging some of their traditional employment venues. Amplification and the loudspeaker meant that the gramophone was employed by public bodies at sports meetings, dirt-tracks, football clubs, skating rinks, cinemas, and large garden

---

[16] See Chapter 8 below for development of these 'Rhythm Clubs'.
[17] *GR*, July 1929, p. 169.   [18] *Records*, Jan. 1927, p. 141.
[19] *MM*, Dec. 1930, p. 1019.   [20] Ibid. 1019.

parties and fêtes. The advantages were numerous. One northern football club secretary explained that, by the use of loudspeakers, 'Everybody, even in the biggest crowd can hear music.' Another commented, 'Amplified records play what we want, when we want, and where we want.'[21] Mechanical music could also perform without breaks, and provided greater variety than the modest repertoire of the average band. The gramophone was thus able to provide music and entertainment in a considerable variety of public locations.

2.2 The music and marketing policies of the gramophone companies

The impact of the gramophone on music and the popular music industry was, to a great extent, linked to its technological progress and to the way in which it was deliberately marketed as a musical instrument. The market for the gramophone had to be newly created at the end of the nineteenth century and, in so doing, the gramophone companies adopted sophisticated long-term marketing strategies. The key to successful sales, the companies thought, was to get people to take the gramophone seriously and to demonstrate successfully its potential as a disseminator of 'high' culture. This search for respectability and the desire to be taken seriously prompted the development of new technology in sound recording and reproduction and had a major impact on the music production policies of the key manufacturers.

When the gramophone first came to Britain in c.1891 it was regarded, at best, as an amusing children's toy. For example, the first gramophones were imported by the toy firm Parkins and Gotto of Oxford Street, London, and one of their adverts for the new contraption typifies the condescending way in which many first treated the gramophone:

We had the pleasure of hearing one of these machines recite 'Twinkle Twinkle Little Star' in tones so absurd, that it was impossible not to laugh. It would prove an excellent antidote to a rainy day in the nursery.[22]

The limitations of technology at the time meant that the quality of sound reproduction was poor, the playing time of the records was short, and the machine had to be cranked continually, leading to fluctuations in the speed at which the record revolved. From these crude beginnings few

---

[21] *MM*, May 1929, p. 507.   [22] British Library, *Revolutions in Sound*, 3.

people would have imagined that the gramophone would have a major impact on musical culture. Indeed, few would have even dared to classify the gramophone as a musical instrument, for it was little more than an interesting piece of technology. The development of technology, aggressive promotion, and the pertinacious courting of the musical establishment by the gramophone companies were to transform its fortunes.

Before the introduction of a viable system of electrical recording in 1925, the gramophone depended on 'acoustic' technology. Many musical instruments, especially strings, could not be recorded properly on the acoustic system due to the limited frequencies that were reproduced; high-pitched women's voices failed to register and many of those instruments that did record were not recognizable. It took several years before the piano could be recorded adequately. Such technical restrictions fostered a considerable number of innovations designed to overcome them. Certain instruments were substituted with those which did record well; for example, the bassoon took the part of the cello, and a brass tuba would play the bass part. In addition, a whole range of musical instruments were developed solely for use on gramophone recordings. The 'Stroh' range of string instruments employed soundboxes and horns, so that sound could be amplified and directed more efficiently into the recording horn used in the recording studio. Orchestras were crammed into tiny spaces to concentrate sound and music stands suspended from the ceiling to prevent vibration. Joe Batten, a recording manager for Columbia, recalls the chaos of these early recording sessions:

The real perplexity of a recording session was to get singer and instrumentalists as close to the all-too-small horn as possible. The singer had the premier place . . . with the violins a foot away, the bassoon midway between his mouth and the recording horn, the clarinets perched on high stools eight feet from the ground with the bells of each instrument six inches away from his right ear, and the flute standing a foot behind him. Only the cornets and the trombone were kept a respectable distance, the cornets standing 10ft away, and the trombones, perched on stools like the clarinets, twelve feet away.[23]

In addition, discs had a short playing time of only three to four minutes. Such limitations impeded artistic freedom and had a substantial impact on the recording output of gramophone companies. Whereas long 'serious' musical works, featuring large orchestras, were virtually impossible to record, certain classical works, such as Bazzini's *Dance of the Elves*,

---

[23] J. Batten, *Joe Batten's Book: The Story of Sound Recording* (1956), 36.

became popular because they were convenient to record. Similarly, large numbers of 'light' recordings were made featuring the banjo, concertina, cornet, glockenspiel, piccolo, and xylophone, all of which recorded well.

Complaints about the technology were widespread. As late as July 1921 Ulric Daubeny, writing in the conservative *Musical Times*, was able to comment:

> In the early phonograph, it may be remembered, all the sounds were absurdly artificial, because lacking in depth. The modern gramophone has enormously improved upon this, but still the fault remains: its tone is palpably artificial . . . when it comes actually to be compared with the pianoforte, the violin, or any other instrument. In what quartet does the [gramophone] 'cello really give the same sensation of deep sound as does an actual 'cello? In what record does the majestic, rich-toned trombone really sound as such? . . . the quartet record is really a high-pitched violin solo, with plenty of surface scratching and occasional indiscriminate mutterings from the 'cello.[24]

Several technical advances made the gramophone a more serious prospect as the period progressed.[25] The development of the spring motor in *c.*1894 by the American Eldridge R. Johnson greatly improved the means of propulsion, allowing a regular speed to be attained, thus improving the fidelity of reproduction. In Britain this was introduced on the 'Improved Gramophone' (known as the 'Trademark') produced by the Gramophone Company from 1900. In 1903 the 'tone arm' was invented (which carried the weight of the horn) improving sound quality immensely and allowing the horn to grow. Pressure grew for the record manufacturers to produce louder, longer, better-sounding products, and progress was rapid. By the outbreak of the First World War, the burgeoning number of gramophone companies had contributed greatly to research and development, and innovations such as the portable gramophone and better recording processes made the gramophone more attractive. Gramophone development after the war was mainly cosmetic, with an increase in the range of machines, from small machines like the Decca portable to the largest cabinet machines (some with electrical motors, but still using acoustic reproduction). There were several improvements in record technology, such as Columbia's 'New Process' laminated record introduced in 1923, which greatly reduced surface noise and made reproduction more realistic. Acoustic machines (still in production until the late 1950s) had, by the end of the 1920s, achieved a

---

[24] *Musical Times*, July 1921, p. 478.
[25] Information in this section is taken from British Library, *Revolutions in Sound*, 10–16.

clarity of reproduction few would have imagined possible in the earliest days of the gramophone.

However, the development of electrical recording was the most important advance. The first commercially viable electric system was released in 1925 and pioneered by the Americans. In that year, Joseph Maxfield developed the 'Western Electrical System' and the first electrically recorded discs from America appeared in Britain. In the same year, the first all-electric disc player, the Panatrope, appeared from Brunswick in America and there was considerable market pressure to incorporate radios into gramophones. The first radiogram in Britain, the HMV model 520, appeared in 1929, to be followed in the 1930s by scores of models at all prices, both from the gramophone companies and from radio companies. The 'record player', a turntable requiring connection to a radio for reproduction and amplification, made its appearance in 1931.

The effects of electrical recording and reproduction on the fortunes of the gramophone industry and on its cultural impact were enormous. The industry witnessed a major revolution as the old technology was replaced by the new records and machines. All the gramophone companies began a major electrical recording programme. Artists and instruments were recorded with greater clarity than ever before and the microphone enabled greater artistic freedom in the recording studio. The result was a rapid expansion of its audience.

In addition to the development of technology, gramophone companies deliberately courted professional musicians and critics in an attempt to improve their sales and gain serious recognition. Concerted efforts were made to acquire 'prestige' and this was done by the development of impressive 'serious music' catalogues. At HMV the main responsibility for this campaign lay with the International Artists Department, under recording manager Fred Gaisberg, who controlled the classical HMV Red Label celebrity series.[26] This label had been created with the specific aim of making the gramophone record, and the Gramophone Company in particular, socially acceptable. Gaisberg, a sound engineer and impresario, toured Europe, India, and the Far East capturing the music of local artists on disc and winning the recording contracts of celebrities for the Gramophone Company. His first major coup was to persuade the Italian tenor Enrico Caruso to allow recordings to be made of him in Milan, in 1902. The effect of this was substantial, as Joe Batten recalled:

[26] For a full discussion of Gaisberg's career see F. W. Gaisberg, *Music on Record* (1946).

Hitherto ostracised by cultured people, the recording of Caruso's voice in 1902 had induced a reversion of taste . . . a new public was being created for the gramophone, a public which cared for music for its own sake . . . Caruso had persuaded a section of the buying public to discriminate in the records it acquired . . .[27]

In the years following the first Caruso recordings, Gaisberg built up HMV's classical catalogue, signing and recording important international performers such as Beniamino Gigli, Nellie Melba, Feodor Chaliapin, John McCormack, and Fritz Kreisler. Such artists were tempted into the recording studio by lucrative royalty based contracts and advances, potential world audiences, and the chance of artistic immortality.

The orchestral repertoire of the gramophone companies was also increased substantially. The first orchestral records in Britain were issued in 1909 but at first only abridged excerpts of musical works were available. Three-minute segments of serious works were not well received. In 1913, Beethoven's Fifth Symphony performed by Nikisch and the Berlin Philharmonic was the first complete symphony to be recorded. Then, in 1915 Kreisler and Zimbalist played Bach's Double Concerto with a string quartet. Such works would be issued on four or five double-sided records, requiring considerable winding of the gramophone and changing of needles. The first complete string quartet to be issued in Britain, Brahms's Op. 51 No. 1, played by the Catterall Quartet, appeared in 1923.

Despite the technical limitations, by the end of the First World War the gramophone was becoming an influence in the musical culture of the country. The rapid developments in technology after the war saw its influence expand further. The musical worth of records was being taken seriously in the press by competent critics who had previously ridiculed them and many artists who had hitherto considered themselves superior to the 'vulgar' gramophone were now eager for contracts. The arrival of the *Gramophone* in 1923 was another major coup for the campaign to give status to the new machine. It was the world's first journal concerned solely with the discussion of gramophone records and provided intelligent and informed reviews of latest record releases and discussion of developments in the industry. Its editor, Compton Mackenzie, established links with many serious musicians and through his devotion to the instrument was able to imbue the gramophone with a degree of cultural respectability previously denied it.

[27] Batten, *Joe Batten's Book*, 37–8.

Yet it was through popular music that the gramophone and recordings eventually became universally popular and it was in this sphere that the industry made most of its profits. Despite this, the relationship between gramophone companies and popular music was an awkward one. The period witnessed a transformation in attitudes towards popular music by gramophone and record companies.[28] During the 1920s, when business was continually expanding, the gramophone companies' attitudes toward popular music must be judged in the context of their search for respectability. Although sales of classical music were generally poor and loss making, such music was central to the industry's long-term strategy of winning over the middle classes. In such a climate, popular music was seen as a 'necessary evil'. 'Necessary' because it sold well, 'evil' because of its associations with 'low' culture and 'vulgarity'. By the 1930s, the attitude was changing, as exemplified by the relative newcomer Decca, which boldly flaunted its popular music catalogue. This was due to the changed circumstances brought about by the depression, by which time the quick profits to be made from popular music recordings were the main target of struggling record companies.

One measure of the earliest attitudes of gramophone and record companies towards popular music can be seen in their classification of particular music genres. In the Gramophone Company, for example, the decisions as to what label different types of music would be released on represented an attempt to categorize music on social grounds. The highest on this scale was the HMV Red Label, which was for classical music, followed by the normal HMV label for lesser classics and superior light popular music then the magenta HMV label for light music, and, at the bottom, the budget Zonophone label for most variety and music-hall records.

As the major gramophone and record companies were centrally managed, the availability of certain music was to some extent dependent upon the tastes of those at the centre. If particular styles of music were disliked by these managers, then not many recordings were made. This was true of jazz music in particular which, although available in Britain on the HMV, Columbia, Parlophone, and Brunswick labels, was poorly represented in terms of volume. Widespread recording and promotion of jazz in the 1920s ran counter to their attempts at 'respectability'.

---

[28] For much of this information I am indebted to Dmitri Coryton and the EMI Music Archives.

Paradoxically, however, the catalogues of all the record companies offered a huge variety of popular and light music styles, and their provision increased as the period progressed. As has been noted, 'light music' initially occupied considerable space in the catalogues of most record companies due to the fact that the instruments associated with its production were among the most easily recordable. Ballads, comic songs, and band records were the mainstay of early record catalogues. Music-hall artists were also amongst the first 'celebrities' who were prepared to record and HMV's earliest catalogues included Dan Leno, Eugene Stratton, Gus Ellen, and Albert Chevalier. Harry Lauder was one of the first performers who saw the potential of records as a fillip to his career and he recorded extensively for the Zonophone label. Popular selections from the musical theatre were also featured heavily in the record catalogues, boosted by a rise in popularity of such entertainment during the First World War (see Plate 4). As the period progressed and the audience for gramophones and records became less exclusive, even more popular music was included in the catalogues of major companies and, as we have seen, new labels were designed specifically to cater for it.

The sale of gramophone records of popular music was greatly aided by the spread of the 'dance craze' following the First World War (see Plate 5).[29] Columbia was one of the first companies to realize the possibilities of the new developments in popular music and the company had an important impact on the spread of new musical styles. In 1912 it issued the first ragtime records in Britain and it remained ahead of most of its rivals in the provision of dance music. Columbia's bands included Billy Cotton, Jack Payne, Henry Hall, Harry Roy, the Savoy Orpheans, Fletcher Henderson, Guy Lombardo, and others. Through the Parlophone label it issued the best in American jazz and dance music, with innovations such as the introduction in 1929 of the first 'Rhythm Style Series'. In November 1919, the HMV label issued recordings of the Original Dixieland Jazz Band, the first ever recordings of jazz. Due to its ties with Victor, HMV had access to some of the finest examples of the new music and this, together with records of British dance bands, laid the way for an explosion in demand for popular music records.

To secure the best possible standards of performance and to enable them to keep abreast of trends in popular music, the record companies employed important popular musicians to oversee production of their popular music catalogues. Carroll Gibbons, the leader of one of the most

---

[29] See Chapters 5, 6, and 7 for a full discussion of the dance craze.

popular dance bands, the Savoy Orpheans, was musical director at HMV from 1928 to 1929, when he was replaced by composer and bandleader Ray Noble, who was musical director until 1934. Bert Firman, another important dance band figure, was musical director for the Zonophone Record Company from 1928 to 1931. Roy Fox was appointed as Decca's musical adviser in 1931 and at Edison Bell, Harry Hudson, a prolific dance band recording artist, was musical director from 1927 to 1934. At British Homophone, Charles 'Nat' Star was dance music director from 1928 to 1934, and Jay Wilbur, another important studio dance bandleader, was musical director to the Crystalate Company from 1930 onwards.[30]

The increasing energy record companies devoted to popular music catalogues was due, principally, to the fact that popular music sold. Popular music was the engine of commercial expansion and profits were used to finance the more prestigious classical recordings described above. Even Sir Hugh Allen of the Incorporated Society of Musicians, a fierce opponent of the gramophone, defended the gramophone companies' popular music policies against criticism that they were 'purposely devised to administer to the poor, but financially secure, taste', with the following justification:

It may readily be admitted that the recording companies have published and sold as many of these 'repellent, devastating and sordid noises' as they could, but it must be remembered that without the financial help of what is loosely called jazz we should never have had the symphonies of Beethoven or Bach's Mass in B minor . . .[31]

Similarly, Louis Sterling of EMI was later to comment 'Boiled Beef and Carrots paid for Beethoven.'

Thus, the record companies reached an uneasy compromise with their recording policies during this period, especially in the 1920s, torn between a long-term 'aesthetic' approach to maximizing profits and one based solely on the short-term profit motive. The former encouraged 'prestige' recordings, the latter pushed popular music for all it was worth. Columbia and the Gramophone Company were particularly schizophrenic, offering plenty of the finest popular music artists, but were more concerned with promoting their classical output. Only Decca was prepared to go all out for brash exploitation of its popular music catalogue

---

[30] See B. Rust and S. Forbes, *British Dance Bands on Record 1911 to 1945* (1989).
[31] *Gramophone*, Feb. 1930, p. 389.

and this was because it was born during the Depression and in part because HMV had the other market cornered. Edward Lewis, after touring the country in 1931 to see how Decca's records were selling with the dealers, believed that the only way to expand business was to sign up big names and advertise them aggressively. His 'big names' were all popular music artists and Lewis spearheaded his promotion campaign in the press with dance band leaders Jack Hylton and Roy Fox, using the slogan 'Leading Artists—Lower Prices'.[32] As the record slump continued, it served to focus the minds of other recording managers and boardroom executives who increasingly abandoned classical catalogues in favour of the better-selling popular music. For a brief period in the early 1930s, the new EMI combine began to rationalize its classical music output and Columbia, in particular, deleted many works and halted major recording initiatives. HMV continued to expand its business in this market but largely because it operated a virtual monopoly over the supply of classical recordings. Thus the 1930s witnessed the increasing primacy of the profit motive and an appeal to 'popular tastes' in this increasingly important area of cultural production.

2.3 The cultural impact of the gramophone

The cultural effects of the gramophone were numerous. The sizeable audience created for the gramophone meant that a huge amount of popular music was available on a scale not seen before. A rapid commercialization and Americanization of the nature, style, and content of popular music occurred and the ascendancy of mechanical music led to less live music making. Both of these developments were seen by many as detrimental to the survival of British musical creativity but in reality a healthy 'native' musical culture was being actively encouraged by the spread of the gramophone.

With the mechanization of music, the productivity of the musician was dramatically altered. Since the eighteenth century, although the Industrial Revolution and mechanization had increased productivity in the majority of industries, the productivity of a string quartet and other musicians had remained relatively unchanged. The only way to increase profits for musicians was either to increase charges or increase audience sizes. Hence, music-hall performers would work relentless schedules,

[32] See E. R. Lewis, *No C.I.C.* (1956), 27–30.

taking on more performances in larger theatres. Clarity of articulation was vital to success and the music-hall artist worked hard to overcome the limitations on productivity and earnings. Once music was mechanized (as it was by the gramophone) then at last the musician could achieve the productivity that the Industrial Revolution had brought to other workers. The gramophone, radio, and talking film revolutionized the economics of the performing arts. For the first time music could be mass produced, standardized, and repeated rapidly and efficiently.[33]

The gramophone widened access to music of all sorts and provided an unprecedented supply of high-quality entertainment at an increasingly affordable price. The gramophone accelerated the pace of the popular music industry and recording catalogues grew quickly as competing record companies tried to offer the best selections of popular music and the best popular music stars. Thus the demand for new material and talent was substantial. Whereas a song could take months and even years to reach a wide audience via the music halls, the issuing of songs on record meant that they were available throughout the country more or less instantly. Sheet music had previously allowed widespread exposure of particular titles but the gramophone record's capacity for such exposure was far greater. Although it was soon superseded by the radio as the major source of new popular songs for the majority of people, for a brief period in the 1920s it was supreme in this respect. Even after radio had developed, the gramophone remained an important medium for the promotion of new stars and new song titles. Indeed, the two media were interconnected and gramophone records were broadcast on the radio from its start. The gramophone was of major importance to the careers of popular music artists. For those already established, a recording career increased revenue and created an opportunity to reach an audience of unprecedented size. Those popular music stars who utilized the gramophone were able to break into markets that previously would have been denied them. Thus, artists with strong regional appeal, such as George Formby and Gracie Fields, were able to become truly 'national' stars with the help of the gramophone. Without the advance audience created by recordings, this would have been a lot more difficult. Significantly, it also gave performers the chance of artistic immortality; their performances would outlive them. New artists were also brought to public attention a

---

[33] For a full discussion of productivity issues in the arts, see W. J. Baumol and W. G. Bowen, *Performing Arts, the Economic Dilemma: A Study of Problems Common to Theater, Opera, Music, and Dance* (New York, 1966).

great deal more effectively and speedily than was previously possible. The vast resources available to the large gramophone companies and their use of sophisticated marketing campaigns allowed certain artists to be thrust into the limelight. Importantly, the decision as to what music and which stars to promote was increasingly taken over by those who directed the gramophone companies. This is particularly significant given the degree of concentration that took place in the industry. Such domination by a handful of companies had far reaching effects on employment patterns and artistic freedom within the popular music industry.[34]

The gramophone also helped to unify and standardize the previously disparate threads of the popular music industry. The creation of large recording repertoires and catalogues by the record companies brought together diverse genres of music and styles of performance and created a 'single' source from which popular music could be selected and chosen at will. The gramophone and gramophone records were also part of an increasing trend towards uniformity in leisure and cultural activities. The gramophone allowed anyone in Britain who could afford it to listen to exactly the same interpretations and selections of musical work as everyone else, regardless of region and class.

The gramophone record also permitted music to cross national barriers more easily than ever before with the result that national and regional cultures became exposed to and mixed with many foreign musical heritages. The largest recording companies, as described, were truly multinational. This was reflected in the cosmopolitan nature of their catalogues. Despite their often conservative policies, the major British companies had, via their ties to American companies, access to the catalogues of the very latest styles and trends in popular music. Columbia, for example, having bought the massive American Okeh catalogues in 1925, was given access to a huge array of popular, jazz, dance, and other American forms of music (see Plate 7). Okeh's artists included Jimmy and Tommy Dorsey as well as Louis Armstrong. It also acquired French popular music artists when it took over Pathé in 1928, including Edith Piaf, Jean Sablon, Lucienne Boyer, Charles Trenet, and Tino Rossi. Decca, too, had access to the new American idiom through its acquisition of the Brunswick catalogue. The Gramophone Company, through its partnership with the American Victor Company, was also able to offer the British public a wide selection of American popular music (see Plate 6). Specialist gramophone shops were also established which imported

---

[34] See Chapter 8 below.

foreign records which were not featured in the catalogues of the British multinationals.

Through the gramophone new musical styles were able to spread more rapidly and more completely than before. Although new popular cultural influences had been brought to Britain through sheet music and musical theatre in the age before the gramophone, the transforming potential of gramophone records was far in excess of anything that preceded it. Jazz and dance music were the first musical forms to be widely disseminated by the two new forms of mass communication, records and radio. There were few visits from American bands, the source of jazz, and the gramophone was thus extremely important in spreading the unfamiliar music. The transforming effect of the gramophone on musical style was pointed out by Edgar Jackson, the pro-jazz critic of the *Melody Maker*, in 1936:

Has it ever struck you that if hadn't been for the gramophone we might still be listening to the Victorian brass and string bands and dancing to the rhythms of the polka and the Viennese waltz?

If you think this is an exaggeration, ask yourself how else the American idiom, on which is based the main portion of our popular music today, would have reached here.

There is the radio, you will say.

Well and good, there is: but where would our radio artists have got the idea from? Listening to American broadcasts? A few might have, but not enough to CHANGE THE TASTE OF A NATION. Nor could the man in the street have familiarised himself with the subject, from the same source, for the times at which American programmes can be heard have not inspired the trade to attempt to make cross-Atlantic reception a universal pastime. It remains even today no more than a hobby for a few enthusiasts with short-wave sets, who are prepared to sit up nightly long after most of us have been only too happy to embrace the comfort of our pillows.

But what about personal appearances by American artists, you may ask?

True, they might have given some of us an inkling to what was happening: but it takes an artist in the flesh a relatively long time to appear before even a portion of the community. Further, it is questionable if more than a handful would have found their way to our shores had not the gramophone created an advance demand for them.

Thus, while a minority of us might have found chances to become intrigued (had we been able to appreciate sufficiently from only a few hearings) by what we would have looked upon as a freak music, the majority would as yet barely have felt its influence, and would probably be wallowing in the aforementioned Victorian instrumentation and its now almost forgotten modes of interpretation.[35]

[35] *MM*, 8 Feb. 1936, p. 11.

The gramophone was able to transform tastes and create an audience for a music based on recordings rather than live performance. This was highly significant for British musical professionals as they had to mimic the style of their American counterparts, whilst also having to learn the new forms from recordings. This led to resentment among older professional musicians whose long-standing training in 'British' styles and methods was soon pushed aside by the large numbers of new musicians who flooded the market in an attempt to satisfy the public demand for jazz.[36] This demand had been created by the gramophone.

Dance music and jazz records, however technically limited, brought American musical styles, American accents, and American vocal mannerisms to the British people long before the talking pictures of the 1930s. The gramophone also preceded the radio as a major disseminator of the American idiom. The gramophone's importance in this process was clear. Valaida, a black American female singer starring in the visiting *Blackbirds* show in 1935, commented:

what amazes me most about England is your knowledge and appreciation of our American music . . . Over here everybody seems to like it, and I have met dozens of English boys who know more about jazz than the people who play it. And it is all because of gramophone records . . . You can guess how surprised I was to find . . . a public that knows all the best musicians and that can recognise their styles of playing just from records.[37]

Despite the major changes occurring in the popular music industry, however, such trends are easy to overstate. Older musical forms did persist and although popular music became increasingly Americanized, a separate British interpretation evolved. The British dance bands appropriated the American idiom and adapted it to the relatively conservative tastes of the British public.[38] The fact that this was also done through the medium of the gramophone record was significant. In the decade after the First World War the gramophone was one of the most important elements in the transformation of British popular music from its Edwardian and Victorian roots to a more American style.

Conclusion

The gramophone and gramophone records, then, became a significant element of both middle and working-class culture in the 1920s and 1930s.

[36] See Chapter 5 below.   [37] *Hot News*, Apr. 1935, p. 10.
[38] See Chapter 8 below.

Arguably, they anticipated the radio in contributing to the movement towards the home and domesticity in the interwar period. An image and practice of intimate and private enjoyment built up around them which served to re-socialize relationships at home and to stabilize and make safe a popular culture that was sometimes regarded as dangerous. At the same time, the portable gramophone enabled recorded music to be taken almost anywhere. Whilst the pleasures of this 'private', 'hobby based' recreation were initially restricted to a middle-class audience, lower prices and rising real wages meant that such 'suburban' lifestyles were able to spread to those lower down the social scale.

The impact of the gramophone on the popular music industry was directly linked to the technical progress of the media and the production policies of the key record producers. Despite a concern to establish cultural respectability, a concern which could have stifled output, the American ties of the largest gramophone and record manufacturers were of major importance to the popular music industry. The gramophone revolutionized the provision of popular music in Britain. It gave rise to an unprecedented supply and variety of music and it also transformed the style and nature of the music.

The popularity of the gramophone meant that music making increasingly became part of the growing consumer economy. In an important sense, the audience were little more than consumers and, as such, their influence over the music went no further than deciding what to buy or what not to buy. If people demanded more of a certain genre, style, or performer, then the market mechanism responded by supplying it. Unlike the music making of the amateur, the gramophone offered a pre-recorded interpretation of a song or tune and there was little room for alternative interpretation. Although various versions of popular songs or classical works were available on records, there was a limited choice. Creativity was not completely eradicated, however, as subversive, counter-cultural versions of popular songs evolved, based on topical events or rude jokes. Despite this, the gramophone record began a process of standardization and commercialization of popular culture— making the once spontaneous into a pre-recorded, packaged product.

The British gramophone industry during the interwar period also transformed the popular music industry by introducing American business methods on a wide scale. The gramophone companies' strategies for marketing and producing popular music were very market driven, despite the notion that popular music output should not upset the drive for respectability. Although the long-term search for respectability by the gramophone companies meant that anything which was morally, socially, or politically unacceptable to the 'elite' was officially not allowed, record companies could turn a 'blind eye'. The production of dance music was a prime example, for although it caused considerable concern amongst the elite, it was the most profitable line in the record companies' catalogues. As the *Gramophone Year Book* for 1920 noted, whatever the moral concerns, the profits to be made from dance music were too good to miss:

The arguments in press and pulpit over the decency or otherwise of certain dances, such as Jazz, the slamming of them by church and society, have all tended to increase interest. Whether it is a good thing for society or not, the fact remains that in many towns and cities, and even in rural communities, interest in dancing has developed into an unprecedented craze. The talking machine business has benefited from this craze as no other business has.[39]

Thus, the gramophone and gramophone record marked a change in the criteria against which certain judgements of cultural worth were made. The production of 'gramophone popular music' ultimately involved the ascendancy of the profit motive over previous criteria based on aesthetic judgement.

[39] Anon., *The Gramophone Year Book and Diary 1920* (1919), 95.

3

RADIO, CINEMA, AND POPULAR MUSIC IN INTERWAR BRITAIN

Introduction

In addition to the gramophone, two other technology based entertainments, radio and cinema, had a significant effect on the popular music industry in interwar Britain. Both of these new media, especially the radio, depended greatly on music for their appeal. Together they were able to provide access to entertainment and music for all but the very poorest members of society, widening the range and quality of musical entertainment for this majority beyond even the gramophone. In addition, they were to transform the world in which music and musicians operated, adding to the commodification of popular music already begun by the gramophone.

Radio in Britain was dominated by the BBC but it was not the only provider. Although commercial broadcasting was forbidden, entrepreneurs and advertisers circumvented restrictions by establishing broadcasts from continental stations, whose signals could be received in Britain. Such stations were run solely to make profit and advertisers discovered that popular music sold products. By focusing on an area where the BBC was seen to be deficient, the commercial radio broadcasters established a reputation for promoting popular music. The output of these stations has previously received only scant attention from historians but it was of great importance to the popular music industry. Also largely ignored is the British film industry's output of musical films. Often of negligible aesthetic quality, British musical films were, nevertheless, an extremely important element of British popular culture during the interwar period and will be considered in detail.

3.1 Popular music and the BBC

The BBC was the main broadcaster in Britain during the interwar period. Officially the sole provider of broadcast programmes, it was established in the early 1920s by British officials who were concerned about the growth of the new radio medium among amateurs and who were determined not to follow America's commercial example. The British government placed broadcasting, therefore, under control of the Post Office. A syndicate called the British Broadcasting Company was formed and made its first broadcast from the London station 2LO on 14 November 1922. In 1926 the company was given a royal charter which instituted the British Broadcasting Corporation. The Corporation was artistically autonomous but dependent for finances on licence fees. Its management—a chairman and eight governors with a director-general as chief executive—was appointed by the Crown. The BBC monopoly was not formally broken until the advent of commercial television in 1954, although it faced a strong threat from commercial radio stations in the 1930s.

The success of radio was phenomenal. In 1922 there had been some 35,000 wireless licences; by 1926 there were already well over 2 million and 9 million by 1939.[1] Initially, radio listening was a cumbersome business involving crystal sets, headphones, and complicated aerials. The attraction of radio grew with the development of the 'valve' set and loudspeakers and, by 1939, the 'friend in the corner' reached almost 34 million people—nearly three-quarters of all households. However, as with the gramophone and other consumer durables, radio sets were at first a luxury item and out of reach of a large section of the population. As production methods improved and technology advanced, prices fell. Another factor in the increasing popularity of radio was the improvement in the choice of programmes which, by the mid-1930s, provided an eclectic mix of drama, classical music and variety, sport, light orchestral music, and dance bands.

From its earliest days, the BBC's broadcasts were dominated by music. Analysis of the output of BBC programmes in selected weeks over the period 1927 to 1938 shows clearly that music was the most widely broadcast type of programme.[2] Non-serious or popular music, as represented

---

[1] A. Briggs, *The History of Broadcasting in the United Kingdom*, rev. edn. (5 vols., 1995), i. 17 and ii. 6.

[2] These and subsequent figures calculated from listings ibid. ii. 34–5, 52.

by the categories 'dance music' and 'light music', was dominant. In 1927 nearly 46 per cent of all programmes broadcast were of popular music. This 'popular' domination was to continue throughout the period. In 1930 'popular music' made up just under a third of the National Programme's output, and nearly 56 per cent of Regional Programme output, falling to over 30 per cent and 46 per cent respectively in 1936. It retained a strong presence on both programmes but fell slightly, to just over 27 per cent and 41 per cent, on National and Regional respectively in 1938. An additional source of music was contained in broadcasts of 'light entertainment' which included music-hall, vaudeville, cabaret, and revue acts. 'Light entertainment' made up a further 5.26 per cent of output in 1927, which in 1938 was 6.84 per cent on the National Programme and 7 per cent on the Regional Programme. If the figures are disaggregated it can be seen that 'light music' was the single most widely broadcast type of music followed by 'classical music' and 'dance music'.[3]

'Light music' was popular with most British listeners, being more populist than 'serious' classical music yet more conservative than modern dance and jazz music. It was a vague and peculiarly British category which included orchestral music, operetta, musical comedy, ballads, and café, restaurant, or cinema organ music and ranged from solo performance and palm court trios to small orchestral ensembles.[4] A range of music was played by such orchestras, from the Viennese waltzes of Franz Lehar to the light classics of Fritz Kreisler and even contemporary popular songs. One of the most popular 'light orchestras' was led by Albert Sandler, a violinist, whose widespread fame was achieved via numerous broadcasts from the Grand Hotel Eastbourne, from 1925 onwards. There were several other popular orchestras, most of which were small. The Gershom Parkington Quintette (the first to broadcast regularly) and quintets led by Lesley Bridgewater and Fred Hartley were particularly popular. Live outside broadcasts were made from orchestras and ensembles in cafés and restaurants throughout Britain. In the summer, regional programmes relayed light 'seaside music' from Whitby, Scarborough, Morecambe, Blackpool, and other seaside resorts.

---

[3] A full discussion of the programme output of the BBC has already been comprehensively handled in the following, from which much of the information in the following sections is taken: Briggs, *History of Broadcasting*, i. 228–70, ii. 24–172 and P. Scannell and D. Cardiff (ed.), *A Social History of Broadcasting* (Oxford, 1991), 181–216, 225–50. Thus only brief summaries are detailed here.

[4] In addition to the sources in n. 3, see also S. Briggs, *Those Radio Times* (1981), D. Gifford, *The Golden Age of Radio* (1985).

Sentimental songs and ballads were also featured widely. The Australian bass-baritone Peter Dawson was one of the most popular artists of this genre, his singing style surviving the huge changes in popular music brought about by jazz. Dawson's repertoire covered light songs, light classics, and music-hall songs. He was featured mainly in gramophone programmes, which had begun seriously in 1925 with the arrival of electrical recordings. The first 'disc jockey', Christopher Stone, started his popular early morning record recitals in 1927. Light operetta styles were also featured in BBC schedules and two of the most popular performers were the duettists Anne Ziegler and Webster Booth.

Military bands and brass bands were also popular. The BBC Military Band was formed under Dan Godfrey in 1924 to supplement the popular recordings by various Guards bands and the RAF band. Organ music was also popular and many cinema organists became household names. The most famous were Reginald Foort, who broadcast prolifically throughout the 1920s and 1930s; Reginald Dixon, who was resident at the Tower Ballroom, Blackpool, from 1938; and the BBC's resident organist Sandy McPherson, 1936–63.

The advent of regular broadcasting in the 1920s also opened the field to dance bands.[5] The first dance music programme went out in early 1923. Many leading hotels had excellent bands and outside broadcasts from hotels were to become the mainstay of dance music output throughout the entire period. The first outside broadcast by a dance band took place in May 1923. In the following year Henry Hall began broadcasting with his Gleneagles Hotel Orchestra and in 1925 Jack Payne was heard regularly with his Hotel Cecil Orchestra. The resident bands of the Savoy Hotel London—the Savoy Orpheans and the Savoy Havana Bands, who broadcast regularly from October 1923, were early favourites.

The BBC did much to sponsor the development of dance music. In 1928 it formed its own resident dance band and Jack Payne was appointed musical director. The band broadcast every weekday afternoon for four years, in addition to numerous evening shows, and Payne became a household name. Later in 1932, Henry Hall was appointed head of a new BBC Dance Orchestra, becoming as nationally famous as Payne had been.

By the early 1930s the BBC was providing a diet of dance music that proved incredibly popular. In regular late afternoon and late night slots

---

[5] In addition to the sources in n. 3, see also Briggs, *Those Radio Times*, A. McCarthy, *The Dance Band Era* (Radnor, Pa., 1982), J. Godbolt, *A History of Jazz in Britain 1919–50* (1984).

(10.30 to midnight), programmes were broadcast every day of the week but Sunday. Each band was allocated its own day and fans tuned in religiously. With a weekly appointment at the microphone guaranteed, the top dance bands were able to develop distinctive sounds and playing styles for themselves, from 'sweet' to 'hot', and from light to serious. The BBC, however, changed this pattern in 1937, aware that the favoured few bands were getting all the limelight. A new schedule was introduced with single compendium programmes starring various bands, but a public outcry forced the BBC to reintroduce its old late-night dance band pattern.

In 1937, the BBC formulated a new policy towards popular music as a whole, with special attention given to standards and taste in presentation. The week's output of dance music, which was around fifteen hours by this stage, was divided into different 'slots' designed to appeal to different audiences: music for dancing, music for entertainment, and music for the connoisseur. 'Music for dancing' was defined as strict tempo, straight, vocalist-free dance music and nightly outside broadcasts from hotel bands continued. 'Music for entertainment' was defined as dance music with unrestricted vocals of any popular songs and recognized the wide appeal of the dance band vocalist. This music was broadcast in the early evening and during the daytime. 'Music for the connoisseur' was in fact 'swing music', which the BBC, correctly, thought a minority taste. After a decade of hostility towards the 'hotter' sorts of music, the BBC wanted to inculcate a standard of taste and appreciation of quality in jazz music. Thus, specialist records were imported from America for a series of afternoon swing record recitals. There were also transatlantic relays of swing broadcasts featuring Benny Goodman, Chick Webb, and Duke Ellington.

The other major area of popular entertainment and music was variety and music hall.[6] BBC broadcasts featured a wide range of comedians, comic singers, impersonators, 'revue' artists, and satirists. Variety productions ranged from live broadcasts direct from theatres and music halls to studio-bound serials and brief sketches. Popular music was a key element in the success of such radio productions as singers and comedians were the most easily adaptable of music-hall performers for the radio.

The BBC had broadcast its first variety programme in January 1923 but early friction between the BBC and music-hall managers severely restricted the radio careers of stage and variety artists during the 1920s.

---

[6] In addition to the sources in n. 3, see also Briggs, *Those Radio Times*, Gifford, *The Golden Age of Radio*.

This ban was eventually lifted, however, and by the mid-1930s, despite further confrontations, the BBC was one of the largest providers of 'variety' acts in the country. The amount of 'variety' broadcast grew enormously. Before 1933, only 16 hours of variety were broadcast from London each month but by 1935 it was 44 hours a month and by 1936 it was 59 hours a month. By the end of the period, programmes such as *Palace of Varieties*, *Monday Night at Seven*, and the pioneering *Band Waggon* attracted large audiences.

The success of the BBC's variety output was largely because of the creation in 1930 of a separate 'Revue and Vaudeville Section' under John Watt. One of the earliest achievements of Watt's regime was the introduction of 'series' programmes. Four new series were developed; *Songs from the Shows* (1931), *Music Hall* (1932), the *White Coons' Concert Party* (1932), and the *Kentucky Minstrels* (1933). These achievements were built on by Eric Maschwitz, who was head of the new Variety Department from 1933 to 1937. Maschwitz developed the 'series' idea even further, commissioning new runs of existing shows and creating entirely new ones, the best known of which was *In Town Tonight*, hosted by Henry Hall. Maschwitz was instrumental in promoting new music-hall and variety stars and performers who made their name with the BBC, encouraged and nurtured by Maschwitz, included Sandy Powell, Clapham and Dwyer, Ronald Frankau, Elsie and Doris Waters, and Tommy Handley. In 1933 Maschwitz also established the new BBC Theatre at St George's Hall, complete with its own variety orchestra. This was used for the staging of variety and music-hall acts, complete with audiences, and provided a valuable source of 'live' material. Specially scripted late-night monthly 'revues' were also featured with sophisticated West End entertainers from the leading night clubs and restaurants providing entertainment. Satire was also introduced after 1934 in the occasional *Little Reviews* and *Monthly Reviews*.

Despite the BBC's excellent provision of popular and light music, there were constant criticisms of the Corporation's attitude towards popular music, both from within the music profession and by members of the general public. Particular areas of disgruntlement included the BBC's output of 'variety', and dance music; its Sunday output; and its general policy of 'educating' its listeners. The 'public service' ethos of the BBC was a source of significant contemporary debate. The development of critical awareness and the philosophy of self-improvement were a vital element of the public service ethos. The BBC wished to 'educate not entertain', advancing the causes of 'refinement' and 'culture', as exemplified by the 'best' in music, literature, art, and science. Access to such 'improving' influences was provided via the BBC's eclectic programming. Thus, although the BBC was a major provider of popular entertainment, it valued it only as part of a wider diet of uplifting and serious material. John Reith's own thoughts on 'entertainment' were set out in his book *Broadcast over Britain*:

To entertain means to occupy agreeably. Would it be urged that this is only effected by the broadcasting of jazz bands and popular music, or of sketches by humorists? I do not think that many would be found willing to support so narrow a claim as this . . . Enjoyment may be sought, on the other hand . . . as part of a systematic and sustained endeavour to recreate, to build up knowledge, experience and character, perhaps even in the face of obstacles.[7]

Many listeners liked such a policy, seeing it as the best way to serve the interest of millions of different listeners. 'FGH' from St Albans, for example, wrote: 'Enough of this perpetual groaning at the BBC . . . Listeners should realise that the BBC has a colossal task to suit everyone's requirements, and I have the courage to put forward the opinion that the programmes are set out with a wonderful sense of variety.'[8] Many others, however, disagreed. 'WB', a listener from Lichfield, complained that the BBC ignored the 'lowbrow':

Our Saturday night programmes are very sadly constructed. Variety always is featured at the wrong time. From the news until the dance music we get talks and heavy music. We have enough of these on Sunday; give us the enjoyment and excitement of a London Saturday night. Remember that there are 6,000,000 licence holders and not all *highbrow*.[9]

So which programmes were seen to be most deficient? Some indication of what radio audiences wanted is given in a *Radio Pictorial* ballot undertaken in 1934. The survey intended to discover readers' tastes in radio programmes and also invited suggestions for 'brightening' BBC broadcasts. The 1,000 plus respondents demanded—in order—more variety, more Sunday dance music, more plays, more running commentaries of public events, less military band music, and, finally, more talks by politicians.[10] More accurate reflections of the public's taste were given by the BBC's own research. Although the BBC kept abreast of the wants and mores of its audience via its journals the *Radio Times* and the *Listener* and

[7] Quoted in Briggs, *Those Radio Times*, 149.   [8] *RP*, 28 Mar. 1934, p. 2.
[9] Ibid. 20.   [10] *RP*, 11 May 1934, p. 21.

via listeners' correspondence, concerted and comprehensive efforts to find out the preferences of its listeners were not started until 1934 when its Listener Research Department was established. Tastes in popular entertainment were established by a 1938 survey of 2,000 listeners undertaken by the BBC's Variety Department.[11] Of those categories with which the majority of people were dissatisfied, the most prominent was 'variety'. This was followed by the organ music of Reginald Foort, a staple of Light Music output, of which people wanted more. There were also considered to be too few comedy programmes, such as *Radio Pie* and *Band Waggon*. Those categories of programmes with which most people were satisfied were musical comedy and dance music. Although this survey is a useful indication of tastes among sections of the BBC's audiences, it must be borne in mind that it was essentially a 'variety' biased audience. Fewer people were content with the BBC's output of dance music, for example, than is indicated in this survey.[12]

It was also the quality of dance music on the BBC which produced complaints. The campaign against the BBC's dance music policy was spearheaded by the *Melody Maker*, the broadsheet of dance band musicians. Since its establishment in 1926, the *Melody Maker* had striven for greater acceptance of dance music and in particular for more 'hot', jazz based music. The *Melody Maker* blamed the BBC's small budget for stifling dance bands' creative and artistic freedom. Dance musicians, via their press, also criticized the BBC for its periodic and often curious restrictions on dance music. For example, temporary bans on vocals were enforced to combat the spread of 'crooning'. Certain dance tunes were banned. The announcing of song titles was banned and in 1935 bans were imposed on 'scat singing' and the use of the word 'hot' to describe jazz.

There were other concerns. Some indications of what the general public considered was missing from the BBC's output can be gained from analysis of a cross-section of letters appearing in the popular *Radio Pictorial* magazine—even though letter writers are self-selecting. Ernest Barnard from London, for example, was concerned that, as the majority of working people left home before the day's broadcasting began and went to bed before the late-night dance music programme, the BBC was denying them entertainment. He continued:

[11] Results featured in *MM*, 18 June 1938, p. 2.
[12] For further views on dance music on the radio see M-O A: Directive Reply: 'Jazz 2, July 1939' and Directive Reply: 'Jazz, Jan. 1939'.

Is it quite fair to the bands to put them on the air when their real public are sleeping? Isn't it about time the BBC realised that the working-class people form a very big majority of their licence holders, and as such should certainly be catered for?[13]

Such sentiments were echoed by 'AKJ' from Woking, who demanded 'breakfast-time dance music':

As I am away from home all day, the only times I can listen-in are after six in the evening and before nine in the morning. I suppose this is the case with the majority of listeners; yet . . . the early morning is about the only time when the BBC is absolutely dead, dark, and silent! Why cannot the BBC . . . give listeners a little entertainment *at a time when they most want it.*[14]

The greatest complaints against the BBC, however, concerned Sunday broadcasting. In the early days of broadcasting there were no Sunday programmes until about 8 p.m., and then usually concerts of a serious nature. The *Radio Times* editorial of 6 February 1925 describes the sombre nature of Sunday broadcasting:

Normally there are no transmissions during church hours. This rule is rarely broken, and then only when a complete religious service is being broadcast. There are two hours of specially chosen music on Sunday afternoons. Then, in the evening, a short religious service is sent out from all studios, familiar hymns or metrical psalms are sung. Usually there is an anthem, and a fifteen minute address.[15]

There was definitely no room for popular or light music within such a scheme. By 1930 the pattern of Sunday broadcasting was beginning to relax a little. Evening orchestral concerts were introduced but they had to be worthy of serious attention. Chamber music, Bach cantatas, and Shakespeare plays were typical. The monotony of Sunday broadcasting was consistently attacked. Even though there was a slightly 'lighter' output as the decade progressed, there were still no Sunday morning programmes other than the Morning Service and the Weather Forecast until April 1938. Even then, the type of music programme transmitted 'represented the BBC's desire to lighten programmes without destroying the special nature of the day'.[16]

Such perceived gaps in provision were met by the commercial radio stations.

[13] *RP*, 9 Mar. 1934, p. 25.   [14] *RP*, 28 Mar. 1934, p. 20.
[15] Quoted in Briggs, *Those Radio Times*, 148.   [16] Quoted ibid. 149.

3.2 Commercial radio

The development of commercial radio broadcasting from the late 1920s provided an additional source of popular music entertainment. Broadcasts to Britain (by British programme makers using British 'stars') from continental stations such as Radio Normandie and Radio Luxembourg had substantial audiences, particularly on Sundays. They were popular throughout the country and not confined to any one region or class. By the mid-1930s they were providing a truly complete and 'national' service that offered a viable alternative to the BBC. Moreover, such stations appealed directly to the tastes of the working and lower-middle-class majority which made up their largest audiences. Popular music was central to this appeal.

Limited but regular commercial broadcasting to Britain began at the end of the 1920s, although occasional one-off broadcasts had been made some years earlier, such as a 1926 concert broadcast from the Eiffel Tower by Selfridges.[17] Despite the limited success of such experiments, in October 1928 a firm of radio manufacturers began a series of $1^1/_2$-hour Sunday concerts of light music from the Dutch station Hilversum, which continued until July 1930. These were followed from 1929 to 1931 with a series of two-hour concerts from Radio Toulouse. The broadcasts went out on Sunday, when the BBC service was most vulnerable. Both programmes were widely advertised in *World Radio* and the *Radio Times* and they gave considerable publicity to the idea of radio advertising. In August 1929, a private company of radio advertising contractors was formed called Radio Publicity Ltd. This was the first agency of its kind, created to canvass potential advertisers and produce programmes to be broadcast on continental stations. Radio Publicity produced an increasing number of sponsored programmes from Radio Paris and elsewhere. In October 1930, Radio Publicity found further stations willing to broadcast sponsored programmes in the Irish Free State. It ran a series of sponsored programmes for an hour a day (including weekdays) from Radio Dublin and Radio Cork.

The number of sponsored programmes grew rapidly in only a few years. Whereas British advertisers had bought a mere nine hours on the foreign air in 1928, by 1930 they were buying nearly 300 hours.[18] The time

---

[17] Much of the information in this section is taken from material in BBC WAC R34/961; E2/2/1; E2/2/2.

[18] BBC WAC R34/961 (1945), 5.

available was still, however, relatively small. Radio Paris never sold more than three to four hours to British advertisers on any single Sunday in 1930; Radio Toulouse never more than two; and Hilversum never more than one and a half hours.[19] Apart from Ireland, there was practically no radio advertising on weekdays. At this stage advertisers were unable to present a serious, continuous alternative programme to those provided by the BBC.

A substantial development in the history of commercial radio came with the formation of the International Broadcasting Company (IBC). The IBC was established in March 1930, financed by the man behind the early Selfridges broadcast, Captain Leonard Plugge (later Conservative MP for Chatham). The IBC's main object was to buy and sell 'time' on the air from foreign radio stations. By June 1930, the *Daily Express* reported that eighteen foreign stations had agreed to broadcast English programmes for the IBC, including Madrid, Brussels, Toulouse, Frankfurt, Milan, and Barcelona. Most of them were received very poorly by listeners in the UK.[20]

Of greater importance was the beginning of IBC broadcasts on a new French station, Radio Normandie, in October 1931.[21] Radio Normandie broadcast from Fécamp on the north coast of Normandy, and its 10 kW transmitter was able to give a good service to the whole south coast of England (its reception was, in fact, better than that of the BBC in these districts). Radio Normandie sold a small amount of time to the IBC, thus creating its first important foothold in the radio advertising field. The IBC's first Fécamp client, Philco, began programmes on Sunday 25 October 1931 consisting of popular gramophone records, presented in what the BBC saw as a 'blatant American' manner.[22] They caused a tremendous response. Early in 1932 the IBC followed up this minor coup by becoming the principal agent for the sale of hours from Radio Paris, securing over half of the English hours available on what remained the most popular Continental station for English listeners. They broadcast on Sundays programmes of dance music and variety, from 2–3 p.m. and 6–7 p.m. in deliberate contrast to the BBC's Sunday output.

The IBC continued to grow rapidly, increasing its foothold with Radio Normandie considerably and experimenting with other foreign stations. By mid-1933, the IBC commanded a significant proportion of time on

[19] Ibid. 6.   [20] Ibid. 8.
[21] BBC WAC E2/2/1, Memo 'Radio-Normandie', 11 Dec. 1935.
[22] Quoted in Briggs, *History of Broadcasting*, ii. 326.

Radio Normandie, Radio Toulouse, Radio Côte d'Azur, and Radio Ljubljana. English announcers were installed at all the stations working for the IBC. Although the number of advertisers was still small, the IBC was now broadcasting a total of sixty-five hours per week. Seventeen of these were on Sunday and forty-eight on weekdays, with Radio Normandie providing most (18½) hours.[23] This made it possible for the IBC to provide a service that could seriously compete with the BBC.

In the meantime, the potential for commercial radio increased substantially with the development of sponsored broadcasts from Radio Luxembourg. On 28 September 1930 the first concession for a wireless station was granted by the Grand Duchy of Luxembourg, with an option to raise revenue through advertising.[24] The transmitter, at 100 kW, was the most powerful in Europe, easily powerful enough to transmit programmes throughout most of Northern Europe, including Britain. The geographical location of Luxembourg was excellent in radio terms as it was at the centre of the region which had the largest radio audience; 80 per cent of the total number of radio sets in Europe were within a 1,000 km radius of Luxembourg.[25] Due to its location, it was initially planned that the station would be a 'European' station, whereby certain countries were allocated one day of the week for programmes—Sunday for Britain, Monday for Italy, and so on. Commercial broadcasters rapidly saw the potential of such a transmitter but they were opposed by many public service broadcasters who feared such a potentially powerful commercial rival. The advent of commercial broadcasting, in general, was met by fierce opposition from the BBC, the Post Office, and the press.

The BBC had two main options available in its campaign against the commercial stations: it could try to halt the broadcast of sponsored programmes through diplomatic channels, centring around the issue of international wavelength allocation, or it could try to compete with them and drive their promoters out of business by providing more popular programmes. Its two main allies in Britain were the Post Office and the press. The Post Office was able to lend its weight to the BBC's international campaigns and it even carried on when the BBC had given up. In addition, the Post Office repeatedly refused to allow the commercial broadcasters land lines between Britain and the Continent, thus making 'live'

[23] BBC WAC R34/961 (1945), 22–3.
[24] BBC WAC E2/2/1 Memo 'English Commercial Broadcasts from Abroad 1928–33'.
[25] BBC WAC E18/283/2, Memo, 24 June 1933.

broadcasts impossible. The press also refused to advertise the sponsored programmes, fearing a loss of advertising revenue.[26]

The long campaign to close Radio Luxembourg by the BBC and the international radio community meant that regular commercial broadcasts did not start until 16 January 1934. They rapidly became a success. The 'European station' concept was gradually dropped and Luxembourg's time became taken over increasingly by British advertising programmes. Radio Luxembourg's great power, together with the large number of hours it had to sell on Sunday (12.25 hours in 1935, rising to 15.25 hours in 1936), soon gave it an unrivalled popularity.[27]

By 1934 sponsored programmes had become established with both the public and advertisers and between 1934 and 1937 Radio Luxembourg and four French stations consolidated their position further. Normandie, Poste Parisien, and Toulouse were joined by Radio Lyons in 1936 and the number of British advertisers using foreign facilities grew rapidly, as did their audiences. The number of hours available for English sponsored programmes each week rose rapidly, from 71 hours in 1933 to 161.25 in 1937. Sunday hours increased from 17 hours in 1933 to 41.75 hours in 1937.[28] As the popularity of the commercial broadcasts grew, the radio advertising business exploded. The amount of money spent on buying time (excluding production costs) rose from £176,000 in 1934 to £315,000 in 1935 and then steadily to over £1 million by 1939.[29] Advertising agencies flourished. In 1936 there were two important agencies, Radio (Universal) Publicity and the IBC. By 1939 there were six. These agencies not only sought out potential advertisers, they also established programme production units. To cater for the expansion in demand from audiences, a new magazine, *Radio Pictorial*, was launched on 31 August 1934, publishing details of English commercial stations from abroad for 3*d*. weekly. By the end of 1938 it had sales of 200,000.

The number of English sponsored programmes continued to expand until the outbreak of the war in 1939; and, surprisingly, a number of new ventures in commercial broadcasting were launched despite the political situation in Europe. A concession from the Republic of Andorra was granted to a British advertising agency in 1939 and Liechtenstein in 1937 also granted a concession to the British owned 'International Corporation Ltd.' to exploit Radio Vaduz, a commercial broadcasting station. In March 1938 attempts were made by Broadcast Advertising Ltd. (London

---

[26] For a full account of opposition see Briggs, *History of Broadcasting*.
[27] BBC WAC R34/961 (1945), 38.   [28] Ibid., Appendix H.   [29] Ibid. 57–8.

agents of Radio Lyons) to establish a station in Iceland. In the same year, an English group was attempting to register a ship under the Paraguayan flag with a view to broadcasting English advertising programmes to Britain from outside the three-mile limit. These were forerunners to the post-war 'pirate' radio stations such as Radio Caroline. In March 1939 the IBC was negotiating in Tangier to erect a short-wave transmitter to broadcast sponsored programmes to Britain and in April of 1939 a new radio advertising agency, Radio Variety Ltd., was registered in London and started construction of a radio station on the Friesian Islands.

Meanwhile, the other main commercial stations went from strength to strength. Radio Athlone (renamed Radio Eireann from February 1938) continued its nightly broadcasts. Radio Luxembourg and Radio Normandie increased their available hours slightly and greatly increased their sales of time. Poste Parisien also increased the number of hours available for English commercial broadcasts substantially from April 1938. In the end it was only the advent of war that halted the continued expansion of the commercial stations and the only commercial station to broadcast English sponsored programmes throughout was Radio Eireann.

The commercial success of these broadcasters was directly linked to their success in attracting large audiences in Britain. The total audience for the commercial radio stations was substantial and increased steadily throughout the period 1932 to 1939. In 1935, the IBC estimated that 61 per cent of those who had radios listened to sponsored English broadcasts from Continental stations. This represented an audience of about 5,300,000 families and a weekly audience of nearly 16 million listeners.[30] The BBC Listener Research Department carried out an inquiry among 2,000 members of the 'light entertainment public' in November and December 1937 which confirmed the IBC's earlier study: 66 per cent listened regularly to foreign stations on Sundays, falling to 22 per cent on weekdays.[31] Perhaps the most comprehensive surveys were those carried out in March and November 1938 by a joint committee of the Incorporated Society of British Advertisers (ISBA) and the Institute of Incorporated Practitioners in Advertising (IIPA). The *Survey of Listening to Sponsored Radio Programmes* estimated that at peak listening times, on Sundays, the four principal commercial stations had a combined audience of over 6 million people.[32] Of these, Radio Luxembourg was the

---

[30] IBC, *Survey of Radio Advertising Penetration* (1935), 3.

[31] BBC WAC R34/961 (1945), 64.

[32] A. Plant, *Survey of Listening to Sponsored Programmes* (Mar. 1938), 6.

most popular. Nearly one in two commercial station listeners tuned into Luxembourg,[33] with a peak Sunday afternoon audience of about 4 million people.[34] Next in popularity was Radio Normandie, with an estimated audience of just over $2^1/_2$ million on Sundays and just over 510,000 on weekdays in 1936.[35] The two other major commercial stations, Radio Lyons and Poste Parisien, had peak audiences of 637,000 and 455,000 respectively in 1938.[36]

Audiences for commercial broadcasts were not, however, consistent. The commercial stations were able to establish themselves by building up audiences at times when the BBC was not broadcasting, or providing only an intermittent service on weekday mornings and on Sundays. Early morning commercial broadcasts were very popular, with the largest audience during the hours before the BBC started its broadcasts at 10.30 a.m. After this time, during the week, BBC broadcasts were always more popular than those of the commercial stations. However, every audience survey of commercial radio stations undertaken before the Second World War shows that the commercial radio stations had their largest audiences on Sundays and that most of these audiences were larger than those of the BBC. This popularity was as a direct result of the BBC's reduced broadcasting time, its sombre output for Sunday, and the commercial stations' bright, lively programmes. The *Survey of Listening to Sponsored Radio Programmes* of November 1938 showed that all of Radio Luxembourg's Sunday programmes before 6 p.m. were more popular than those of the BBC.[37]

The commercial radio stations provided an alternative source of popular music and entertainment on a *national* scale. The popularity of certain stations and of sponsored radio as a whole, however, did vary regionally. One problem of broadcasting from stations on the Continent was that certain parts of Britain were unable to receive the programmes with sufficient clarity to make regular listening feasible. Initially there were considerable technical problems but after 1935 advances in the quality of reception were rapid. In terms of signal strength, the most complete 'national service' was offered by Radio Luxembourg, whose reception was strong in most parts of the country, even the North. Radio Normandie's reception was extremely good in the London area and most of

[33] BBC WAC R34/961 (1945), 64.   [34] Plant, *Survey* . . . (Mar. 1938), 6.
[35] Ibid. 6.   [36] Ibid. 6.
[37] A. Plant, *Supplementary Survey of Listening to Sponsored Programmes* (Nov. 1938), 23 and 25.

the south of England but was negligible in the Midlands and the north of England. Reception in Scotland, however, was very good. Poste Parisien was better received in the northern half of Britain. Together, the various stations provided all parts of Britain with at least one, and usually a choice of two or more, commercial, popular music-oriented radio programmes.

There were significant regional variations in audience size.[38] In 1938, for example, average listening to Radio Luxembourg was highest in the north-east of England, followed by South Wales and London. Radio Normandie was most popular in the south of England, with its highest audience in the area from Southend to Bournemouth, Poste Parisien was most popular in the London area and the eastern Midlands, and Radio Lyons and Radio Toulouse were most popular in the south-west.[39] The commercial radio stations were particularly popular with the working and lower-middle-classes, who also made up 75 per cent of the BBC's listeners. The proportions of each social class listening to the programmes declined as income rose and the commercial stations deliberately aimed their programmes at working and lower-middle-class audiences.[40] In addition, the times at which the commercial stations broadcast were arranged not only to coincide with silent spots in the BBC output but also with these groups' early work routines. Radio Normandie, for example, began broadcasts at 7 a.m.

The commercial radio stations were more popular with women than men.[41] Among age groups, the young were the most regular listeners to commercial stations, though the appeal of such stations spanned age divisions. In 1938 average listening to all radio stations, including the BBC, was greatest among the 35–40 age group, closely followed by the 14–20 and the 21–34 age groups. For Radio Luxembourg and Normandie audiences, however, a higher proportion of the 14–20 and 21–34 age groups listened than any other age group.[42]

The commercial radio stations, therefore, had a huge audience throughout Britain. Sponsored programmes were popular among all sections of society but its most avid listeners were the working and lower middle classes, particularly young females. What did this audience listen to?

The commercial radio stations aimed their programmes directly at the audience for popular and light entertainment which it considered the

[38] IBC, *Survey of Radio Advertising Penetration*, Appendix II, 1935.
[39] Plant, *Survey* . . . (Mar. 1938), 57–58.
[40] IBC, *Survey of Radio Advertising Penetration*, Appendix I.
[41] Plant, *Survey* . . . , 7 and 54.   [42] Ibid. 55.

TABLE 4. *Content of English sponsored programmes broadcast on Radio Normandie for October 1934*

Programme type	Radio Normandie English sponsored broadcasts for 1–31 October 1934 (total = 152 hours)	
	Hours broadcast	Proportion of total (%)[a]
'Popular' songs	31	20
Comedy songs	9	6
Dance music	62	41
Light orchestra	27.5	18
Military bands	6	4
Total popular music output	135.5	89
Drama	0.75	0.5
Special features	0.25	<0.5
Variety	0.75	0.5
Children's hour	6.75	4.5
Religion	2	1
Total non-music output	10.5	7
Classical music	6	4

[a] Percentages are approximate.

Source: Calculated from programme listings in *RP*.

BBC was failing to satisfy. The popularity of the commercial programmes was due to the high proportion of popular music broadcast and the stations used popular music and a 'popular' style of delivery to create a distinctive image for themselves: Table 4 shows the extent to which the English sponsored programmes broadcast by Radio Normandie in October 1934 were overwhelmingly popular music. Approximately 89 per cent of the programmes broadcast for this month were programmes of popular music, with a playing time of 135½ hours. If the figures are disaggregated it can be seen that, of the different types of popular music, programmes of dance music were the most common, followed by programmes of 'popular songs', then 'light orchestral' music programmes and finally programmes of 'military band' music. Non-music output was small by comparison.

Sunday output, having the largest audience, was different but, again, was dominated by popular music. Table 5 shows the content of English

TABLE 5. *Sunday output of English sponsored programmes broadcast on Radio Normandie, Radio Luxembourg, and Poste Parisien for January 1935*

	Radio Normandie (48.75 hrs)		Radio Luxembourg (52.5 hrs)		Poste Parisien (16.25 hrs)		Total (117.5 hrs)	
	Hours	%	Hours	%	Hours	%	Hours	%
Popular songs	14.25	30	16.75	32	3.5	22	34.5	29
Comedy songs	4	8	8	15	5.5	34	17.5	15
Dance music	6.25	13	12.5	24	3	18	21.75	19
Light orchestra	13.75	28	10.25	19.5	2.25	14	26.25	22
Military bands	3.5	7	0	0	0.25	1.5	3.75	3
Total popular music	41.75	86	47.5	90.5	14.5	89.5	103.75	88
Drama	0	0	0.25	0.5	1	6	1.25	1
Special features	1	2	0.25	0.5	0.75	4.5	2	1.75
Variety	0.25	0.5	0	0	0	0	0.25	0.25
Children's hour	1	2	2	4	0	0	3	2.5
Spoken word	0	0	2.25	4	0	0	2.25	2
Outside broadcasts	2	4	0	0	0	0	2	1.75
Religion	2	4	0	0	0	0	2	1.75
Total non-music	6.25	12.5	4.75	9	1.75	10.5	12.75	11
Classical music	0.75	1.5	0.25	0.5	0	0	1	1

Source: Calculated from programme listings in *RP*.

sponsored programmes broadcast by the three principal commercial radio stations on Sundays. Out of the 117½ hours broadcast by all three stations, 103¾ hours were made up of programmes of popular music, representing 88 per cent of the month's total Sunday output. The station with the highest proportion of popular music broadcast and largest number of hours played was Radio Luxembourg. Interestingly, the table reveals that popular music output on Sundays was different from that for the week as a whole. Whereas dance music programmes were most common on weekdays, on Sundays 'popular song' programmes were the most featured. Dance music was still popular, however, and usually broadcast after 9 p.m. All three stations provided considerably more of this sort of music than the BBC. For Sunday broadcasting the popular music was of a 'lighter' variety than during the rest of the week. Poste Parisien, for example, which only broadcast approximately four hours of English programmes on Sundays, devoted most of its time to programmes of 'comedy songs'.

Taking each of the stations analysed, on average the audience could expect to hear nearly four hours of popular songs, about three and a half hours of light orchestral music, and just under two hours of dance music on Radio Normandie each Sunday. On Radio Luxembourg audiences could hear over four hours of 'popular songs', three hours of 'dance music', and two and a half hours of light orchestral music, with further popular music output to complement quiet spots on Poste Parisien. Again, non-music output was small.

The programme makers deliberately contrasted their programmes with those on the BBC. In 1930, E. Woolf, publicity manager of the Decca Record Company, said that, 'None of the music in our programmes is either religious or classical. This is its secret.'[43] Other advertisers also made the most of the popular music content of their programmes. In July 1933 the radio manufacturers Philco launched a programme on Radio Normandie, advertising it as 'a much needed programme of light, cheery music every morning from 11 am till noon'.[44]

The high proportion of popular music contained in the programmes broadcast on the commercial radio stations was, in part, because of the Post Office's refusal to grant them land line facilities. This meant that all programme material had to be pre-recorded and had an important effect on the output of the stations.

Until 1935 the majority of programmes broadcast on the commercial radio stations was made up of selections of commercially available gramophone records. Gramophone programmes were cheap and easy to produce and provided the latest popular songs by the most popular dance bands without the expense of hiring performers. As a result, a large amount of broadcasting time was occupied with music. The radio stations actually insisted on a quota for the minimum amount of music permissible in each programme. To give the impression that performances were actually being broadcast from the studios, stations such as Radio Normandie and Radio Luxembourg would use a series of turntables and 'dub' over recordings of applause or laughter. The fact that records were being used was often not announced to listeners. The BBC attempted to stop the commercial radio stations from using recordings of its own artists and protested to the record manufacturers but with little success.

---

[43] *World's Press News*, 8 May 1930.   [44] IBC, *IBC Programme Sheet* (July 1933), 7.

British record companies were closely associated with the new commercial radio stations and they had been among the first sponsors of programmes from the Continent. Radio Toulouse, for example, began broadcasts in English in 1929 with programmes sponsored by British gramophone companies. EMI and Decca sponsored many early programmes of gramophone records and the record companies reached agreement with the commercial stations over the broadcasting of records as early as 1934. Radio Luxembourg approached the new gramophone combine EMI and, although not legally required to do so, offered to pay EMI every time a record was played and broadcast.[45]

This concentration on the use of gramophone records and recorded programme material gave rise to the full development of the 'disc jockey'. Christopher Stone, who worked initially with the BBC, was the first person in Britain who developed this style. Programmes of gramophone records, with a different theme, were presented and discussed each week. Stone also wrote reviews of gramophone records for *Gramophone* and the *Daily Express*. Before long he began to compère similar programmes for the newly created Radio Luxembourg while still working for the BBC. Although the BBC at first accepted this, it was later to terminate his contract. At the BBC, each excerpt of music broadcast had to come to a clear finish before a short statement was made, with an interval of one second before the next selection could be played. This formality was typical of the BBC's output. At Radio Luxembourg, however, Stone was free to develop fully the 'disc jockey' style into one which is still the predominant form of music broadcasting today. Stone and others used the less formal 'voice over' technique and even greeted listeners by name if they had written. The more relaxed, convivial style on commercial radio was perfect for their largely popular music-oriented output and was an important element in their success. One listener writing in *Radio Pictorial* in 1934 said: 'Mr Christopher Stone . . . delights us not only with his masterly selection of records but the charm of his friendly manner is also very attractive to the listener. We can picture him sitting there, puffing away at his pipe and beaming genially through his glasses.'[46] Developments in recording technology enabled the commercial radio stations to pioneer a number of other programme developments. By 1935, new recording processes had been developed on film, disc, and Philips-Miller tape. The use of film and tape improved sound quality and enabled longer recording

---

[45] BBC WAC E18/283/3, Interview with A. Clark, 17 Sept. 1934.
[46] *RP*, 25 Jan 1935, p. 35.

sessions. Advertisers and their agents began to spend an increasing amount of money on their programmes and several programme units were established in London by companies such as IBC, who launched the Universal Programme Corporation in 1935. The large advertising agencies J. Walter Thompson, Erwin Wasey, Lord Thomas, and the London Press Exchange also opened studios in London. Advertisers strove to improve the quality of their programmes and first-class dance band and variety programmes, serials, and other features were produced by these units. Recordings were made in London on film, disc, or tape and dispatched for transmission to the Continental stations. This made it possible to give listeners entertainment specially provided by the most expensive artists and bands and specially presented by popular compères, without the companies having to send artists and orchestras abroad. In fact, no British star, band, or other performer ever performed 'live' from the studios of the commercial radio stations on the Continent. The sound quality of the film was so good that commercial radio stations were able to convince listeners that they were broadcasting 'live' performances of popular artists from Britain. In addition, the film process enabled 'scrapbook' type programmes to be made more easily. Some of the most popular programmes on Radio Normandie were those such as *Talkie Time* which contained excerpts from the latest cinema releases, together with reviews and interviews with the stars. *What's On* on Radio Normandie, also gave details of events on the stage and elsewhere for the week ahead in London; broadcasts of recorded live programmes from London theatres proved to be very popular. 'Outside Broadcasting' material was also obtained by special recording vans that toured provincial seaside resorts and theatres recording concert programmes. The commercial radio stations thus created a number of original programmes that tapped directly into the general public's desire to hear news and gossip from the world of entertainment.

One of the most important factors in the success of the commercial radio stations was the way in which, by concentrating on star artists, they used popular music to attract audiences. As audiences grew and advertising revenue increased, the budgets available to programme makers also increased, enabling them to offer top-ranking entertainers fees large enough to attract them away from the BBC and the theatres. It became a common policy of the bigger advertisers to associate their products with the names of single 'stars', rather than with various artists. Such 'stars' were usually film actors, comedians, variety entertainers, singers, and dance bands. This 'star' policy gave the commercial radio stations wide variety in their popular music and light entertainment programmes and also attracted 'devotees' of particular artists. In 1939, for example, the ninety-two regular sponsored programmes broadcast weekly on Radio Normandie included the *Rinso Radio Revue* with Jack Hylton and His Band, Tommy Handley, Bebe Daniels, and Ben Lyons; the *Kraft Cheese Show* with Billy Cotton and His Band; the *Feenamint Laxatives Show* with George Formby; the *Cookeen Cooking Fat* programme with Carroll Gibbons and His Orchestra; Cadbury's *Songs to Make You Sing* and *Cadbury Calling* with pianist Charlie Kunz and His Orchestra and the Atora Shredded Suet programme *Around the World* with comedian Sandy Powell.[47] The belief in the power of stars was so great that in November 1936 Radio Luxembourg, in conjunction with Wireless Publicity, launched a series of unsponsored *All Star Concerts* on weekday evenings between 6.45 and 7.15. These all-star shows were designed to raise the profile of weekday broadcasts and attract potential advertisers. The stars featured included Gracie Fields, Evelyn Laye, Stanley Holloway, and Maurice Chevalier.[48] The proliferation of dance bands was one of the commercial stations' biggest advantages, especially on Sundays, as the *Advertisers' Weekly* was able to comment:

A Sunday's sponsored broadcasting from Luxembourg, Normandie and Lyons often contains more stars than the BBC broadcast in a whole week. Take dance bands alone. Every Sunday you can hear Billy Cotton, Ambrose, Marius B. Winter, Debroy Somers, Geraldo, Billy Reid, Billy Bissett, Sidney Lipton, Jack Payne, Lew Stone. Beat that, BBC![49]

Standards for these 'star' programmes were taken seriously by the commercial radio stations. Radio Luxembourg, for example, specified that 'it is essential that all Sunday programmes between the hours of 9.00 a.m. and 10.00 p.m. should consist of material specifically recorded by the artists for the programme concerned', i.e. no-gramophone record programmes. Repeated material was also forbidden and advertisers were asked that 'programmes should provide as great a contrast as possible, particularly on Sundays'.[50] The association in the minds of the general public between 'stars' and the commercial radio stations was soon made.

The BBC was so concerned at the large number of these stars and their success in attracting audiences that it launched a campaign to try and

[47] See IBC, *Radio Normandy Programme Book* (Jan. 1939).
[48] Wireless Publicity Ltd., letter to potential advertisers, 7 Nov. 1936.
[49] *Advertisers' Weekly*, 27 May 1937, p. 5.
[50] BBC WAC: R34/149 Memo, 'Pre-War Commercial Broadcasting', no date.

stop the commercial stations from 'pilfering' what the BBC considered to be its own artists. Many of the 'star' artists appearing on the commercial radio stations also had contracts with the BBC and they monitored the content of commercial programmes closely for the appearance of 'BBC performers'. The first person to suffer from the BBC's crackdown on appearing on commercial radio was Christopher Stone, one of the BBC's most popular attractions, whose contract with the BBC was terminated on 29 August 1934 and was not renewed. No detailed explanation was given to Stone himself but the fact that he had close links with commercial broadcasting served as a warning to other artists. Following Stone's dismissal, the employment of other artists was placed under review and they were also threatened, as a memo of August 1934 illustrates:

A friendly and informal warning to be disseminated among Variety artists to the effect that they cannot run with the hare and hunt with the hounds, i.e., that they will be prejudicing their position with the BBC by broadcasting from Luxembourg.[51]

Several artists found their engagements with the BBC in jeopardy. Those affected included the popular performers Stanley Holloway, Flanagan and Allen, and Jessie Matthews. A large number of artists turned down offers of work from Luxembourg; a policy that often meant substantial financial sacrifices. By 1935 this policy of 'guerrilla warfare' was being questioned. The entertainment executive of the BBC was concerned that it was making the brief careers of music-hall artists unnecessarily difficult and harming their livelihood. By 1937 it was clear that the threats from the BBC were not working. Not only did most artists simply ignore these warnings but also, when action was taken, the BBC merely made the contrast between itself and Radio Luxembourg even sharper, as they admitted in March 1937:

Those broadcasting from Luxembourg fairly regularly are the people we want ourselves and include several of the most prominent dance bands; so far as I can see only the BBC suffers if they are banned. On the whole, I do not think that we can adopt any procedure over artists which can combine advantage to ourselves and disadvantage to Luxembourg.[52]

The policy was thus reversed and outright bans became rare, confined to those who actively participated in the affairs of sponsored radio, although the BBC continued to monitor the appearance of 'star' artists on the commercial radio stations.

[51] BBC WAC E18/283/3, 'Luxembourg programmes', 29 Aug. 1934.
[52] BBC WAC E18/283/6, Memo, 8 Mar. 1937.

The commercial radio stations soon became an important employer and an influential part of the popular music industry. They provided a large amount of popular music and became inextricably linked with vested interests in the popular music industry. Various programme production companies, musicians, variety and stage artists, music publishers, and authors and composers had an interest in seeing the commercial stations succeed. One early investor in commercial radio programmes, the theatrical producer and composer Gordon Sherry, saw them as an important new employer and rival to the BBC. Speaking to the *Sunday Dispatch* in November 1928 he argued, 'everybody in the entertainment business feels that no portion of it should be a monopoly. One ought to be able to take one's goods not only to one market but to an open market . . . An open market is better for the listener, better for the artist and better for all the arts—music, singing, and drama.'[53] These early hopes were soon realized. In 1934 *Melody Maker* praised commercial radio for creating greater employment prospects and better pay for dance musicians, predicting an 'era of prosperity' as Radio Luxembourg and others grew in popularity. It contrasted the commercial stations' treatment of artists with that of the BBC:

As things are in this country, the BBC's amateur showmen can present their programmes as they like, sheltered from all competition, and so impecunious in their financial resources that they find it necessary either to grind down the artists' terms or else engage inferior talent.[54]

These feelings were echoed by the *Radio Pictorial* in the same year:

Advertising on the air is good for the artists, because it means that they will be paid according to their merit, and a public favourite will be able to command a far higher salary than he will ever get from the BBC.[55]

By 1938, it was estimated that the various programme production companies, musicians, variety and stage artists, music publishers, authors, and composers were receiving about half a million pounds each year from the commercial radio stations.[56] When the Incorporated Society of British Advertisers Radio Defence Committee launched a new campaign to defend Radio Normandie and Radio Luxembourg in February 1938, one of its main arguments was the employment levels for popular

[53] *Sunday Dispatch*, 4 Nov. 1928, p. 1.   [54] *MM*, 29 Dec. 1934, p. 1.
[55] *RP*, 24 Aug. 1934, p. 8.
[56] Incorporated Society of British Advertisers Limited: Radio Defence Committee, *Statement on Sponsored Programmes* (9 Feb. 1938), 1.

musicians created by the radio stations. The Committee's *Statement on Sponsored Programmes* argued:

The Dance Band Directors' Association has stated that many of their members depend entirely on commercial radio for their livelihood. BBC engagements are few and far between and when obtained often the fees paid barely cover expenses. In the variety and theatrical fields sponsored programmes have helped many artists to augment their incomes, and a number of performers can be said to owe their success to their activities in sponsored radio where they have established their reputations with millions of listeners.[57]

Yet it was not only dance musicians who had benefited. A large number of professional and trade associations from the popular music industry were members of the Radio Defence Committee. These included the Musicians' Union, the Music Publishers' Association, the Society of Popular Music Publishers, the Variety Artists' Association, the Concert Artists' Association, and the British Authors' and Composers' Association.[58]

The success of the commercial radio stations, though not sufficient to bring improved working conditions for most entertainers at the BBC, was sufficient, however, to influence its output. The commercial radio stations' attitude toward popular music greatly affected that of the BBC and the success of sponsored programmes prompted a series of stylistic changes in programmes and an alteration of broadcasting hours.

To the BBC, at least publicly, the commercial stations were illegal and amateurish organizations broadcasting cheap and vulgar programmes. A good indication of the BBC reaction to the early commercial programmes is a 1933 report on the IBC programmes on Radio Athlone, Dublin, Cork, and Fécamp. Of the actual programmes, it was reported:

These are of little account and . . . are of a musical nature, principally of the very light popular type . . . During the eight occasions on which I listened to these concerts, I heard nothing that could be called a first class concert. . . . Quite frankly I can't imagine a great deal of interest being taken in these programmes. They are far too dull and there is a good deal of enterprise lacking in programmes, presentation and advertising.[59]

Lord Reith recoiled at what he described as 'the monstrous stuff that Luxembourg is putting out'[60] and the BBC was so concerned by the

---

[57] Ibid.   [58] Ibid.
[59] BBC WAC E2/365/1, 'Report on IBC Transmissions', A. C. Shaw, 1933.
[60] BBC WAC E18/283/4, Memo, Director-General to Controller (A), 14 Oct. 1935.

question of 'good taste' that it monitored both Radio Normandie and Radio Luxembourg specifically for vulgarity and for blatant advertising. Although it seldom found anything of an offensive nature, the monitoring continued. One of the BBC's principal objections to the standard of sponsored programmes was the large amount of popular music and other material of popular cultural origin. As late as 1945, the BBC summed up the content of commercial programmes thus:

> The sponsored programmes from abroad varied vastly in cost and entertainment quality but their nature was always the same. They presented one long orgy of variety, popular music and 'singing' and melodramatic serials, punctuated by the smartness of compères and an occasional feature like 'Teaser Time' from morning until night. . . . They were determined to 'give the public what the public wants' and that public was mainly drawn from the lower and lower middle class.[61]

This attitude towards the popular nature of the commercial stations' programmes was also shared by other radio authorities. In 1932 the British general secretary of the Union Internationale de Radiodiffusion, A. R. Burrows, complained to his friends at the BBC that, in terms of musical prowess, 'the good name of England' was being damaged by the programmes. Commenting on a sponsored programme of gramophone records broadcast on Radio Paris in October 1932 he wrote:

> A more disgusting display of musical depravity could not be conceived. One song was supposed to represent a prisoner praying to his 'Gawd in 'eaven' and moaning to his 'muvver'. Another record had the classic title 'You are lazy, you are lousy, but I love you' and there were several more of the same order . . . There is on the continent of Europe an idea, false but understandable, that the English are not musical themselves and have no taste for music. The BBC, I like to believe, has done something to disprove this belief, but I cannot conceive anything more calculated to create a profound contempt for English taste than yesterday afternoon's programme of records . . . It seems to me a very great pity that if the continental peoples have to listen to English commercial programmes on Sunday afternoons, they should have given to them, not the best possible programmes but almost the worst conceivable.[62]

This attitude, however, slowly began to change. The rapid success of the commercial radio stations, especially Radio Luxembourg and Radio Normandie, shook the BBC considerably. It gradually became clear that the BBC must compete with sponsored radio on its own terms. In June

[61] BBC WAC R34/961 (1945), 62.
[62] BBC WAC E2/2/1, Letter: A. R. Burrows to C. F. Atkinson, 10 Oct. 1932.

1933 the director of Information and Publications wrote to the director-general arguing that, apart from the legal and international pressure being brought to bear by the BBC, 'Our only other weapon appears to be that of studying all these programmes, both in hours and material, and manipulation of our programmes to compete with them, driving them out by our superior merit.'[63]

The process was slow. Initial reactions did not foresee a dramatic alteration of programme policy nor a change in the attitude towards popular music and 'popular' programmes, but the continued success of sponsored programmes eventually brought about considerable change by the BBC. This took two forms. First was a series of extensions in the number of hours that the BBC broadcast, chiefly on Sundays. The second was to change the nature of programmes to appeal more directly to the sort of listeners who were switching to the commercial radio stations.

Although there were no fundamental changes in the BBC's programme policies for Sundays or other days, considerable effort was made to lighten the content of Sunday programmes. The Music Department was at the forefront. From March 1934, the categories of 'light music' allowed on a Sunday were extended to include selections from musical comedies and light operas. The Music Department was also told to provide 'light and popular' material before 4.30 p.m. using 'popular titles'.[64] The BBC's own ban on current dance music on Sundays, however, remained and, therefore, it had to rely on more old-fashioned genres, such as the organist Reginald Foort and the light orchestra of Albert Sandler, to provide most of its light music material. It also provided concerts of national airs, brass and military bands, and gramophone recitals. The changes were a start but were a compromise which failed to please either the 'brighter Sunday' lobby or the Church. Further changes were made in 1938, coinciding with the further extension in Sunday broadcasting hours. The BBC's Religious Advisory Council remained an effective force, however, especially in Scotland, and it insisted that only light music programmes be broadcast during the new hours.[65]

The BBC realized that light music on its own was not sufficient to beat off Luxembourg competition and considered several options, including interspersing light music programmes with variety acts and 'scrapbook' programmes. Neither were acted on as the Religious Advisory

[63] BBC WAC E2/365/1, Memo, 'International Broadcasting Club', 7 June 1933.
[64] BBC WAC R34/961 (1945), 38.   [65] Ibid. 45.

Committee objected to any changes to the usual programming before 12.30. Certain other changes were considered and the BBC decided to adopt some of the techniques of the commercial stations. For example, it was decided that programmes should be featured regularly and at fixed times, and that on Sundays programmes should change every half hour. The principle of listener loyalty to certain programmes was now accepted. Of greater importance was a new emphasis on the style of the programmes. By January 1938 it was considered that '*popular* presentation is of the utmost importance', signalling an end to the ordinary announcer style.[66] With this in mind, in October 1938 the Variety Department took charge of certain light music periods with a view to better presentation. Moreover, the BBC decided 'That the regular appearance of popular personalities, both as characters within a programme and as compères of programmes, script readers, etc., is desirable. This particularly applies to Sunday programmes, but popular personalities should also be a feature of weekday programmes.'[67]

The bans on sport, political controversy, dance music, straight variety, and full-length musical comedy remained strictly in force. Successive changes in programming had, however, lightened the BBC's programmes on Sundays. Even more important was the new attitude towards popular personalities and popular styles of presentation. Whereas popular music and the performers of such music had once been sneered at, they were now considered essential to the success of the BBC at times when competition from commercial radio was at its fiercest. This competition had thus forced the BBC into direct changes based on the commercial radio stations' style of programming.

Together the BBC and the commercial radio stations meant that radio was a major force behind popular music sales and in the generation and promotion of stars and songs. By the mid-1930s, the BBC was the largest single employer of musicians in the country, able to direct the terms and nature of musicians' careers. Such was the power of radio that sections of the popular music industry used the new media to further their own commercial interests and the BBC was accused of 'song-plugging'.[68] The effect of the new media in determining tastes and trends in popular music was substantial.

---

[66] BBC WAC R34/607, Memo, Controller of Programmes to Director-General, 17 Jan. 1938, p. 1.
[67] Ibid.   [68] See Chapter 8 below.

3.3 The cinema

The cinema was the dominant non-domestic leisure activity in Britain during the 1930s and accounted for nearly two-thirds of all entertainment admissions and expenditure. The cinema offered unprecedented luxury for everyone, with lavish surroundings and warm, comfortable seats at cheap prices. There was a slow growth in attendances from annual admissions of 903 million in 1934 to 990 million in 1939 when average *weekly* admissions were estimated at 23 million. The increase in the number of cinemas was also substantial, from an estimated 3,000 cinemas in 1926 to just under 5,000 in 1939.[69] Cinema was popular at all levels of society and virtually all of the contemporary surveys on the subject conclude that it was particularly popular among the working class, which made up the majority of the audience. The cinema was affordable entertainment enjoyed by some of the poorest members of the community, including the unemployed, though they were not great attenders proportionately.

Importantly, the cinema also offered state of the art audio technology. At the cinema, backed by the huge multinational film industry, audiences could hear the most modern equipment. Cinema not only looked good, it *sounded* marvellous. Given the enormous popularity of the cinema, it is particularly significant that popular music featured widely in films and that 'musical films' were among the most popular. The cinema was a very powerful and influential source of popular music. 'Musical films' took a variety of forms, from basically 'conventional' films with an occasional song or the appearance of a musical personality added, to large scale musical extravaganzas.

That some of the most popular film stars of the period in Britain were the stars of musical films is a good indication of the popularity of the genre. Films stars whose careers were closely associated with popular music were consistently popular in interwar Britain. Two of the most popular, George Formby and Gracie Fields, for example, were inextricably linked to a music-hall tradition, with their appeal based directly on popular songs. An important indication of tastes among cinema audiences was gathered in a Mass-Observation survey of Bolton audiences of March 1938.[70] Asked which their favourite types of film were, the largest

---

[69] J. Richards, *The Age of the Dream Palace* (1984), 11–12.

[70] Results in J. Richards and D. Sheridan (ed.), *Mass-Observation at the Movies* (1987), 33–41.

single category favoured was 'musical romance' with 30 per cent of respondents naming it their favourite. This was considerably ahead of the next favoured category, 'drama and tragedy' with 18 per cent. Although 'musical romance' was the most popular single category for both men and women, such films found relatively greater favour among women: 24 per cent of men but 43 per cent of women named 'musical romance' their preferred choice in films. Cinema managers' reactions are also important. The manager of the Embassy cinema in Bolton remarked that 'Musical pictures in Lancashire go the best for any [sic]' and pointed to the devotion of fans of musical films who, given a good musical, 'won't only go once, but two and even three times'. Such preferences do not appear to be confined to the north of England. In the East End of London 'Good action pictures and good musicals seem to top the list in every cinema.'[71] Of the East End's favourite films for 1936 three out of seven were musicals; they were the American *Follow the Fleet* and *Top Hat* with Fred Astaire and Ginger Rodgers and *The Broadway Melody of 1936*. Similarly in Winifred Holmes's study of an unnamed Southern English town, the manager of the working-class cinema, the Grand, declared: 'Musical comedy is the best bid and I must say that Jessie Matthews and Gracie Fields are among the greatest draws. Jack Hulbert, Cecily Courtneidge [sic] and Charles Laughton are other popular British stars.'[72] All, with the exception of Laughton, were popular musical artists. Individuals' comments, as revealed by the Mass-Observation survey of cinema habits in Bolton in 1938, are particularly illuminating in understanding the wide appeal of musical films. One middle-aged male observed that 'bright musical films make one feel that an hour at the cinema has been well spent and a tonic'. Another stated that a musical 'always gives you something interesting . . . there never seems to be a dull moment'. Others enjoyed them because of their 'good singing' and 'good story with lovely scenery'.[73] One 33-year-old female who was a regular cinema-goer remarked, 'I like the Musical Romance type of film best because "It's Romantic, it's Superb, it's Colossal." To find yourself singing the catchy tunes the next morning, then you know you get the utmost pleasure out of the films. They just relive in your memory.'[74] The escapist appeal

[71] R. Carr, 'World Film News', Jan. 1937, p. 9, quoted in Richards, *Dream Palace*, 27.
[72] 'World Film News', Dec. 1936, pp. 3–4, quoted in Richards, *Dream Palace*, 28.
[73] Replies quoted in Richards and Sheridan (ed.), *Mass-Observation at the Movies*, 41–135.
[74] Quoted ibid. 125.

of musical films was important to their audience. A 45-year-old woman commented: 'Musical films are usually good entertainment. One does not expect anything true to type—just good singing and pretty or spectacular scenes: things do not need tiring concentration.'[75] A 36-year-old working class male, with a preference for musical films, observed that they provided 'that relaxation which people need after a day's work. An excursion into that world of make-believe which we each have a longing to explore but seldom do. It is also a pleasing sense of "well-being" to be amused.'[76]

For such a new genre, film musicals had caught on remarkably quickly with cinema audiences and the studios were quick to respond to this demand. With the coming of sound films at the end of the 1920s, a whole new world was opened to film makers. In the first days of the new technology there was a large output of 'musical' films drawing directly from a variety of musical influences. However, Hollywood gradually began to evolve a distinctive musical film style. The first important example was Irving Thalberg's *The Broadway Melody* (1929) made at MGM which employed composer Nacio Herb Brown and lyric writer Arthur Freed to write an entirely original score for the film. Its success encouraged the major film studios to establish units specializing in the creation of film musicals. Specialist directors, choreographers, composers, and writers were employed to work solely in this field. As a result the 1930s were highly productive and led to the 'golden age' of the Hollywood musical. Busby Berkeley's lavish productions such as *42nd Street*, *Gold Diggers of 1933*, and *Footlight Parade*, all from 1933, took the genre to new heights of elegance and ingenuity. The great popular composers such as Richard Rodgers, Lorenz Hart, Cole Porter, Irving Berlin, and the Gershwins were enrolled in production. Plots, direction, and music improved dramatically and stars such as Fred Astaire and Ginger Rodgers, Jeanette MacDonald and Nelson Eddy, Eleanor Powell, Eddie Cantor, Judy Garland, and Mickey Rooney added new vigour to the films. With their lavish art deco sets, fantasy romantic storylines, escapist themes, and first-rate musical scores, Hollywood musicals rapidly became strong favourites with British cinema audiences during the 1930s.

Despite the preponderance of Hollywood musicals, the British film industry during the 1930s did produce its own contribution to the genre and were among the biggest attractions for cinema audiences. Though much has been written on Hollywood musicals, the British musical film

[75] Quoted ibid. 130.   [76] Quoted ibid. 98.

has only recently attracted attention. As Stephen Guy argues to ignore British musical films is to fail to see their importance in popular culture.[77]

Although they might be thought mere adjuncts to the 'main feature', British musical films occupied an important position in British film studios. Analysis of the output of the British film industry in the sound era reveals the high numbers of musical films produced. Historians of British cinema have assessed the output of British studios with reference to the pioneering work of Denis Gifford who listed all entertainment films made in Britain from 1895 to 1970.[78] An analysis of the output, notwithstanding Gifford's somewhat narrow definition of 'musical films' ('comedy, drama or romance with an *above average* quota of songs'), suggests that the percentage of British musicals produced throughout the thirties was moderately high. In 1930, for example, around 18 per cent of British films were musical films, rising to a peak in 1936 when 48 British musical films constituted about 22 per cent of all releases. By 1939, this had fallen to just over 5 per cent. However, the figures are not really representative. Gifford's categorization is necessarily restrictive and omits a large number of films which were partly musical. Stephen Shafer, for instance, includes films classified by Gifford as 'Revues', which, he points out, almost invariably include a large proportion of 'songs, sing-alongs, and musical numbers'.[79] Yet even this is insufficient to gauge comprehensively the range of British musical films. First, the large number of short films that were very definitely based on musical performance must be included. Secondly, the areas of comedy and music also overlapped considerably, especially as many British musical films drew heavily on a music-hall and variety tradition. Thus the films of George Formby, for example, are included here as 'musical films' not only because of their substantial musical content but also because there is evidence to suggest that one of their main areas of appeal was music. Thirdly, musical stars often appeared in films to provide extra box-office attraction and to add a casual musical element. Thus radio personalities, dance bands, and artists like Paul Robeson added a musical dimension to films whose importance should not be discounted.

Using this broader definition of 'musical films' the proportion of 'musical-type' films produced is more impressive. In 1930, the year when

[77] S. Guy, 'Calling All Stars: Musical Films in a Musical Decade', in J. Richards (ed.), *The Unknown 1930s: An Alternative History of the British Cinema 1929–39* (1998), 99–118.

[78] D. Gifford, *The British Film Catalogue 1895–1985*, 2nd edn. (Newton Abbot, 1986).

[79] S. C. Shafer, *British Popular Films 1929–1939* (1997), 22–5.

American musicals flooded British cinemas, around one-third of all films produced in Britain were musical films. The only other category with such presence was 'comedy' films. Although this high proportion of musical films dropped back to a quarter in 1933, by 1936 over ninety musicals, revues, musical shorts, and musical comedies were produced in Britain, representing 36 per cent of all the films released that year. Musical films, therefore, represented a substantial proportion of British film studios' output, providing further evidence of the enduring popularity of the genre among British audiences.

Broadly speaking, there were four main types of musical film produced in Britain. The first was musical 'shorts' of around ten to fifteen minutes in length, which were little more than film records of individual acts. Second were 'revue' films, longer films featuring a procession of different acts. Thirdly, there were cinematic 'vehicles' for particular musical artists; and finally full-length feature 'musicals' which were more like their American counterparts. Such films drew from a wide range of existing musical traditions, predominantly music hall, but also the 'legitimate' musical theatre and even operetta.

Short films featuring musical artists were among the earliest forms of sound film made. Experiments in sound, with films being synchronized with gramophone records, were made as early as 1900. A variety of systems, such as Gaumont's Chronophone and Walturdaw's Cinematophone recorded many performers, especially music hall acts. The limitations of the system were obvious, however.[80] With the introduction of true sound film in the late 1920s, 'musical shorts' became even more numerous. The production of shorts was enhanced by 1927 legislation to protect the British film industry and which set quotas for the proportion of British films shown in cinemas. So-called 'Quota Quickies' flourished. Several studios produced series of 'shorts' of this nature, which were shown in advance of the main feature. Most British musical shorts were music-hall and variety performances. The easiest way of presenting music-hall stars and songs was simply photographing their acts with no attempt to adapt the entertainment to the new genre of film. In the early 1930s artists like George Robey, Robb Wilton, Nervo and Knox, and Harry Lauder made a large number of such shorts. They were cheap and quick to produce and remained popular throughout the period. Trends in popular music were well catered for in such films and the popularity of dance music is

[80] A. Medhurst, 'Music Hall and British Cinema', in Charles Barr (ed.), *All Our Yesterdays: 90 Years of British Cinema* (1996), 175.

reflected in the large number of short films in which it features. In January 1930, for example, Gainsborough studios produced a series of fifteen *Gainsborough Gems*, of about ten minutes' duration each featuring, among others, Martini and His Band, Hal Swain and His Sax-o-Five, and Lewis Hardcastle's Dusky Syncopators. In 1936 there was a series of nine *British Lion Varieties*, which included the dance bands of Roy Fox and Joe Loss, and in 1939 musical shorts included *Radio Nights* with Eddie Carrol and His Boys and *Tunes of the Times* with Alfredo Campoli and His Orchestra.

The second genre of musical film, the 'revue film', was cinematically little more advanced than these shorts. The 'revue' or 'parade' film was one where several different musical acts were patched together. The crudest were simply longer versions of the musical shorts, containing virtually no plot at all. *Radio Parade* (1933), for example, merely presented series of acts strung together with no plot and featured Roy Fox and His Band, comedienne Florence Desmond, comic duo Elsie and Doris Waters, singers Elsie Carlisle and the Carlyle Cousins, and singing partners Flotsam and Jetsam. *Variety Parade* (1936) was a similar offering with the dance band of Mrs Jack Hylton and Her Boys, crooner Sam Browne, xylophonist Teddy Brown, and the jazz-inspired Nat Gonella and His Georgians. Other films in this genre did develop plots further, but most were weak. One gimmick, borrowed from America, was to give films a show business setting—radio stations, recording studios, stage shows, film or television studios—in order to account for the prevalence of musical entertainment in such films. *Limelight* (1936), for example, was the story of a girl who helps a busker become a star of the musical stage and features Anna Neagle with twenty-four 'Hippodrome girls', American singer Arthur Tracy, and Geraldo and his 'sweet music'. Other examples of this genre include *Elstree Calling* (1930), which advertised itself as 'all-star vaudeville and revue entertainment' and had a plot based in a television studio. The film was a medley of musical, dance, and comedy performances by variety stars Jack Hulbert and Bobbie Comber, music-hall veteran Will Fyffe, radio star Tommy Handley, and international cabaret star Anna May Wong.

Perhaps the most popular use of music-hall and variety talent, however, was in the creation of cinematic 'vehicles' created to exhibit the talents of individual stars and artists. The most successful were the films of George Formby and Gracie Fields (see Plates 8 and 9).

Fields and Formby were the most popular cinema stars in Britain during the 1930s. In the *Motion Picture Herald*'s list of British box-office attractions for 1936, Formby, after only two years in the cinema, was already fourth. By 1937 he was second to Gracie Fields, and from 1938 to 1943 inclusive he was first.[81] Formby made twenty-one films between 1934 and 1946, and nearly all of his pre-war films were 'hits'. Fields made ten films between 1931 and 1939, the final three for the American studio Twentieth Century Fox.[82] For all their other qualities—their comedy and their warmth—it is clear that the main appeal of such films is their music. Formby himself thought that the insertion of songs halted the momentum of his films and would have preferred to exclude them but his producers anticipated public outcry at this. Michael Balcon, who produced Formby's later films at Ealing Studios, testified to their importance, when he wrote: 'We used to gnash our teeth at . . . the difficulty of integrating these numbers into the film. We even tried leaving them out, but the Formby public would not have it. No comedy songs, no audience.'[83] There is some evidence to support this hypothesis. Mass-Observation carried out a detailed survey of audience reactions to the 1940 George Formby film *Let George Do It* indicating that the songs themselves became very popular.[84] A majority approved of the musical content of Formby films, with 45 per cent saying that they did like him singing in his films and a further 20 per cent saying that they usually liked him singing but not the songs featured in this particular film. Twenty-eight per cent disliked Formby's singing and 7 per cent were of no opinion.

Yet Formby and Fields were not the only stars who had musical vehicles built around them. Jack Hulbert, Cicely Courtneidge, and Jack Buchanan were in a similar position. *Jack's the Boy* (1932) was a huge commercial hit. In the 1930s, the heyday of the dance bands, bandleaders, singers, and star instrumentalists, film producers rapidly realized their potential for film making. Several dance bands had vehicles specifically tailored for them. Jack Payne appeared in *Say it with Music* (1932), Jack Hylton appeared in *She Shall Have Music* (1935), and Henry Hall in *Music Hath Charms* (1935). In addition to these starring roles, dance bands also made brief appearances in other feature films in order to ensure box-office success. The 1930 *Symphony in Two Flats* by Ivor Novello, for example, featured Jack Payne and the BBC Dance Orchestra and the 1933 non-musical *The King's Cup* featured Lew Stone and His Band.

[81] Richards, *Dream Palace*, 198.   [82] Ibid. 177–90.   [83] Quoted Ibid. p. 193.
[84] M-O survey results in Richards and Sheridan (ed.), *Mass-Observation at the Movies*, 331–49.

The last category of British musical films were full blown 'musicals'. Many British film musicals relied heavily on the theatre, and were essentially film versions of stage productions, often using the original cast. *Digging for Gold* (1936) for example, was even filmed in the Windmill Theatre. One of the most up to date was *The Lambeth Walk* (1939) a film version of *Me and My Girl* (1937) which had introduced the song and inspired Adele England's dance. Like the stage version, Lupino Lane starred. Other productions were adaptations, altered for the new medium, such as *She Knew What She Wanted* (1936) based on *Funny Face*, by Fred Thompson. As Stephen Guy has noted, European operetta-style musicals, a musical style with a popular following, were also produced in Britain, though not in large quantities. They were set in exotic locations with lavish sets and costumes and were also a continuation of an old genre, musical comedy and light opera, where British composers had established a successful niche for themselves. The titles of such films revel in this exotica. From 1933, for example, was *Prince of Arcadia*, a musical set in Ruritania, Noel Coward's *Bitter Sweet* set in Vienna in 1875, and *Waltz Time* starring Evelyn Laye and based on Strauss's *Die Fledermaus*. Among the biggest successes were *Goodnight Vienna* (1932) starring Jack Buchanan and Anna Neagle and *Blossom Time* (1934) based on the life and music of Franz Schubert. In addition to using stars of the popular musical theatre such films also featured popular classical singers. The most popular was the Austrian tenor Richard Tauber who had a wide repertoire and a large popular following. He also recorded widely.

The nearest British studios got to matching the critical success of Hollywood musicals was in the films of Jessie Matthews. Lavish art deco sets, with plots taking place in a stylized world laden with the icons of interwar culture-nightclubs, ocean liners, newspaper offices, and radio studios. Well-written musical scores and a star as sumptuous as any Hollywood leading lady made the Jessie Matthews musicals popular on both sides of the Atlantic. In the *Motion Picture Herald's* popularity polls, Matthews was consistently highly rated, being second in 1936, third in 1937, and fourth in 1938. In all she starred in nearly twenty films between 1931 and 1939, ten of them musicals. Her most successful musicals were *Evergreen* (1934), *First a Girl* (1936), *It's Love Again* (1936), *Head over Heels* (1937), and *Gangway* (1937). It was through these films that Jessie Matthews made numerous hit songs. Such was her success in America that several attempts were made by American studios to get her to partner Fred Astaire but nothing came of them.

The enormous popularity of musical film stars like Matthews gave film studios considerable influence in the popular music industry. The cinema's pervasive influence in peoples' leisure, especially among the working class, enabled it to shape trends in popular music. The extent to which the cinema could direct tastes in popular music can be seen in the Appendix, which lists the most popular tunes for each of the years 1919, 1925, 1930, 1935, and 1939 arranged month by month. By 1930 it appeared that the British popular song was in danger of being washed away in a tide of American songs, most from the new medium of the talking film. Nearly half of the most popular tunes of 1930 (45 per cent) had first been heard in films. Of the film successes of 1930, for example, were *Gold Diggers of Broadway* which introduced 'Tip Toe through the Tulips' and 'Painting the Clouds with Sunshine'; *Sunny Side up* with 'Sunny Side up', 'I'm a Dreamer' and 'If I Had a Talking Picture of You'; *The Love Parade* with 'Dream Lover', 'Nobody's Using it Now' and 'My Love Parade'; and *Chasing Rainbows*, with the depression song 'Happy Days are Here Again'. Hollywood began to have as important an influence on British popular music as America's Tin Pan Alley and jazz had had a decade earlier. After 1930, despite a large decline in the number of popular hit songs originating in films, the cinema retained its importance. By 1935, a quarter of the most popular songs came from films, and this proportion was to remain constant, with the 1939 figure almost the same, at 23 per cent. (See Plates 10 and 11.)

Indeed such was the success of the cinema in promoting sales of popular music that *Voice* advised gramophone and music shops to promote 'tie-ups' with the cinema. The fillip that cinema had given to the industry was clear, as *Voice*, journal of HMV gramophone dealers, commented:

the Talkie has given to the mighty stream of the gramophone record industry an enormous and ever growing tributary. And it has come to stay. You know perfectly well that a large proportion of your last year's business was done in records of theme songs from Talkie Films.[85]

Methods for promoting gramophone–cinema 'tie-ups' were numerous. Gramophone companies produced a range of advertising paraphernalia for their dealers, with streamers and leaflets referring to individual films, general 'Talkie Streamers', and special catalogues of recordings from films. Dealers were also asked to approach cinema managers to ask them for film stills to make window displays. As early as 1929 arrangements had

---

[85] *Voice*, Mar. 1930, p. 1.

been made with Associated British Cinemas Ltd. for an announcement to be shown on the screen of each cinema stating that the 'song-hits' from the film were available from the local dealer. In turn the HMV dealers were advised to create window displays advertising the records of the song hits featured during the week the films were showing.

Conclusion

The impact of the radio and cinema on interwar society, culture, and popular music in particular, was great. The radio and cinema, as the gramophone had done before them, provided an unprecedented supply of music to the British people. As Edward German commented in 1935, the new media were largely responsible for music's ubiquity:

Music, like the poor, has always been with us, and never more so than to-day, when the miracle of broadcasting places the works of the world's greatest composers, living and dead, at the disposal of us all.

The possession of a comparatively inexpensive radio-set enables any music lover to satisfy his soul with all the music, and any form of music, that he requires. He may breakfast to music, if he so morbidly desires, and in the privacy of his home he may dine and dance and read and even talk to music, and, by tuning into foreign stations, enjoy a musical accompaniment to life during twenty-four hours of every day . . . music has never before been so popular or been made so lavish a use of as it is to-day.[86]

Such media constantly required huge amounts of fresh material, thus creating a large demand for new hit songs. The *Voice* observed this rapid turnover of hits in the cinema:

The theme song may have a short life, but it is certainly a merry and busy one, and there are so many of them. No small cinema holds a film for more than a week. Every Talkie has one big theme song, many have four. This means that in your particular neighbourhood there will be created a demand for records of at least one new theme song per week.[87]

All three of the musical mass media were interlinked, with the radio, cinema, and gramophone part of an increasingly sophisticated entertainment industry providing ready-made popular music for a growing audience. Many feared such concentration of power. The cinema and radio, like the gramophone before it, were accused of killing off sales of sheet

---

[86] Anon., *Radio and the Composer* (1935), 28–9.   [87] *Voice*, Mar. 1930, p. 1.

music and threatening the survival of live music. In fact, the radio and
cinema were responsible for widening the appeal of music in Britain and
the BBC in particular was responsible for a transformation of musical
appreciation. The radio and the cinema were also unifying and standardizing cultural entities to an extent not seen before. Dance music, for
example, was played by the best bands, to society audiences in London's
leading hotels, and relayed live into the humblest homes throughout the
country. The same dance band and the same music were accessible by
rich and poor alike. Both the cinema and radio were affordable to all but
the very poorest members of the community and they provided a standard and range of entertainment of unprecedented quality.

Part Two

THE 'LIVE' POPULAR MUSIC INDUSTRY

4

DEVELOPMENTS IN 'LIVE MUSIC' 1918 TO 1939: FROM 'PERFORMERS' TO 'LISTENERS'

Introduction

Between 1918 and 1939, the sphere of 'live music' underwent a dramatic transformation. There were two main pressures on live music; one internal and the other external. Internally, the period saw a huge shift away from private performance in the home and a rapid increase in the public performance of live music. The general public became listeners rather than performers, reflecting the growing commercialization of popular music. By the end of the period there was a vast quantity of 'live music' being heard in theatres, public houses, cafés, restaurants, hotels, and public parks throughout Britain. This shift created widespread disruption to the established worlds of music publishing and musicianship. As the Performing Right Society put it in 1932:

There can be little doubt that thirty or forty years ago nothing like the present number of public musical entertainments were taking place. On the other hand, private performances . . . have diminished over the same period in inverse ratio, judging from the rapid falling off of sales of printed music for home use. It is common-place that at the beginning of the present century almost every family had one or two members who made some pretension to musical attainments, either as vocalist or instrumentalist, with the result that there was always a ready market for the printed sheet. Nowadays the majority of our citizens are listeners rather than performers—a fact which does not by any means indicate a diminishing interest in music, but which has naturally produced a most profound change in the fortunes of those who create and publish it.[1]

[1] *PRG*, Apr. 1932, p. 67.

The second pressure on live music came from outside forces. Audiences rapidly abandoned live music of all kinds in favour of the radio, gramophone, or cinema and this threatened to destroy 'live music' completely.

This chapter is divided into two sections. The first will look at the place of self-made music, where the general public is an active performer. The second section will look at the spread of ready-made musical entertainment where members of the general public were predominantly listeners to 'live music'. The development of the dance band, which was to the twentieth century what the 'brass band' was to the nineteenth, is so important that it merits a separate chapter of its own. Similarly, dance halls, one of the most widespread venues for the performance of 'live music', are also dealt with separately.

4.1 Self-made 'live music': the public as performers

Self-made music, where the public were performers, was centred in the home. As the availability of musical instruments and sheet music were vital to the production of such live music, the fortunes of both the music publishing industry and the music instruments trade are a key to estimating the popularity of domestic music making in the interwar period. It must be borne in mind, however, that the sale of musical instruments and sheet music was in no way limited to individuals for domestic use. Professional dance bands, orchestras, and various string quartets and trios all provided light, popular, and 'serious' music in public and accounted for a large proportion of sales. Also, some forms of music making, such as choral music, did not require instruments. However, certain instruments, notably the piano, had substantial domestic markets. Indeed, since the nineteenth century the piano had been crucial to the popular music industry. Importantly, what Cyril Ehrlich has called the 'piano culture'—a culture based around the use of musical notation via sheet music and the widespread use of pianos—was transformed during the interwar period. Prior to this, the piano was at the centre of domestic musical entertainment in (largely middle-class) homes of all sizes. Since the availability of cheap uprights in the 1830s, the piano had become an increasingly important factor in the dissemination of popular music. By the Victorian period, falling prices and rising incomes moved the piano into the home and it rapidly became a focus for domestic music making. The popularity of the piano in Britain was far greater than elsewhere in Europe. The new, piano based ragtime music which emerged just before the First World War actually encouraged the growth of the piano rather than killed it off. The piano encouraged the growth in the number of piano teachers, made music reading an essential element of popular music, and thus led to huge sales of sheet music. As Cyril Ehrlich has said, 'The piano was the centre of domestic entertainment, music shops were familiar in every high street, and sheet music was regularly purchased, by people of all ages and at every level of society.'[2] The interwar period, however, saw a rapid transformation of this situation. The popular music industry, and live music in particular, were revolutionized by developments in technology. The musical instrument and sheet music trades were subject to the onslaught of mechanical competition in the form of gramophones, radios, and sound films. Both were altered permanently.

Sales of musical instruments in the early part of the twentieth century were high and the sale of musical instruments continued to grow strongly before and immediately after the First World War. Changes in domestic musical habits did not manifest themselves clearly until the mid-1920s. After this, the musical instruments trade contracted considerably, especially between 1930 and 1935. According to the various Censuses of Production, the value of the output of the musical instruments trade, without the gramophone, was £1,784,000 in 1907, rising to £5,202,000 in 1924.[3] By 1930, output had fallen to £3,630,000, falling again to £2,473, 000 in 1935, before rising to £3,674,000 in 1937.[4] The reasons for these changes were chiefly a result of the impact of broadcasting, electrical reproduction of the gramophone, and the sound film. Despite the changes, however, the musical instrument trade was worth nearly twice as much in 1937 as it was in 1907.

If the figures are disaggregated it can be seen how certain sections of the musical instrument industry fared. Most importantly, the interwar period saw the end of the piano culture's predominance in popular music. The number of new pianos produced in Britain rose from 58,100 in 1907 to 79,600 in 1912 and rose further to 95,010 in 1924.[5] This represents an increase in output of 37 per cent between 1907 and 1912 and by over 19 per cent between 1912 and 1924. After this date, output of pianos fell

---

[2] C. Ehrlich, *Harmonious Alliance: A History of the Performing Right Society* (1989), 5.

[3] *Final Report on the Third Census of Production of the United Kingdom 1924* (1931), Part IV, 398–9.

[4] *Final Report on the Fifth Census of Production 1935* (1940), Part IV, 545 and *Final Report on the Census of Production for 1948* (1951), Part 5L, 2.

[5] *Third Census of Production*, Part IV, 398.

dramatically, falling to 53,822 in 1930, stabilizing at 51,309 in 1935, and dropping slightly to 48,263 in 1937.[6] This pre-dated the downturn in the rest of the musical instruments trade. Such dramatic changes of fortune meant that the piano's place in the home was greatly reduced. Indeed, the piano culture was virtually dead by 1939.

Changing tastes in popular music accentuated this decline and there were a number of trends in the sale of other musical instruments. The ukulele, for example, was in vogue in the 1920s. It was popular in the new dance music and during the 1930s the popularity of George Formby encouraged a boom in sales. Most sheet music gave ukulele fingering, reflecting its position as a rival to the piano. Other entertainers also affected the sales of instruments. In 1938, for example, there was a craze for the harmonica, as a result of the success of Larry Adler. There were also crazes for accordions, maracas, and kazoos. The most enduring influence on the sales of musical instruments was the popularity of dance music, which particularly encouraged the sale of saxophones and trumpets. Large numbers of amateurs joined a growing number of professionals to form dance bands,[7] which gave the wind instrument sector of the musical instruments trade a certain resilience in face of the changes described above.

The wind sector of the musical instruments trade was the largest. The value of wind instruments and parts produced in Britain in 1907 was £73,000, rising to £158,000 in 1924 and continuing to rise to £166,000 in 1930.[8] Although output fell back to £89,000 in 1935, it soon recovered to a respectable £115,000 in 1937.[9] String instruments and parts produced in Britain in 1907 had a value of £15,000, rising to £66,000 in 1924.[10] By 1930, the value of output had fallen to £48,000 and by 1935 it was £25,000, still larger than at the start of the century, however.[11] The value of 'other' musical instruments and parts was £18,000 in 1907 rising to £99,000 in 1924. Production fell back rapidly to only £19,000 in 1930, before rising to £88,000 in 1935; nearly five times the value of production in 1907.[12]

Although such statistics indicate substantial sales of musical instruments, it was increasingly clear that the piano was no longer central to popular music making and that other instruments were beginning to take

[6] *Fifth Census of Production*, Part IV, 547.   [7] See Chapter 5.

[8] *Final Report on the Fourth Census of Production 1930* (1935), Part IV, 253.

[9] *Census of Production for 1948*, Part 5L, 6.

[10] *Third Census of Production*, Part IV, 398.

[11] *Fifth Census of Production*, Part IV, 547.   [12] Ibid.

its place. Interest in music making remained high, however, and music shops, for example, remained a familiar feature of the interwar high street.

Music shops catered directly for the demand for home music making and from the end of the nineteenth century they were a familiar feature of every high street. A snapshot of the number of music shops throughout Britain during the height of the sales of musical instruments in this period (1925) shows just how much musical instruments had become part of life in Britain. The number of music shops selling pianos, gramophones, music, orchestral instruments, and accessories listed in the 1925 *Directory of the British Music Industries* was much larger than it is today.[13] In London there were 551 shops, indicative of the growing centralization of the music trade in the capital. In major provincial cities the provision was also large, however. Manchester had 72 shops, Glasgow 51, Birmingham 49, Liverpool 45, Bristol 39, Leeds 32, Portsmouth 30, Edinburgh 26, Bradford 23, and Cardiff 22. In large towns there was also provision; Huddersfield had 17 shops in 1925, Northampton 15, Aberdeen 13, and Croydon 13. Even small towns were well catered for. Hereford had 6 music shops, Crewe had 5, Gillingham also had 5; Liskeard in Cornwall with a population of just 4,376 had 5 music shops.

Clearly, interest in music making was still high in interwar Britain. However, although the music instruments trade in general was bigger at the outbreak of the Second World War than it was at the start of the century, the data related to the sheet music industry suggests that this was in some part a reflection of the large number of public performances of live music rather than the survival of home music making.

Popular music publishing had developed as a separate entity at the end of the nineteenth century when growing affluence created a commercial demand for printed music. Prior to this, apart from the success of Chappells and Boosey with the ballads market, music publishing had been predominantly concerned with 'serious' music. The first popular songs printed widely were comic songs, the demand for which was created in the various 'Pleasure Gardens' and music halls which were popular in the mid-nineteenth century among an increasingly working-class audience. There was soon a substantial market for copies of the songs that were heard in the halls and established publishers like Chappells and Boosey began to provide popular sheet music.

---

[13] Federation of British Music Industries, *The Directory of the British Music Industries, 1925* (1925).

Popular music publishing expanded rapidly beyond being a mere 'side-line' and by the late nineteenth century it was a distinctive form of music publishing, with several publishers devoted to working specifically in this field. Hopwood and Crew were early pioneers in this respect, and they increasingly focused on popular songs. The first successful firm catering *exclusively* for popular music was Francis, Day, and Hunter, established in 1877. This was joined by Bert Feldmans in 1896 and later by Lawrence Wright and a host of others. The success of Francis, Day, and Hunter is indicative of the growing strength of the popular music publishers at the end of the nineteenth century. Francis and Day was set up in 1877 by brothers William and James Francis and friend Harry Hunter to exploit the songs of their own minstrel troupe. They appointed David Day, who worked for Hopwood and Crew, to run the publishing business, initially to publish their minstrel songs. Day expanded the repertoire of the business and developed close connections with the music hall, its representatives touring the halls for new songs and new talent. It also published the latest ballads from America. On the death of James Francis, Harry Hunter was made a partner and the name of the business changed to Francis, Day, and Hunter. A growing school of writers was employed to cater to the demand from music-hall artists for songs and the success of the business saw the firm expand and move into premises in Charing Cross Road in 1897. Between 1900 and 1910, Francis, Day, and Hunter were publishing, on average, between 40 and 50 songs per month, sometimes 80 or 90.[14] The firm began to cater for a mass market and in the same period it found new outlets in the developing multiple chain stores and employed dozens of exploiters to tour public places of entertainment selling the company's products.

The increasingly international nature of the music business saw Francis, Day, and Hunter opening offices in New York in 1905, with the double purpose of selling British numbers there and also bringing in American numbers and catalogues for the home market. The rapid influx of American songs was to have far reaching effects. In Britain a special department was established to deal specifically with developments in America. Francis, Day, and Hunter were one of the first firms to introduce ragtime to Britain and after the First World War they regularly visited the United States to get new material. Offices were also opened in Paris and Berlin.

Francis, Day, and Hunter's rapid growth was evidence of a healthy market for popular music. The demand for sheet music in Britain before

---

[14] J. Abbott, *The Story of Francis, Day & Hunter* (1952), 21.

the First World War was huge. By the end of the nineteenth century, annual sales were estimated to be some 20 million pieces with 40,000 new titles, each printed in runs of at least 200. Popular hits often sold 200,000 copies. Simple piano pieces and piano tutors, scales, and exercises were another large sector of the industry.

As the demand for sheet music grew, the popular music publishing business became increasingly organized and concentrated in central London. The large amount of business generated by the pre-war craze for ragtime helped to formalize the industry. In a small side street off Charing Cross Road called Denmark Street, a host of publishers settled to form London's 'Tin Pan Alley', the name consciously borrowed from America. Francis, Day, and Hunter had been the first to move to this part of London, establishing itself in Charing Cross Road in 1897, but the first firm to move into Denmark Street was Lawrence Wright Music Co., who set up business in premises at No. 8 in 1911. With the success of ragtime and the demand created by the First World War, Tin Pan Alley became extremely prosperous and more firms moved there. By 1938 around 300 people were employed in the music publishing business in this little area of London.[15] Although less concentrated than America's Tin Pan Alley— at least three of the biggest song publishers still had premises elsewhere as late as 1937—this particular area of central London became a focus of the entertainment world.[16] London's major theatres were situated nearby in Shaftesbury Avenue and Leicester Square. Adjacent to it, in the night clubs of Soho, was the centre of Britain's developing dance music and jazz scene while later the British Film Industry established itself next to Denmark Street, in Wardour Street.

The market for sheet music continued to grow rapidly and was boosted by the jazz and dance crazes of the post-war years. The output of the musical instruments trade and sales of pianos continued to expand every year after the First World War until the mid-1920s. In this period a number of individual songs achieved impressive sales. In 1919 Lawrence Wright, for example, had one of his biggest successes with 'That Old Fashioned Mother of Mine' which, although not an overnight success, eventually sold over 3 million sheet music copies. Wright followed this with 'Wyoming' (1920), which sold 3 million sheet music copies and records, 'Pasadena' (1924), which sold a million sheet music copies, and 'Among My Souvenirs' (1926), which made over £20,000.[17] This growth was not continuous, however, and from the mid-1920s onwards, there

---

[15] M-O A: MDJ, 5/B, A. Hurley, 'Interviews: Denmark Street', 9 Dec. 1938, p. 18.
[16] *Songwriter*, June 1937, p. 14.   [17] E. Rogers, *Tin Pan Alley* (1964), 47–8, 51.

was a dramatic collapse in sheet music sales, reflecting a huge change in domestic musical entertainment.

The collapse of the market is graphically illustrated by the world sales returns of nine representative music publishers (including Lawrence Wright, Francis, Day, and Hunter, and B. Feldman) from 1925 to 1935. In 1925 sales of sheet music for these nine publishers were £566,549, falling to £453,564 in 1929, £284,564 in 1933, and £217, 632 in 1935.[18] In just one decade their sales of sheet music had reduced by more than half. The collapse of sheet music sales is also reflected in the experience of Keith Prowse and Co. Ltd, a large retailer of sheet music with numerous branches throughout London. Keith Prowse sold sheet music from the catalogues of all the major music publishers. Sales to music retailers throughout the country, plus sales in its own branches, virtually halved, dropping from £40,992 in 1921 to £21,434 in 1935.[19]

Amid this general malaise, the 'popular ' publishers were particularly hard hit. In 1921 the Lawrence Wright Music Company had sales of sheet music of £71,047, haemorrhaging to £13,831 in 1935. Francis, Day, and Hunter saw their sales drop from £88,072 in 1921 to £32,549 in 1935. Sales at B. Feldman and Co. fell from £67,206 in 1921 to £25,082.[20]

Prior to the collapse in sheet music sales, profits had been dependent on the high sales from a relatively small number of 'hit' numbers. By the mid-1930s, however, the pattern was inclined towards the sale of fewer copies of a higher number of different songs—increasing considerably the costs of production. An examination of the sheet music sales of the six most popular works in the catalogues of three of the major publishers of popular music from 1921 to 1935 shows that the sales of individual 'hit' songs decreased dramatically.[21]

In 1921, the sales of B. Feldman's six most popular works earned £15,006; by 1935 the corresponding figure was £4,262. Whereas Feldman's best-selling number in 1919, 'I'm Forever Blowing Bubbles', made

[18] PRS A: 'Memorandum D: Statement of Decrease in Royalties on Sales of Sheet Music and Gramophone Records' from 'Memorandum prepared by the Society for use before the Broadcasting (Ullswater) Committee 1935' (June 1935).

[19] PRS A: BBC Arbitration 1937: 'Prove of Ernest John Morriss, Accountant of Keith Prowse and Co. Ltd.' (1937).

[20] PRS A: BBC Arbitration 1937: 'Comparative Statements Relating to the Sales of Sheet Music, Mechanical Royalties, Performing and Broadcasting Fees of Publishers and Composers' (1937).

[21] PRS A: BBC Arbitration 1937: 'Statement Shewing Sheet Music Sales and Mechanical Royalties of the Six Most Popular Works in the Catalogues of Certain Publishers of Light Music for the Three Years 1921, 1929 and 1935' (1937).

£7,212, by 1935 its top draw, 'Lullaby of Broadway', made only £1,299. Francis, Day, and Hunter witnessed a similar collapse of sales. Every title, with the exception of 'Dapper Dan', in their 1921 top six had sales of over £2,000, with the most popular number, 'Peggy O'Neil', reaching sales of £10,590 and number two, 'Coal Black Mammy', £7,580. By 1935 every number was selling less than £1,000 worth of sheet music, with the exception of 'When I Grow Too Old to Dream' which had sales worth £5,976.

The decline in sheet music sales was particularly marked between 1929 and 1935. At Lawrence Wright Music Co., for example, sales for 1929 show that there was still a considerable profit to be made from popular music. Its best-seller for 1929 was 'Carolina Moon' which had sheet music sales of £8,701. This was followed by 'Happy Days and Lonely Nights' with sales worth £5,340; 'Glad Rag Doll' £4,397; 'Girl of My Dreams' £3,118; 'Just Plain Folk' £2,637; and 'Shinaniki-Da' with sales worth £1,613. These six most popular works had sheet music sales totalling £25,806. By 1935, however, no single work made more than £1,000 and the total return for the top six songs was a mere £3,304. Even the top-selling song of 1935, 'Love is Everywhere', only made £882, and number six, 'Look up and Laugh', sold a paltry £266 worth of sheet music.

The causes of this collapse in sales were the changes that were taking place in the entertainment industry as a whole, reflecting the availability of greater choice and improved living standards for the majority of people in Britain. The sheet music industry was dealt a double blow in this period. The first occurred during the 1920s when the number of public locations for the performance of popular music mushroomed enormously.[22] In cafés, theatres, concert halls, village halls, and public parks, the number of performances of live music increased rapidly. Music was everywhere, creeping into areas of life it had previously not entered. The resulting shift from private to public performance is described in 1928:

less sheet music is sold now than formerly, and it must necessarily follow that there has been a corresponding decrease in the number of performances taking place by means of sheet music. But where has this decrease manifested itself? Surely not in the number of public performances, which are far more numerous today than ever before, as the hundreds of cinema and dance halls which have sprung up all over the country during the Society's life-time bear witness, and

[22] See above.

also the increasing prevalence of music in hotels, restaurants, etc. The diminution has occurred, then, in the number of private performances . . . This points to the inevitable conclusion that less sheet music is sold for private performances than hitherto, but whether less sheet music is sold for public performances is very much open to question.[23]

Dance bands needed sheet music, cinema orchestras needed sheet music, and café trios needed sheet music. Thus, the growing public performance of live music partially compensated for the reduction in sales for domestic use. However, one dance band playing to several hundred people at a dance hall required less sheet music than if the dancers were to make their own music at home. The irony for the music publishers and composers was that although music sales were falling, more people than ever before were actually hearing their compositions. This logic was to increase the power and influence of the Performing Right Society.[24]

The second and more important setback came at the end of the 1920s and the 1930s when the threat from 'mechanical music' developed fully. In the home, the gramophone and the radio began increasingly to replace the piano as the chief source of musical entertainment and neither required sheet music. Becket Williams of the Musicians' Union described the effects of 'the rise of mechanical music':

the outlook for the creative musician appears very bleak indeed. We live in a chaotic age. Old conventions and usages are going by the board . . . I do not propose to moralize, but the world is lazy and indolent. And, after all, why should a new generation trouble to learn to play the piano, now the reproducing instruments have arrived at such a pitch of perfection? Why should my sons and daughter take singing lessons when a gramophone record gives much more pleasure?[25]

The rise of the gramophone from scientific novelty to Britain's first musical mass media form had a serious effect on the sheet music industry. Prior to 1911, the gramophone offered no real threat but by this time it had become a practical instrument and the sales of gramophone records were affecting sheet music sales. This fact was recognized by the legislature in the Copyright Act of 1911 and a royalty was payable on all records of copyright musical works to compensate for the loss in revenue to composers and authors. The sales of gramophones and records steadily increased until 1925, when electrical recording and reproduction were launched. Between 1925 and 1929 improvements in electrical

[23] *PRG*, Oct. 1928, p. 351.
[24] For development of the PRS see Ehrlich, *Harmonious Alliance*.
[25] *PRG*, Apr. 1926, p. 85.

recording brought about a boom in the sales of gramophones and gramophone records. It was in this period that the sheet music industry really began to feel the competition of its new mechanical rival. The gramophone, however, was tolerated by the composer and author of popular music because of the copyright arrangements made under the Act of 1911. As long as gramophone sales increased, composers saw a corresponding increase in their royalties, which partially compensated for the drop in sheet music sales. This boom in gramophone record sales was, however, cut short by the world depression and by the development of another mechanical threat—radio.

When broadcasting was launched in 1922 it posed little threat to sheet music sales. Receiving instruments were expensive and inconvenient, the quality was very poor, and the programmes very limited. Improvements in broadcasting were rapid, however, and by 1925 it was having a noticeable effect on sheet music sales. The radio became increasingly affordable and established itself quickly as the chief source of musical entertainment in the home. By 1929 it was beginning to affect both the sales of gramophone records and sheet music. Its convenience and value for money compared favourably with the more time consuming and expensive process of individual music making. Whereas playing from sheet music required musical skill, expensive instruments, and sheet music, the radio provided a vast range of music at the switch of a button and for a small annual fee. As William Charles Ward, general manager of the Lawrence Wright Music Co. Ltd, stated in 1937, 'The continuous performance of music by the best bands and artists available "on tap" throughout the day has to a very great extent killed the desire of self-performance (or expression) by the individual in the home.'[26]

Broadcasting had other consequences. The effect of radio was to shorten the life of the 'hit' song and thus to reduce the time during which publishers could exploit its success. Radio transformed the domestic habits of Britons of all classes, in all regions, turning them, at a stroke, from 'performers' to 'listeners'.

'Mechanical music' was, however, not alone in doing this. Of equal importance were the nation's changing habits. The increasing popularity of bicycling had affected the popularity of the piano in the nineteenth century by taking women (the largest group of piano players) out of the home. Considerably more people were able to spend more time and

---

[26] PRS A: BBC Arbitration 1937: 'Evidence of William Charles Ward of Lawrence Wright Co. Ltd', (1937), 4.

money on leisure from the 1920s onwards and this had an even greater effect on domestic music making. A large number of highly commercialized alternatives to home entertainment developed. The cinema, dance halls, ice rinks, speedway tracks, and so on, all offered well-run and cheap alternatives to household music making. The example of the cinema is particularly pertinent, for not only did sound films take their toll directly on the sales of sheet music but indirectly on the habit of individuals' making their own music. The coming of sound films in 1929 removed at a stroke one large market for sheet music completely and forever. As Cyril Ehrlich has observed:

Almost overnight there was no longer any need for a large and steady supply of 'photoplay' or background scores and instrumental scores, to thousands of British cinemas, as distinct from a handful of sound recording studios. Huge stocks . . . accumulated in warehouses, never to be used again, and were eventually destroyed.[27]

The new luxury cinemas changed people's entertainment habits. The cinema offered a world of diverting, ever-changing entertainment in warm, comfortable surroundings at a cost that represented exceptional value for money. With such alternatives, it was not surprising that parlour sing-songs around the piano declined. The sheet music industry and domestic music making centred around the piano were casualties of the new-found diversity of choice in leisure pursuits.

Although for some firms the decline in sales was almost permanent, there were others who were able to survive and flourish. The Lawrence Wright Music Company, for example, was at its most influential during the 1920s and 1930s. Lawrence Wright first set up a business selling music in 1906 in the Market Hall, Leicester. His business flourished and his entrepreneurial skills enabled him to open stores all over the East Midlands in a few years. Wright, under various pen names, usually 'Horatio Nicholls', was also a composer of songs and he had a keen sense of what the public wanted, acquiring particular success with topical numbers. He moved to Denmark Street in 1911 and there he built up his business shrewdly, swiftly, and systematically. He developed an impressive catalogue of ballads and comedy numbers and became associated with a string of hits. After the First World War he opened up demonstration shops in Blackpool and at various other coastal resorts. In 1924, with large royalties coming in, he turned to show business and presented *On*

---

[27] Ehrlich, *Harmonious Alliance*, 66.

with the Show, a showcase for contemporary popular songs from both sides of the Atlantic (see Plate 12). The show was a regular feature at the North Pier, Blackpool, where it ran for thirty-two years until 1956. In 1933 he bought the Prince's Theatre in Shaftsbury Avenue for £140,000 with the aim of bringing *On With the Show* to the West End. In 1926 he had founded the *Melody Maker* as the firm's house magazine and although he ceded control in 1927, he had managed to launch one of the most influential popular music journals of the period.

Lawrence Wright became associated with American style promotion of songs, spending heavily on publicity and doing much to improve trade in the popular music publishing industry as a whole.[28] That he spent heavily throughout the 1920s and 1930s suggests that he believed sheet music sales could be sustained. Wright also recognized the value of big American hits and he spent more than any other publisher in buying up the British rights to US songs. He signed up the popular American writer Walter Donaldson for three years at a cost of $50,000.[29] He also bought the British rights to Hoagy Carmichael's 'Lazybones' and 'Stardust'.

After several lean years, as testified by the evidence above, British popular music publishers saw a slight revival in fortunes in the mid-1930s. With the worst of the depression over and disposable income starting to rise, popular songs began to sell again.[30] In 1935 Lawrence Wright launched a new series of promotional campaigns, declaring that he believed that the slump in sheet music sales was over and predicting a new era of prosperity for the music trade and sales of sheet music. He told the *Melody Maker*:

Personally I am going all out for British songs, plugged one at a time with all the strength of my organisation and backed by the best publicity that money can buy. I believe that the trade generally will follow my example and . . . we can make people buy the kind of songs they like in greater numbers than ever before. I am back with my coat off, and believe me I will want some stopping.[31]

Although levels of business never returned to their former heyday, there was sufficient business for several new popular music publishers to enter the field.

One of the most important new popular music publishers, the Peter Maurice Music Company, was founded in 1930 by Jacques Koch de

[28] See Chapter 8 below.
[29] Donaldson hits include: 'Yes Sir, That's My Baby' (1925); 'My Blue Heaven' (1927); 'Makin' Whoopee' (1928), and 'My Baby Just Cares for Me' (1930).
[30] *The Songwriter*, June 1937, p. 15.   [31] *MM*, 19 Jan. 1935, p. 1.

Gooreynd, a member of the Belgian Royal Family. From 1933 the professional manager of the company was Jimmy Phillips, a successful songseller, who was hired to salvage the firm, which had debts of £100,000. Phillips changed the publishing policy of the company, taking the focus away from jazz and dance music and moving it to ballad style songs.[32] The firm's fortunes were transformed by one single British song, 'The Isle of Capri', which was written by Jimmy Kennedy and Will Grosz. It sold over 1 million copies in Britain and the USA (see Plate 11). Jimmy Kennedy was subsequently contracted to Peter Maurice, where his hits included 'Red Sails in the Sunset' (1935), which sold 420,000 copies; 'Serenade in the Night' (1936) and 'Harbour Lights' (1937), with sales of 140,000 copies. Other hit successes for the firm included 'Did Your Mother Come from Ireland?' (1936) with sales of 175,000 and 'Misty Islands of the Highlands' (1936) which sold 120,000 copies.[33] Indeed, Jimmy Kennedy, together with partner Michael Carr, was, more than anyone else, responsible for a revival in the fortunes of the sheet music trade in Britain during the 1930s. Their hits, together and with other writers, included 'The Teddy Bears' Picnic' (1932) which sold over a million sheet music copies, 'Old Faithful' (1933) which sold 800,000 song copies, 'Play to Me Gypsy' (1933) (which the *Melody Maker* said had 'electrified the music business')[34] one million copies, 'The Coronation Waltz (1937) 100,000 copies, and the most popular, 'South of the Border' (1939), over 1 million.[35] Such was their success that Peter Maurice established agents in sixteen countries world wide, including the USA, Australia, France, Italy, Spain, Switzerland, Poland, Germany, and the Balkan States.[36] By 1938, Peter Maurice's total British sales were averaging 1.5 million pieces per year.[37]

Songs like these played a big part in the revival of the sheet music industry's fortunes and illustrate that there was still a substantial audience for sheet music. As the *Songwriter* put it in 1937:

The million sale has not come back to be an almost commonplace thing in Tin Pan Alley, but the ten firms who publish the bulk of the popular music in England are experiencing brighter times. If they don't sell as many copies of their music there are radio, films, gramophone records, commercial broadcasting and vastly increased performances to make up for it.[38]

[32] M-O A: MDJ, 5/F: A. Hurley, 'Interview: Jimmy Phillips', 1 Dec. 1939.
[33] *RP*, 3 Sept. 1937, p. 22.   [34] *MM*, 28 Apr. 1934, p. 9.
[35] Rogers, *Tin Pan Alley*, 6–7.
[36] M-O A: MDJ, 5/C: Letter, Jimmy Phillips to Tom Harrison, 9 Dec. 1938.
[37] M-O A: MDJ, 5/C: Tom Harrison, 'Song Sales', 8 Aug. 1938.
[38] *Songwriter*, June 1937, p. 15.

The success of Peter Maurice was not unique. Equally successful was Campbell Connelly. This firm was founded by singer-songwriter Jimmy Campbell and his friend, the pianist Reg Connelly, on the back of one single song, 'Show Me the Way to Go Home' (1925). Having co-written the song with Canadian Hal Swain, the pair were convinced of its potential but could not get anyone to publish it. They decided to set up their own firm to do so and rented two rooms on Tottenham Court Road in 1925. The song was a huge success on both sides of the Atlantic and sold 2 million copies within one year. The firm grew rapidly and in 1926 they moved to Denmark Street, with a staff of twelve. Connelly was a shrewd businessman and Campbell a resourceful song plugger. Business expanded at a rapid rate. They collaborated with Ray Noble on 'Goodnight Sweetheart' (1931), 'By the Fireside' (1932), and with Harry Woods on 'Try a Little Tenderness' (1932) and negotiated exclusive tie-ups with American companies. In 1936, Campbell Connelly formed a new company with Gaumont-British, called Cinephonic, with the aim of linking up film and sheet music and cornering the song output of British musical films. Connelly had realized the importance of film as a medium for popularizing songs and had made numerous contacts, signing up writers wholesale. They also published the music of other film companies and had early successes plugging the material of Jessie Matthews.[39] Campbell Connelly developed into a powerful publishing organization, with fourteen associated companies and branches in Europe, America, and Australia.

Other firms formed during this period included Cameo Music Publishing Ltd., Cecil Lennox Music Company, and Noel Gay Music Co. Cameo was founded in 1929 by Will Haines, a former music-hall performer who had collaborated on many songs written for Gracie Fields. The Cecil Lennox Music Co. was founded jointly by songwriters Tolchard Evans, Harry Tilsely, Stanley J. Damerell, and Robert Hargreaves. They wrote and published their own tunes and successes included 'The Lady of Spain' (1931), a worldwide hit; 'Let's All Sing Like the Birdies Sing' (1932), which sold half a million copies between November and Christmas; 'Unless' (1934); and 'There's a Lovely Lake in London' (1935). The Noel Gay Music Company was founded in 1938 by the highly successful songwriter Noel Gay, following the spectacular success of his song 'The Lambeth Walk', and it prospered.

[39] *MM*, 20 Feb. 1937, p. 11.

It is likely that the reasons for this renewed demand were due to the great popularity of a string of individual well-written 'hits' from Jimmy Kennedy and others. Whatever the reasons, there was sufficient demand in the sheet music trade during the 1930s for a number of cheap magazines to be launched giving the sheet music of six well-known numbers plus articles, for the remarkable value of 3*d*. Thus, as late as 1934, *Popular Music and Dancing Weekly* was relaunched, having first appeared in 1924. *Popular Music and Film Music Weekly* followed in 1937. These magazines were sold at news stalls and newsagents and reached sales of over half a million.[40] Sheet music was also published regularly in several newspapers, including the *News of the World*.

This revival however, was a belated attempt to save the remnants of a collapsed industry. The death of the piano culture was almost complete by 1939. New sales of sheet music were more likely to have been due to their use by dance bands and by the popularity of other musical instruments, part of the transition away from the piano and toward its replacement by the 'guitar' culture of the 1950s and beyond. Music publishing and domestic music making had been transformed. By the end of the interwar period, successful music publishers were more likely to gain their revenue not from the sales of sheet music, but from fees collected on the performance of their works. Public performance, either 'live' or via radio and cinema, was now vital to success.

4.2 Ready-made 'live music': the public as listeners

The interwar period saw a notable shift towards the public performance of live music, where audiences were charged for their entertainment. This shift reflected the growing commercialization of the supply of popular music and the collapse of the old do-it-yourself piano culture. The variety of venues for the performance of live popular music between 1918 and 1939 was wide. Despite the new attractions of radio and cinema, live musical performance survived in many of its traditional public venues and also ventured into new ones. As the period progressed, the principal indoor venues—theatres, music halls, cinemas, and concert halls—were joined by an increasing number of small venues such as cafés, restaurants, and tearooms, where patrons were provided with a 'café-orchestra', string quartets, or pianists. Hotels, for a long time a source of live music,

---

[40] *MM*, 6 Nov. 1937, p. 1.

became increasingly important as providers. Other businesses also began to provide musical entertainment. Even skating rinks, particularly popular in the 1920s, hired orchestras, usually to play dance music. Most of the shift in public provision of live music was accounted for by dance music. Indeed, it was only here that there was an increase in the popularity of live music. The great popularity of dancing after the Great War saw demands for dance bands in a whole range of venues, not least of which were the new dance halls developing in every town and suburb.[41]

The burgeoning presence of live music in so many different venues called for adaptability on the part of musicians. To cater for this, music publishers provided a whole range of music for the small café and restaurant ensembles. In 1922 the *Performing Right Gazette* remarked:

An important feature of the modern arrangements is their general adaptability for performance by either small or large orchestras . . . The growth of arena orchestras and bands for performance at restaurants, cafés, and other public places, has brought about within recent years a new form of orchestral publication . . . the specially arranged salon edition, which is so scored that it enables almost any small combination of players to give a most effective performance.[42]

To cope with the increasing shift to the public performance of music and to protect the interests of composers and publishers in the face of mechanized competition, the Performing Right Society took on an increasingly important role. Performing right fees had long been collected for the performance of foreign opera and foreign plays but not for British musical works. The collection of fees for the many performances of music that took place daily, in so many venues, was an administrative problem that deterred composers and publishers from claiming their rights. Whereas it was relatively easy to collect fees from very popular performers, the hundreds of smaller performances by 'unknowns' up and down the country presented a considerable problem. With the steady increase in number of public performances of music all over the country, it soon became apparent that the problem could only be solved with the formation of a central body which would be empowered to deal with the whole situation on behalf of all owners of musical copyright. Thus in 1914 the Performing Right Society (PRS) was established in order to grant licences and collect fees for the public performance of copyright musical works.

This represented a fundamental economic shift in the music industry. Whereas previously music publishers and composers had paid entertainers

---

[41] See Chapters 5, 6, and 7.   [42] *PRG*, July 1922, p. 15.

to sing their songs (particularly in the music hall) in order to increase sheet music sales, now they were charging them to sing them. Thus, money was made from *performance*, not sheet music sales, recognition of the changes occurring elsewhere in the music industry. This shift away from 'domestic' to 'public' was vitally important.

Analysis of the Performing Right Society's licences illustrates the diversity of venues for public performance. The Society issued licences at all places of public performance and all venues were included, whether admission fees were charged or not. The number of premises licensed for the public performance of music grew rapidly. In 1919 the PRS issued licences to just over 4,000 premises. By 1927 this had risen to 7,600 and by 1938 there were over 41,000 premises in the British Isles licensed for the performance of music.[43] Even allowing for the fact that there were 5,000 cinemas in Britain in 1938, this is still a substantial number. The process of issuing licences was, of necessity, a gradual one. Although large numbers voluntarily applied for licences, many more had to be convinced of their responsibilities under the 1911 Copyright Act. Thus, at least part of the increase in the number of licences granted reflects the growing effectiveness of the Performing Right Society in encouraging premises to take out licences. It is significant that the Performing Right Society was concerned with *all* types of music, not just popular music. Between 1919 and 1926, popular music publishers were not members of the PRS. However, the rapid growth in the number of premises licensed after 1926 reflects the ever increasing number of venues where popular music was performed. In addition, the premises covered also included those where radio, gramophones, and other forms of non-live music performance were given.

Further analysis of Performing Right figures indicates the most popular venues for the public performance of music. The *Performing Right Gazette* listed annually some of the premises for which new licences had been granted. Although these lists do not give comprehensive statistics, they do highlight certain trends in live music provision. Of the 208 new licences granted and listed for 1922, hotels were the largest growing sector accounting for 22 per cent, followed by 'cafés and restaurants' with 21 per cent. Music hall accounted for 20 per cent, cinemas 18 per cent, theatres for 13 per cent, and then dance halls and concert halls for 3 per cent each.

---

[43] *PRG*, Apr. 1924, p. 171; July 1927, p. 216; Oct. 1938, p. 127.

The burgeoning number of different venues for the performance of music illustrates the fundamental economic shift away from private domestic performance to public performance of music. However, many traditional venues for live music also suffered during the interwar period. From the end of the First World War to the start of the Second, British musical theatre underwent a rapid and wholesale transformation. The music hall, having reached the height of its popularity in the late Victorian and Edwardian period, was in decline and by the beginning of the Second World War it was virtually extinct. The influence of the music hall on British popular music remained strong, however. The new media of radio, cinema, and gramophone absorbed much of the creative talent from British music hall, in addition to taking most of its audience. All three of these media offered a huge supply of music-hall based performances. Various other forms of live musical theatre did develop throughout the 1920s and 1930s, however. 'Variety' theatre became increasingly popular, really a more elaborate and spectacular version of music hall, and 'revue' also flourished. As the period progressed, the British musical theatre also developed a series of musical comedies and musical plays that owed much to the music-hall tradition.

The music hall was one of the most important native developments of popular music in Britain and it was from the music hall that the twentieth-century popular music industry was born. Music hall was popular with a wide range of social classes and in all parts of the British Isles. However, it was among the working classes that it had its greatest appeal, described by Ashley Dukes in 1930 as 'the one genuinely popular art of the English theatre'.[44] The music hall has already received considerable attention by scholars and it is, therefore, not within the scope of this study to chart in detail its rise and fall.[45] It did, however, remain important to the popular music industry at this time and so is outlined here.

The music hall proper had begun to decline before the huge changes in the popular music industry of the interwar period. It was irredeemably altered in 1914 when the London County Council introduced new regulations banning eating and drinking in the auditorium because of a large number of music hall fires. This took much of the unique atmosphere

[44] A. Dukes, 'The London Scene', *Theatre Arts Monthly* (New York), June 1930, p. 206.
[45] See P. Bailey, *Music Hall* (Milton Keynes, 1986); D. Cheshire, *Music Hall in Britain* (1974); E. Lee, *Folk Song and Music Hall* (1982); and R. Poole, *Popular Leisure and the Music Hall in Nineteenth Century Bolton* (Lancaster, 1982).

away from the music hall and forced it to become more like other ordinary theatres. The musical theatre that replaced music hall was to have decreasing audience participation and the audience became further removed from the source of their entertainment. This reduced its appeal considerably.

The music hall, however, was still popular in the early 1920s. The *New Survey of London Life and Labour* showed that, since 1891, the total seating accommodation of theatres and music halls in the county of London had actually increased from 115,000 in 1891 to 142,000 in 1931, in spite of the competition from 344,000 cinema seats.[46] The accommodation was almost the same as in 1911, when there were 141,000 seats. In 1929 there were 82 theatres and music halls in the county of London, rising to 92 in 1931.[47] This was partially because the leisure time filled by the cinema had either been non-existent before, or was spent in the pub or on the street corner. Nor had the 'talkie' reached the peak of its popularity in 1931. However, by then, as the *New Survey* points out, music halls in London had a predominantly middle-aged audience and had little appeal for younger audiences. Although prices were similar to those of cinemas, from 4*d.* to 2*s.* 6*d.*, their facilities were nowhere near as luxurious and the attraction was not considered comparable. In Liverpool too, there was a sharp decline in the popularity of the music hall but it seemed to maintain a stronger attraction for younger audiences than in London. In 1913 there were eleven theatres and music halls in Liverpool. By 1934 the *Social Survey of Merseyside* found that nearly half of these had closed, with only three music halls and three theatres left. At those surviving, audiences were greatly reduced. In other parts of Merseyside there were another seven theatres remaining, six of which were music halls. The seating capacity of these seven Liverpool theatres and music halls was 10,000 or, allowing for repeat performances, from 100,000 to 110,000 per week. Average weekly attendance at Liverpool theatres was estimated at about 50,000 persons, or just under 6 per cent of the total population.[48] On Merseyside, the audience was greatest amongst clerks, shopkeepers, and shop assistants (class B), as manual workers (class C) preferred the cheapness of the cinema. The Merseyside audience for cinema was also predominantly young.

[46] H. Llewelyn Smith, *The New Survey of London Life and Labour* (1930–5), ix. 9.
[47] Ibid. 47.
[48] D. Caradog Jones, *The Social Survey of Merseyside*, (Liverpool, 1934), iii. 278–9.

Cinemas offered a direct challenge to the music hall, as films were first shown as 'acts' in the halls. Entertainment circuits soon realized that cinemas were considerably cheaper and easier to run. The huge increase in demand for the new entertainment meant that one by one music halls were converted to cinemas.

Radio was another key element in the huge change in entertainment habits which took place between the wars but, paradoxically, it also helped the music hall tradition survive. Radio's effect on music hall was complex. 'Variety', which was neither cabaret nor American show business, flourished on the radio. Variety came from the tradition of music hall, without the stage and footlights and refined to suit the BBC's standards. It provided new employment opportunities for many of the displaced personalities of the halls, in addition to building up new stars and audiences. George Robey, one survivor of the old tradition applauded the radio:

I have never regarded those two interests to be diametrically opposed. It is true that while people are listening to broadcast performances in their homes they are not spending money in music-halls, yet I cannot believe that the one replaces the other. . . . To-day the position is that the music-hall feeds the wireless studios, and the studios feed the music-hall. Clearly, there is no case for rivalry, but for close co-operation. As I see it, the future progress of both interests will lie along these lines of friendly interchange. It is a future which I applaud and recommend.[49]

A clear example of this 'interchange' was the opening in 1938 of the New Hippodrome in Coventry, a new £100,000, 2,000-seat 'palace of variety' theatre, which included a BBC studio for relays to the BBC Midland station.[50] It was, however, unrepresentative of the general trend in tastes which meant that by the end of the period, save for a number of highly popular radio programmes, music halls were all but dead.

Despite the decline in the music hall, however, the musical theatre remained a popular source of musical entertainment. The working-class audience which had previously attended the music hall could find similar entertainment in the large number of variety theatres that replaced them. For the middle class, revue, cabaret, and musical comedies grew in popularity.

'Variety' had always been an alternative name for the music hall but it gradually became associated with a distinctive form of entertainment that

---

[49] *RP* 24 Sept. 1937, p. 5.   [50] *RP* 25 Feb. 1938, p. 12.

grew out of music hall. Variety was more sophisticated than music hall, was better packaged and presented to its audiences, and took advantage of the popularity of jazz and dance music. It was also more suited to the large 'Palaces of Variety' that developed in the twentieth century. The top dance bands were a regular feature of the variety circuit and they appeared alongside troupes of chorus girls, comedians, crooners, and instrumentalists. Working-class artists such as George Formby, Gracie Fields, Max Miller, and Flanagan and Allen continued in the music-hall tradition but they also made much of their success through the new mediums of radio, cinema, and gramophone.

'Revue' developed from music hall and by the turn of the century had started to become a distinctive entertainment. Being more 'intellectual' than music hall and frequently satirical, it appealed more to middle-class audiences. Revue first became popular among wider audiences with the influx of American productions that came to Britain just before the First World War. The first hit revue was Irving Berlin's *Everybody's Doing It* (1912), which introduced ragtime to Britain. It was followed by the elaborate American shows *Hullo, Ragtime!* (1912) and *Hullo, Tango!* (1913). British productions fought back, however. Charles B. Cochran was a major British producer of popular revue and launched such stars as Binnie Hale, Beatrice Lillie, Jessie Matthews and Gertrude Lawrence in productions like *Cheep* (1917), *Buzz-Buzz* (1918), and *Tails Up* (1918). After the war Cochran worked with Noel Coward and Ivor Novello. They were joined by André Charlot, Oswald Stoll and Alfred Butt, all providing a range of lavish, chorus girl packed entertainment.

Cabaret was a more intimate form of popular musical entertainment than variety and revue and it developed in the leading night clubs and restaurants of London's West End during the 1920s. Cabaret evolved as a way of attracting customers when the jazz band and dancing were insufficient. It was a mixture of variety and dance with dance bands and variety stars such as Ronald Frankau and Sophie Tucker. It was not designed for the ordinary man or woman. In 1941 Thomas Burke observed: 'It was not the casual cheap cabaret of Paris: it was a "luxury restaurant" affair, and its model was the sophisticated and elaborately dressed (or undressed) floor-show of America . . . it was instantly popular with everybody except gourmets.'[51] Several leading restaurants refused to allow cabaret to intrude on the pleasure of diners but the majority of the smartest restaurants did. By the end of the 1930s, cabaret

---

[51] Thomas Burke, *English Night Life* (1941), 140.

was firmly established and had become largely standardized in form and presentation. The London Casino was spending £1,400 per week on cabaret entertainment in 1938, the Savoy Hotel £220 per week, and the Dorchester and the Trocadero were also spending freely upon the cabaret turns. It was estimated that there were at least thirty restaurants, hotels, or night clubs in London where cabaret was on every night of the week by 1938.[52]

That the musical theatre was still a potent source of entertainment is reflected in the fact that between 1918 and 1939 some 462 different musical productions were presented on the London musical stage. The most active years were 1925 and 1926 when 28 and 29 musical plays were produced in each year respectively. The semi-depression years of 1922 and 1929 saw the least activity with 19 and 18 different plays; 1931, the year of the international financial crisis, and the war year 1939 had 19 musical productions each.[53]

It was not only in London that musical productions thrived. Musical plays, revues, and comedies featured in London often toured the rest of the country at the end of their run. Some were given trial performances in larger provincial cities such as Manchester and Liverpool. Variety acts were even more adaptable for touring and the well-known stars could easily move around the country. Variety theatres and music halls had been major employers of dance band musicians since the arrival of the Original Dixieland Jazz Band at the Hippodrome Theatre in 1919. 'Show bands' increased in popularity throughout the 1930s and most of the popular dance bands toured the country in variety theatres.

Such productions were, on the whole, a far cry from the music-hall performances of earlier days. The slick, lavish spectaculars that graced the musical stage were as 'stage managed' as any other theatrical production, if not more so. Gone was the spontaneity and interaction of the music hall; audiences were expected to be quiet, respectable, and courteous whilst performances were under way. The largest shows were treated increasingly as investment opportunities for the many theatrical speculators who emerged after the First World War. The new music theatre of the 1920s and 1930s was an ever more pre-packaged and commodified form of entertainment and did not escape the notice of contemporary observers. In 1930 American commentator Ashley Dukes observed:

---

[52] E. Short and A. Compton-Rickett, *Ring up the Curtain* (1938), 299.
[53] Calculated from B. Rust, *British Musical Shows on Record 1897–1976* (Harrow, 1977).

Of all theatrical productions today the big musical show most easily becomes a commodity, an article of commerce without any pretension to artistic integrity or a soul or purpose of its own . . . Its stars are the spoiled darlings of the entertainment world as far as salaries are concerned . . . Its underlings are . . . young people without professional prospects, mechanically going through a certain number of evolutions in the name of vanity or necessity. Its managers are mostly common tradesman, few of them can read a script intelligently, much less a musical score . . . All they know is that night after night a large and fairly stupid public will present itself at their doors; and if they are lavish enough they can satisfy its appetite for entertainment. Their backers are speculators uniting hopes of gain with a desire to thrust this or that artist into public favour . . . From first to last it is hard to find anything in the world of musical showmanship that is done for the sake of theatre and theatrical credit, not to say theatrical art.[54]

One widespread source of live musical performance that escaped such artistic pretensions was music in pubs. Public houses remained one of the most important sources of live popular music, outside the theatre. However, in common with other developments in the popular music industry, they too increasingly became subject to a commercialization of music supply.

Mass-Observation's *The Pub and the People* found that 'pub music' played an important role in the life of Bolton's 300 pubs. Most pubs had pianos in their parlours which customers were free to play, and much pub music was provided by enthusiastic amateurs. Increasingly, however, pubs would hire professional variety artists and entertainers for their patrons. Music and singing could be heard on most evenings and pub concerts were a popular attraction. Such concerts provided an important focus for the community and were a unique working-class entertainment. As Mass-Observation noted, music was:

a vital element in pub culture, one which each evening transformed the individual units of drinkers in all rooms into a harmonising whole, who send themselves into a sweat with laughter and melody. Worktown people love music of a simple sort. They love singing. There is nowhere else where they may sing the songs of their own choosing.[55]

Rowntree's survey of York also found that public houses were a great source of popular musical activity. Out of 156 public houses in 1938, 23 had music licences.[56] In 'traditional' pubs, found in the older parts of the

[54] A. Dukes, 'The London Scene', *Theatre Arts Monthly* (New York), June 1930, p. 210.
[55] Mass-Observation, *The Pub and the People* (1987), 259.
[56] B. S. Rowntree, *Poverty and Progress* (1941), 351.

city, large numbers of pubs had separate singing or music rooms to cater specifically for the provision of popular music. There was even more musical activity in the city's 'modern' public houses, the large elaborately furnished pubs found in the city centre and new housing estates. Many of these pubs had musical licences and a special room set apart for concerts, seating from 100 to 250 persons. A few pubs even had permanent orchestras of two to three musicians and engaged special entertainers every week. In pubs with concert rooms the musicians had to be adept performers, as one such employee wrote in the *Melody Maker* in 1934:

> To play in a concert room you must be able to play jazz and straight stuff, be able to transpose, read at sight, be a lyric writer and every other darned thing in the musical line. I will describe briefly a night's work in a concert room. First of all the pianist opens with a couple of selections, then one of the artists gives a song (there are generally two or three artists, chorus, comedy and a 'straight' singer). Invariably they ask us to stick it up half a tone, or down, as the case may be . . . Next come a couple more selections on the piano, followed by another song, and so on through the night.[57]

Such facilities were used by breweries in order to attract younger drinkers, whose numbers had been steadily decreasing for several years. It appeared to work, as the York survey found that the majority of those present during special musical concerts were aged between 18 and 25, mostly working class, and included a higher proportion of women and girls than in the rest of the pub.[58]

Social clubs also provided a range of opportunities for listening to live music in an atmosphere similar to that of the pub. Rowntree's *Poverty and Progress* pointed to the importance of social clubs as a source of musical activity and focus for working-class leisure. In 1938 York had 29 licensed clubs with 11,600 members, equivalent to 35 per cent of the total male population over 18 years old and estimated to be 60 per cent of the working-class male population of that age. Such clubs were open from 9.30 a.m. to 10.30 p.m. Over half of the clubs (16) organized weekly concerts for members and their wives for which professional entertainers were engaged. These cost over £2,000 per year. Typical performances included mostly comedians and singers (classified as 'baritone', 'tenor' 'soprano', etc.) and occasionally dance orchestras, performing light music, variety, and more up-to-date dance music. Many of the performers worked wholly on the club circuit and developed a distinctive style and

---

[57] *MM*, 4 Nov. 1933, p. 17.   [58] Rowntree, *Poverty and Progress*, 358.

presentation, rooted in music hall and working-class culture. Several of the women's lounges at these clubs also had wireless sets where music was provided. Such musical attractions were popular with members, as one who was unemployed commented:

We have some grand concerts on Sunday nights, and sometimes we get as many as 500 people. We can bring our wives, and we all have our favourite seats. I bring the missus with me regularly. It's the only night in the week that she gets out and we have some grand times.[59]

Joining these more traditional venues for the performance of live music, was the newly popular cinema. Before the advent of talking pictures in the late 1920s, the cinema was an important source of live popular music.[60] Cinemas provided an enormous stimulus to the music market during the 1920s. They were largely responsible, together with the gramophone, for the fact that more live music was being performed by professional musicians than at any other time in the country's history. At a gathering of cinema musical directors in January 1927, attended by popular music industry representatives, Alex Cohen, musical director of the Futurist Cinema, Birmingham, was able to boast:

the cinema is now, through its orchestra, the principal propagator of music in every civilised country. Incomparably more people listen to music when associated with films than listen to music under any other conditions.[61]

Films were silent, but they required a constant background of music which could not yet be provided by machines. Indeed the association between films and music was strong in the minds of the general public. The *Performing Right Gazette*, for example, believed that a film without music was inconceivable. It wrote:

There is little doubt . . . that a continuous strain upon the sense of sight alone would soon become undesirable and produce restlessness and headache among the audience. Under the circumstances music in the cinema is clearly a necessity . . . happily the modern tendency is to lift such music above . . . mere mechanical accompaniment, and to make it a thing so wedded to the film that the two together produce the effect of one harmonious whole.[62]

Until the autumn of 1929, suppliers of music, therefore, enjoyed a golden age. Every cinema, however small or remote, needed the services of

[59] Ibid. 360.
[60] See C. Ehrlich, *The Music Profession Since the Eighteenth Century* (1988) and *Harmonious Alliance* for further discussion.
[61] *MM*, Feb. 1927, p. 158.   [62] *PRG*, Jan. 1925, p. 243.

at least a pianist for long hours throughout the week. Many of them employed up to a dozen players and 'super cinemas' in the larger towns and suburbs engaged near full sized stage orchestras. The cumulative effects on the demand for music and musicians was, therefore, enormous. Instrumentalists enjoyed the benefits of an industry which provided some 80 per cent of their jobs and publishers were similarly well placed. The cinema's demand was heavily concentrated on the light music and popular classics. Whole catalogues of 'mood music' were created for accompaniment to films. The choice of music was considered vital to the success of films, giving musical directors and orchestras in cinemas considerable importance. As G. H. Clutsam wrote in 1927:

> The selection and arrangement of items for the progress of an ordinary film programme is a more serious and difficult business than is generally realised. There are usually two lengthy films in a programme. With the topical and extra items, the round of entertainment will involve the choice of something in the neighbourhood of a hundred excerpts . . . The secret of perfect musical accompaniment to a picture . . . lies . . . in a subjective direction and a deliberate reticence in expression. There is no better medium for attaining this than the orchestra.[63]

Despite their importance to the cinema, however, the arrival of talking film made many musicians instantly redundant. Sound cinema caused major changes to the structure of the music profession and unemployment was high. Live music in cinemas, did, however, make a small comeback. The introduction of 'ciné-variety', where musicians and variety acts were provided during intervals, plus the popularity of the large Wurlitzer-type cinema organs in large cinemas, meant that music survived the transition to sound, though on a vastly reduced scale.

Conclusion

The plight of cinema musicians was symptomatic of the wider, fundamental changes in Western music occurring in the post-First World War era. The world of professional musicians was transformed by three influences coming together. The application of technology to music-making—the gramophone, radio, and sound cinema—not only transformed the way in which music was produced and received, it also altered established patterns of employment. Technology destroyed the

---

[63] *PRG*, Apr. 1927, p. 188.

link between the demand for music and the simultaneous employment of musicians. The result was that, despite new opportunities for live music in hotels, restaurants, and so on, these musical media became the largest patrons of music in the country. By the early 1930s, the BBC was the largest single employer of musicians and the gramophone companies had a significant impact on the careers of individual musicians. In addition, the rapid decline in domestic music making decreased the demand for widespread musical training and encouraged the move away from live music making.

The impact of changes in technology were sudden and dramatic and created widespread fears amongst musicians for the survival of live music making. That so much live music making did survive, either by individuals' entertaining themselves as performers, or, increasingly, by going to listen to others, is evidence that such fears were not wholly realized. For the general public, a shift away from making their own music did not mean a corresponding decline in the supply of live music. If anything it increased. Thus, despite creating a revolution in music making and employment, the new media did not replace the older forms of live music completely, although they increasingly came to dominate it. Such changes, however, meant that the sheet music and musical instrument industries witnessed turbulent times, with output rising until the mid-1920s and then falling back dramatically from 1930 to 1935. Despite some recovery in the late 1930s and the success of individual companies, music publishers were increasingly reliant on revenue from performance rather than the sale of sheet music.

5

'LIVE MUSIC': DANCE BANDS, DANCE MUSIC, AND DANCE MUSICIANS

Introduction

Dance music and dance bands were at their most popular in the period 1919 to 1939. The names and music of dance bandleaders Jack Hylton, Henry Hall, Jack Payne, Ambrose, Roy Fox, and Harry Roy were known to millions of households throughout Britain. A 'dance music culture' quickly developed which assumed great importance in the popular culture of the period. The media of the gramophone and the radio combined with live performance at the dance hall to provide an unprecedented supply of this form of popular music. It was not uncommon for young working-class people to come home from work, listen to dance bands on the gramophone, go out for an evening's dancing, and return late to a programme of dance music on the radio. This dance music culture was particularly prevalent amongst younger sections of the population. In fact, the popularity of dance bands and their music was sufficiently great to encourage hundreds of enthusiastic amateurs to play the music for themselves and many turned this hobby into a source of income.

Although there are several fascinating antiquarian works on the popularity and lifestyles of the famous dance bands, little has been written about the amateurs, nor the way in which dance music affected the general public and the wide audience which it had.[1] Cyril Ehrlich's excellent *The Music Profession Since the Eighteenth Century*, touches briefly on the subject but the ordinary dance band and its musicians, the provincial and suburban

---

[1] See A. McCarthy, *The Dance Band Era* (Radnor, Pa., 1982); J. Godbolt, *All this and 10%* (1976); B. Amstell, *Don't Fuss Mr. Ambrose* (Tunbridge Wells, 1986); B. Rust, *The Dance Bands* (1972).

dance bands which the majority of people danced to, have remained hidden. This chapter is the first of three dealing with the dance music culture. It deals with the provision of 'live' dance music and will look at the rank and file musicians of the dance band and the problems and opportunities that these new musicians faced. The remaining chapters will examine the importance of the dance halls to this aspect of popular music.

5.1 The size and scope of the dance music profession

The dance music profession, incorporating both professionals and semi-professionals, was sufficiently large to provide a source of live dance music in virtually every community in Britain. The types of venue were varied: dance bands played to most social groups, from society circles in London's West End to rural communities in village halls.

The history of the arrival of jazz music from America into Britain is well documented.[2] This chapter will focus primarily on its effects on the music profession and general public and in this context will consider, first, ragtime. Ragtime, the precursor of jazz, had invaded Britain, promoted by sheet music and gramophone recordings, before the First World War. By 1913 there were two ragtime bands active in London, performing at the 400 Club and at the Murray Club. In 1915, the Savoy Hotel, in the first of a number of appointments that were to place it at the heart of modern popular music for many years, hired a ragtime band. This was Murray's Savoy Quartette, which proved to be hugely popular with its patrons. London, and to a lesser extent the rest of Britain, became fascinated with ragtime. It enjoyed enormous wartime popularity on music-hall and theatre stages and through gramophone recordings. Several American ragtime bands came over to play in Britain, the best known being led by Art Hickman, Murray Pilcer, and Dominic la Rocco. In 1917 a new music, jazz, burst onto the music scene in Britain, arriving with the American troops. Gramophone recordings and press reports of its popularity in the United States created an interest even before the arrival of the real thing. One of the earliest American bands to play the new music was the all-white Original Dixieland Jazz Band which, after appearing for one night at the London Hippodrome on 7 April 1919, moved to the Palladium and then for a nine-month residence at the newly opened Hammersmith palais-de-danse. They stayed for a total of fifteen

---

[2] See J. Godbolt, *A History of Jazz in Britain 1919–50* (1984).

months and, despite some criticism from older music-hall performers (notably George Robey), received a generally tumultuous reception. The Original Dixieland Jazz Band was followed by other American bands, notably Sidney Bechet and his Southern Syncopated Orchestra in 1920.

British bands rushed to imitate the new music, principally from gramophone recordings. Most merely modified existing styles but were widely popular. The music was seen as refreshing, fast, and exhilarating. During the 1920s the differentiation between 'dance bands' and 'jazz bands' in Britain was blurred. Dance bands were those bands which played the newest 'jazz' and popular music from America. They played the foxtrot and the quickstep, not the valetta or the polka. There were few, if any, real 'jazz' bands on the American model, although there were many who called themselves such. By the 1930s, the Golden Age, the 'dance band' was the common name for exponents of modern dance music. Swing music and 'hotter' types of music were also performed but there were few bands who played this type of music exclusively.

By the mid-1920s, dance bands were a very important part of the music profession. The *Census for England and Wales* estimated that there were approximately 22,600 professional musicians in 1921, rising to 25,900 in 1931.[3] There were no separate census figures for dance musicians but, in 1930, the *Melody Maker*, journal of the dance band musician, estimated that there were about 100,000 performers of dance music in Britain.[4] The huge discrepancy between this and the census figures is due to the large numbers of semi-professionals on the dance band scene. As the average dance band consisted of between five and eight musicians, this means that there were approximately 12,500 to 20,000 dance bands operating throughout the country in 1930. By 1935, after several years of rising unemployment amongst musicians, the estimate had fallen to about 10,000 dance bands.[5] The largest concentration of dance bands was to be found in London, where a 1933 survey found 1,000 dance bands (thought to represent 75 per cent of the London total), with a personnel of 6,000–7,000.[6] Census figures estimated 3,155 professional instrumentalists (excluding pianists) in London in 1921 and 1,264 in 1931.[7] The 1932 *Musicians' Directory* listed approximately 1,400 professional dance musicians in London and disaggregated them according to instruments played.[8]

---

[3] C. Ehrlich, *The Music Profession Since the Eighteenth Century* (Oxford, 1988), 235.

[4] *MM*, July 1930, p. 581.   [5] *MM*, 9 Feb. 1935, p. 10.

[6] *MM*, 27 Jan. 1934, p. 13.   [7] Ehrlich, *The Music Profession*, 237.

[8] Anon., *Musicians' Directory Incorporating the Dance Musicians' Directory* (1932).

They included 244 saxophonists, 212 trumpet players, 131 trombonists, 240 drummers, 71 guitarists, 102 clarinettists, 123 bass and sousa players, and 237 pianists. In Manchester in 1934 there were approximately 2,000 dance musicians. Liverpool, Birmingham, Glasgow, Edinburgh, and Leeds also had large numbers.[9]

Of these dance bands, only a minority of several hundred were made up of fully professional musicians. The vast majority were semi-professional, run by and composed of men who had other, more permanent jobs. The *Melody Maker* estimated that semi-professionals outnumbered professionals by a margin of at least twenty to one. In Leeds in 1934, for example, out of a healthy community of dance band musicians, only 50 were fully-fledged professionals. The census estimated that there were 87 professional musicians in Leeds in 1931, not all of whom played in dance bands.[10] Large numbers of keen amateurs coexisted alongside a small coterie of highly skilled musicians (see Plates 14–17).

At the summit of the dance music profession were London's leading dance bands, who performed in West End hotels, night clubs, and restaurants, and in the larger dance halls and variety theatres. The Mayfair Hotel, the Savoy Hotel, Monseigneur Restaurant, and the Café de Paris were among the most exclusive venues and they catered for the most exclusive dancers. They were the first to experiment in the new forms of dance music and to introduce the new styles to Britain. Leading bands also performed elsewhere. In November 1929, for example, the *Melody Maker*'s 'Who's Where' feature reported that Billy Cotton and His Savannah Band were appearing at the Astoria Dance Salon, Charing Cross Road, whilst the extremely popular Jack Hylton and His Orchestra were appearing in vaudeville. The stage was a major attraction for the biggest bands—in the same month, for example, Percival Mackey and His Band were at the New Dominion Theatre. As the period progressed theatre work became even more widespread. In Manchester in April 1934, for example, no fewer than seven leading bands were appearing on stage. As *Melody Maker* reported:

Never before has the music 'fan' in Cottonopolis been treated to such a galaxy of real talent as in recent weeks. Seven first-class orchestras have drawn record audiences from all parts of Lancashire . . . Billy Cotton set the ball rolling when he fulfilled a week's engagement at the Ritz dance hall. He was followed by Lew Stone's outfit, who broke all records for the hall. Meanwhile the management of the Paramount Theatre, Oxford Street, were busy signing up Roy Fox and Jack

[9] *MM*, 24 Nov. 1934, p. 9.   [10] Ehrlich, *The Music Profession*, 236.

Payne. Not to be outdone, the Capitol Theatre decided to innovate variety, and chose Debroy Somers as the 'top'. The show was so successful that it was retained for a second week . . . Mrs Jack Hylton was rushed to the Hulme Hippodrome, where 'America Calling' proved to be a big draw, and this week we have Cab Calloway and his Cotton Club Orchestra at the Paramount.[11]

Broadcasting and recording work for the gramophone companies also provided considerable income for these leading bands (see Plate 18) and in the survey of bands in November 1929, Jack Payne and His Dance Orchestra were at the BBC.[12] Below these top-line bands there were the secondary London bands performing at second-class hotels, restaurants, brasseries, lesser night clubs, and the principal West End dance halls. They were followed by dance bands working in small West End cafés, clubs, and dance halls and, finally, those bands playing in the suburban palais-de-danse and other dance halls.[13] In the provinces the hierarchy was similar, with a distinction between central and suburban work. Although dance music appealed to all classes there was nevertheless a hierarchy of performers linked to the social status of their audience.

A survey of leading professionals illustrates this diversity.[14] In 1929 out of 51 top provincial and London professional dance bands listed in the *Melody Maker*'s 'Who's Where' section, a third were performing in dance halls, 27 per cent were appearing in night clubs and restaurants, 18 per cent in hotels, 14 per cent in theatres and vaudeville, and 8 per cent elsewhere. If these figures are disaggregated it can be seen that there were differences between the provinces and London's West End. From 1929 to 1932, the majority of leading professional dance bands in the provinces were to be found in dance halls (59% in 1929, 53% in 1930, 67% in 1931, and 47% in 1932) whilst in London the most popular locations were night clubs and restaurants (32% in 1929, 42% in 1930, 34% in 1931, and 40% in 1932), followed by hotels and then dance halls.

Next in the dance musicians' hierarchy were 'gigs'.[15] These were temporary engagements such as society and hunt balls, college dances, middle-class parties, and those dances organized by factories, offices, and various social and political clubs. Though professional bands did perform at such occasions, during the 1920s most of the work at the less

---

[11] *MM*, 7 Apr. 1934, p. 2. [12] 'Who's Where', *MM*, Nov. 1929, p. 1008.
[13] This classification is based on those drawn up by the Musicians' Union in June 1935 when establishing rates of pay for dance musicians.
[14] See 'Who's Where' in *MM*, Nov. 1929; Mar. 1930; Mar. 1931; Aug. 1932.
[15] The use of the word 'gig' possibly derived from the use of transport for such engagements; a 'gig' was a two-wheeled, one-horse carriage.

important gigs was taken by the semi-professional dance musician. By the 1930s, the whole gig market had become increasingly dominated by semi-professional musicians. Proprietors of dance halls and dance promoters also made increasing use of this cheaper source of talent for other work and by the end of the 1930s semi-professional dance bands were working in suburban palais-de-danse, restaurants, hotels, and even occasionally broadcasting or appearing on the variety stage.

The growing number of dance bands gave rise to several journals, which catered for their interests. The first and most influential was the *Melody Maker*, established in 1926, initially as a house magazine of the Lawrence Wright Music Publishing Company, but then as a dance musician's journal published by Odhams Press. It had a readership of 25,000–30,000 by 1939.[16] A rival, *Rhythm*, was launched in 1927 by the musical instrument manufacturer John E. Dallas. Other journals included *Musical News and Dance Band*, *Ballroom and Band*, *Swing Music*, and *Hot Music*. These journals give details of dance musicians' activities in various regions of Britain and from them two distinct seasons of work can be identified. The main season ran from September to June, with a quieter summer season from July to September. A survey of dance band activity in major cities in November 1935 illustrates the type and number of engagements encountered.[17]

With nearly 2,000 dance musicians, Manchester was a major centre for dance music. There were, according to official census figures, 567 professional musicians in Manchester in 1921, falling to 291 in 1931.[18] This was the largest number outside London. In November 1935, the *Melody Maker* reported that the dance music business was booming. At the Ritz Ballroom, Ivor Kirchen and His Band were being supported by a five-piece band led by Freddy Waites, whilst in the Plaza Ballroom Harry Godfrey and His Boys were sharing the work with an eight-piece band, Tommy Smith and His New Oxford Band. Other ballroom work included Norman Collins's Band at the new Lido in Sale. At the prestigious Midland Hotel, Joe Orlando and His Band were performing and Henry Crousdon's Rhythm Boys were at the Press Club annual ball. Of additional interest to dance band musicians was the opening that month of an extension to Manchester's largest musical instrument store, Mameloks on Oxford Road. The store had a ballroom, café, lounge, and

[16] M-O A: MDJ: 5/A, 'Associate Editor: Melody Maker', 28 Mar. 1939, p. 3.
[17] The following is taken from *MNDB*, Nov. 1935 and *MM*, 2–30 Nov. 1935.
[18] Ehrlich, *The Music Profession*, 236.

teaching rooms. The Dance Band and Variety booking agencies on its premises made it a centre for 'gigsters'.

Birmingham was also well provided for. As early as 1928 observers commented that:

Birmingham may now be fairly regarded as one of the most advanced cities—syncopationally speaking, outside London. The progress during the last two or three years has been remarkable . . . the style . . . of the playing . . . has improved and continues to improve month by month.[19]

Census figures put Birmingham's total number of professional musicians at 201 in 1921 and 197 in 1931; there were considerably more semi-professional dance musicians. In November 1935 Birmingham's ballrooms had music provided by the bands of Ernie Rose at the Tower Ballroom, Phillip's Dance Band at the Albert Hall, and Tony's Red Aces, led by a 17-year-old, at Tony's Ballroom. At the Birmingham palais-de-danse two bands were performing every night, with Stan Hudson's resident band complemented by Jack Groom's 'Selmner' Band. Jack Dale and His Band were also performing to large crowds at the Masque Ballroom, Walford Road.

In Glasgow that month (137 professionals in 1921, 127 in 1931),[20] Charlie Harkinn and his Kit Kat Band were fully booked with engagements at St Andrew's Hall, together with the Philco Dance Band. At the New Locarno dance hall was a band from the Isle of Man led by Doug Swallow. Alec Freer was at the Locarno, Jimmy Love at the 'F and F' Palais, Sammy Blue at the Revellers and Gordon Ballrooms, and Jack Chapman at the Albert Palais, from where he was broadcasting on the BBC. Elsewhere, Joe Orlando and His Band were appearing at the London, Midland, and Scottish Railways' Central Hotel and Pete Low was providing teatime dance music at the St Vincent Tea Rooms, with Lester Penman at the Du Barry Café. Tex O'Brien's band was busy with many gigs in the city and at the Alhambra Theatre there was a visit from top London bandleader Debroy Somers and His Band.

In Nottingham in November 1935, Ambrose and His Orchestra were at the Victoria Ballroom, where the resident band the Serenaders was also performing. Eric Harrington and His Band were at the Ritz ballroom and George Colbourn's Band and Ivor Kirchen's Band from London and Manchester respectively were at the County Ball. In Leeds the cinema circuit Gaumont British was installing dance orchestras in its cinemas,

[19] *MM*, Apr. 1928, p. 410.   [20] Ehrlich, *The Music Profession*, 236.

with the Majestic and Coliseum both receiving fifteen-piece orchestras. George Adamson and His Aristocrats were in the Palais-de-Danse in South Parade, Harry Booth at the Harehills Palais, and Toni Rice at the Boston Ballroom. The Victory Hotel had just installed Archie Joyce and His Orchestra.

The second season for dance band employment was in summer. During the summer season many dance halls in urban areas closed but there was still considerable work available in holiday resorts. The *Melody Maker*'s 'Who's Where' section for July 1931 shows that out of 37 provincial professional bands performing that month, 20 were engaged at seaside holiday resorts.[21] A survey of Torquay, Devon, and Newquay, Cornwall in August 1935 reveals the extent to which work could be found in hotels during the summer season. The two principal venues open to the public in Torquay, a place 'exceptionally well served in the way of dance bands', were the St James Hotel Ballroom, where Charlie Rowe and His Orchestra were playing, and the Marine Spa Ballroom run by the local Corporation, with Bunny Rowe and His Boys.[22] There were also bands at the Palace Hotel, the Grand Hotel, the Imperial Hotel, the Roslyn Hall, the Belgrave, the Park Hall, the Victoria and Albert Hotel, and the Torbay Hotel. The *Melody Maker* commented:

Newquay is the dance musician's Mecca in Cornwall during the summer season, and all the large hotels employ resident bands, who play for a continual round of dances from one week to another. Whilst the large hotels employ an exclusive resident orchestra, it is the practice here for the smaller establishments to share an orchestra, the boys playing at different hotels on alternate nights.[23]

On the East Coast, summer work could be found in the new holiday camps. One Norfolk camp at Caister, north of Great Yarmouth, was attracting up to 40,000 holiday makers per year by 1935, and Percy Cohen's Band played to a packed ballroom of up to 1,500 dancers nightly.[24] Further north, dance bands on the Lincolnshire coast found most of their business in cafés and restaurants. For example, in Cleethorpes in 1935 there were dance bands at the Café Dansant on the Promenade. In Skegness, bands played at the Imperial Café, the Tower Café, and the Piazza Café, whilst Chapel St Leonards had bands in its Café Mimosa and Café Marina. *Melody Maker* observed:

[21] *MM*, July 1931.   [22] *MM*, 17 Aug. 1935, p. 3.
[23] *MM*, 31 Aug. 1935, p. 11.   [24] *MM*, 17 Aug. 1935, p. 3.

Find a café and you will find a dance band! In fact, it would be quite as difficult to take a meal without music as it would to find a spot exclusively devoted to dancing . . . few places make a cover charge for entry, and it is quite possible to dance to one's heart's content for the price of a cup of coffee, but that the idea pays is proved in that there are so many bands in such a sparse area.[25]

Hotels, seaside dance halls, cafés and restaurants thus provided the mainstay of summer work in Britain's holiday resorts.

There were, however, significant regional variations. There were more dance bands on the whole in the north of the country than in the south, with the exception of London. Many of the personnel of the top West End bands had come from the north and the Midlands. The most popular bandleader of the period, Jack Hylton, was originally from Bolton. The traditionally strong musical activity of Northern England found a new outlet in dance music. In 1935, for example, the majority of professional dance bands (outside London) advertising themselves in *Ballroom and Band*, came from Northern England. Out of 100 bands advertising in 1935, although 27 per cent were from London, 23 per cent were from Yorkshire and Lancashire.[26] In the south, particularly sparse areas of dance band activity included the Eastern Counties of England and West Kent. In these areas, a few dance bands would travel long distances to gigs, but their proximity to London meant that many dance music fans went outside of their own locality for music. In Norfolk, apart from a few bands in holiday camps and in Norwich, the county was poorly catered for. The West Coast of Kent was virtually barren of dance bands. At Dover, in 1935, the only regular 'live' musical entertainment was provided by a single military band, whilst in Folkestone there were only two dance bands. The *Melody Maker* commented: 'if one were to commence at Deal or Dover and travel round the coast westwards until the Kent-Sussex border was reached, he would have about as much chance of finding any dance bands as a traveller in the Sahara has of finding an oasis!'[27]

There were hundreds of small towns and villages throughout Britain which had to rely on visits from dance bands based in the nearest large town or city. Remoteness or a small population did not necessarily mean a lack of dance band activity, however. In Cornwall, as we have seen, the main areas of dance band activity were centred around the large holiday resorts of Newquay and St Ives. These centres were exceptional and

[25] *MM*, 21 Sept. 1935, p. 3.   [26] *BB*, Mar. 1935, p. 49.
[27] *MM*, 7 Sept. 1935, p. 12.

acted as a magnet for dance band activity, providing a large number of bands who also toured smaller towns and villages. Considerable coverage was provided by 'gigging' bands. In 1934 one such band, Billy Tanner and the Rhythmonians, though based in St Ives, were prolific tourers.[28] The availability of portable amplifying equipment meant that gig bands could provide a show more or less wherever they chose to stop. The band estimated that, from 1930 to 1934, it had undertaken 600 touring engagements in West Cornwall, including Penzance, Redruth, and Truro.

5.2 Dance band musicians

Dance band musicians came from a variety of different musical backgrounds. Apart from the highly skilled musicians in the leading professional bands, most of whom had a traditional musical training, one of the most striking features of dance band music was the large number of enthusiastic amateurs. As befitted the more spontaneous type of music that they were playing, entry into the dance band scene was less rigid than into other parts of the musical profession. This meant it was able to grow rapidly, attracting large numbers of people who would previously have had limited contact with music. Although this enabled the further spread of the new musical style it also created considerable friction within musicians' circles.

Hero-worship of famous band leaders was a common reason for playing, as Spike Hughes, writing in *Rhythm* noted in 1936:

Most of you took up dance music because you heard a record, or a broadcast. You had 'an ear for music;' you could imitate what you heard so you learned some instrument to imitate it on . . . You took up an instrument so that you could play like somebody or other earning a fabulous salary at some swell hotel. This hero worship is a common thing in this age. The modern youth would rather be a crooner or a bandleader than anything. The jazz merchant is the idol of the people. Don't you believe me? Then go as I did to Margate or Southend in the summer and notice the young men walking about. They talk pseudo-American they learned at the movies and they sing with all the mannerisms of our better known crooners. *Vox populi* in the 1930's is the voice of Bing Crosby and Harry Roy.[29]

Apparent financial rewards were a clear incentive. The press particularly encouraged dance music fans to believe that there were rich rewards

[28] *MM*, 6 Oct. 1934, p. 2.   [29] Spike Hughes, *Rhythm*, Jan. 1936, pp. 20–1.

for those who wanted to play. In the 1920s when the 'jazz' band was something new and shocking, the press was fascinated by its top exponents, on both sides of the Atlantic and the salaries of Jack Hylton, Paul Whiteman, and Jack Payne were public business. In 1927 Ambrose was earning £10,000 per year at the Mayfair Hotel and Jack Hylton could afford to turn down an offer of £40,000 per year in 1928.[30] Although the economic reality for most musicians in the dance music scene was considerably harsher, for many enthusiastic young fans stuck in low-paid jobs the attraction of these salaries was strong. The *Radio Magazine* commented in 1934:

Many . . . have extravagant ideas about the money that dance band players earn. They have been fed by a popular press which has never been able to forget that, in the halcyon days of 1920 to 1925, the mere possession of a saxophone led to a well-filled pocket on every weekly ghost night. The top liners made £80 a week and spent it with the utmost indifference . . . Every minor professional dance musician aspires to become a member of one of the show West End bands, those you inevitably hear from 10.30 to 12 p.m. every night on the Regional and National transmitters. He, too, thinks that such a position soon leads to rows of houses and thousands in the bank.[31]

Several sections of the popular music industry were quick to exploit the interest in dance music among amateurs and a large sub-industry grew up, providing everything from bandstands to uniforms and, as the majority of those taking up dance music had little or no musical training, various companies began to adapt their products for these novices. The large numbers who flooded the dance band scene in the 1920s and 1930s found the transition between amateur and professional status both easy and fast. This transition was made quicker by the fact that the most popular instruments (saxophone and clarinet) were easy to pick up. Dance bands needed fewer instrumentalists than other orchestras and so lent themselves to small groupings which were easier to assemble from friends and within a small locality.

Music publishers produced a series of self-tutor books designed to give amateurs a musical grounding in their chosen instrument. Available at prices from 4s. 6d. to one guinea, these books provided affordable tuition for the beginner. Weber's, for example, ran a 'Modern Dance' series for the clarinet, piano, saxophone, and cornet and musical instrument manufacturer Selmer enrolled the help of leading dance band instrumentalists for its self-tutor series. The amateur market that publishers were aiming

---

[30] McCarthy, *Dance Band Era*, 52, 96.   [31] *Radio Magazine*, Apr. 1934, pp. 46–7.

for is clearly illustrated in a 1935 advertisement for Ben Davis's Selmer Saxophone Tutor:

The reader who wishes to take up the study of the saxophone, peruses my book like he would read a novel. It interests him because it is written in non-technical language, and because the fundamentals of music theory which he must acquire are given to him sugar-coated so that he does not realise he is being taught so dry a subject.[32]

The *Melody Maker* was also an important source of instruction. It ran several monthly musical courses for each instrument, written by leading professional dance musicians, published orchestrations for the latest dance tunes, step-by-step instructions on how to play 'hot' and 'sweet' choruses and there was also a technical question and answer service whereby aspiring musicians could ask the experts about playing technique and advice on instruments.

The necessity for advanced musical knowledge was reduced further by the availability of ready-made arrangements from the music publishers, who arranged their latest numbers especially for dance bands, complete with orchestrations for each instrumentalist. Until the mid-1930s the music publishers, keen to have their songs publicized, gave these orchestrations away free to dance bands, but as radio developed the practice eventually stopped. Publishers' 'Subscription Clubs' kept prices for these orchestrations as low as possible. Membership of clubs was yearly or half-yearly with a subscription fee of between 10s. 6d. and £1 securing six months issues for a small orchestra.[33] This allowed the band to receive all the dance numbers published by the particular music publisher for that period. For those who wanted an individual arrangement, professional arrangers advertised in the various music journals such as *Melody Maker* and *Rhythm*.

The gramophone also made the job of the new dance band musician easier. The gramophone helped the spread of this new musical style immeasurably. Gramophone recordings of the top British and American dance bands could be used to give an idea of how to play correctly. In February 1932, the *Melody Maker* started a section 'Learn from Others', listing records from which to copy, with subsections for 'Hot Arrangements', 'Slow Rhythm Arrangements', and individual instruments including the clarinet, saxophone, trumpet, string bass, trombone, and

---

[32] *MM*, Dec. 1932, pp. 1008–9.
[33] S. Turnbull, *How to Run a Small Dance Band for Profit* (1937), 48.

drums.[34] In March 1936 Brunswick Records, with the support of *Melody Maker* and *Rhythm*, produced a series of 'Accompaniment Records' for dance band instrumentalists to play and practise with and vocalists to sing along to.[35]

Instruction was also available through the numerous dance band contests that were held throughout the country. *Melody Maker* had been officially organizing semi-professional contests since 1926 and rival contests were held by the magazine *Rhythm*. The popularity of such contests is shown by the fact that, for the month of April 1934, *Melody Maker* was holding contests in Leeds, Birmingham, Rugby, Reading, Southport, Margate, Nottingham, Oxford, Oldham, and Belfast.[36] Judging was carried out by the editors of the *Melody Maker* together with instrumentalists or leaders from top British bands, with a famous guest band performing. By 1939, *Melody Maker* was running over thirty of these contests each year.[37] The climax of this contest activity was the All Britain Dance Band Championship and enthusiasm for such contests amongst amateurs and semi-pros was intense.

There was tension between dance bands and 'straight musicians' however. The straight musician in the 1920s and 1930s also played popular music but with a repertoire of light orchestral and traditional music performed in a traditional, non-dance style. This category included cinema musicians, light orchestras, brass bands, and the ubiquitous café trios and quartets. Despite differences in delivery and repertoire, there was overlap between the work of straight musicians and dance band musicians. At most dances organizers would require non-'jazz' tunes, and there was a vogue for 'old-time' dancing in the mid-1930s which required a knowledge of older tunes and older playing methods. Similarly, those orchestras providing music in restaurants, cafés, cinemas, and theatres, would often be required to play in the style of the 'jazz band'. In the 1920s, when the jazz band was still new, there was even a fusion of the two musical styles, with some bands playing both.

By the mid-1930s, with so many competent semi-professional dance bands available, straight musicians could no longer attempt to provide both forms. There was a continuing interest in more traditional styles of popular music throughout the period but a decreasing amount of work. During the 1920s a significant amount of work was transferred

[34] 'Learn from Others', *MM*, Feb. 1932, p. 161.
[35] *MM*, 14 Mar. 1935, p. 1.   [36] *MM*, 17 Mar. 1934, p. 6.
[37] M-O A: MDJ: 5/A, 'Associate Editor: Melody Maker', 28 Mar. 1939, p. 3.

away from light orchestras toward dance bands. This caused much hostility.

5.3 Dance bands, employment, and employers

The complex relationship between amateur and professional and the easy access to the dance musicians' world caused problems for those involved in the dance band scene. As the popularity of dancing and dance music grew, businessmen realized that there was money to be made, and employment of musicians was increasingly taken over by large entertainment circuits. The inability of professional musicians to impose any formal musical restrictions on those entering dance band music greatly weakened their position in relation to employers.

When a dance hall, hotel, theatre, or other venue wanted to employ a dance band, it had one of three options. The first was to approach one of the many dance band agencies which dealt with the business of securing engagements and promoting their own bands. The majority of such agencies were small and handled under ten bands at any one time. The 1932 *Musicians' Directory* listed sixty booking agents in the Greater London Area and similar agencies were found in any town or city in which there was a sizeable community of dance musicians.[38] For a fee, the agencies would offer one of the bands on their books. The second option for the venue was to arrange its own auditions, which was a time-consuming process and one in which only local bands usually became involved. The third option was to book blind, based on the recommendations of others.

The majority of engagements were made through independent employers or these small to medium sized band agencies. As with other sections of the popular music industry, however, dance bands became the focus of increasing syndication on the part of employers. The largest of these employers was the Mecca Agency. Founded in 1933 by Carl Heimann and Byron Davies as a subsidiary to their dance hall circuit, by 1938 it controlled 300 bands playing in some 2,000 establishments and operating from the World's Band Centre in London. In 1934 Mecca launched their 'Blue Star Flying Visits' scheme, whereby top dance bands were engaged to tour their circuit of dance halls.[39] Mecca sent 'advance travelling managers' to feed local managements with all the necessary publicity matter and they paid large sums to get the names they

---

[38] Anon., *Musicians' Directory*, 61.   [39] *MM*, 3 Feb. 1934, p. 11.

wanted. Billy Cotton, Lew Stone, Alfredo, Ambrose, and Roy Fox were among their star performers and in June 1934 Mecca engaged the visiting American Coleman Hawkins to play in its dance halls for one week. Mecca was aiming to imitate the hugely successful Mills Artist Bureau of the United States. Run by Irving Mills, this controlled a substantial number of dance orchestras and had handled nearly all the great jazz musicians at one time or another. In August 1934, Mecca launched a series of National Band Trade Shows designed to give it a major control over the booking of dance bands.[40] Mecca toured the UK inviting potential band bookers to the Band Trade Shows where they were entertained by dance bands who were available for employment. Special rooms were allocated for the discussion of business between the band bookers and Mecca, as promoters of the scheme, received a commission of 3.75 per cent from the bands if, and only if, contracts were secured. The dance bands on the lists provided at these shows were to have their publicity and advertising controlled by Mecca. The first show was held at the Streatham Locarno on 25 September 1935 and attracted some 2,000 potential bookers. The scheme was later extended to the north at the Ritz dance hall, Manchester. The scheme reduced the 10 per cent commission usually taken by agencies, eliminated the expense of hiring auditions rooms, and brought employer and employee together in well-equipped venues. However, the odds were clearly stacked in favour of the band bookers and Mecca. After the Musicians' Union attacked the Band Trade Shows for making the dance bands perform without fees and for giving the employer the upper hand, the scheme eventually collapsed. By the end of the 1930s, however, the Mecca Agency controlled more dance bands and more musical venues than any other single agency.

The Mecca Agency was not the only large circuit employer in Britain. Variety theatres and music-halls had been major employers of dance band musicians since the arrival of the original Dixieland Jazz Band at the Hippodrome Theatre in 1919. 'Show bands' increased in popularity throughout the 1930s and most of the popular dance bands toured the country in variety theatres. Cinemas had also been major employers of musicians since they first developed and by the 1920s were one of the largest employers in the country.[41] The coming of sound destroyed virtually all of this work. There had been little work for jazz and dance bands in the cinema, however, and it was not until the early 1930s that the newer, more fashionable dance bands were provided by cinema owners in

---

[40] *MM*, 11 Aug. 1934, p. 1.   [41] See Chapter 4 above.

response to demands by audiences. Dance bands began to appear as part of the stage shows that the larger cinemas provided prior to the showing of films and during intervals in the programme.

The use of dance bands in the cinema meant that a large number of musicians were being employed by a handful of powerful cinema circuits which developed in the 1930s.[42] During the 1920s cinema circuits were small and the majority of cinemas independent. In 1920 the largest circuit, Provincial Cinematograph Theatres, had only sixty-eight cinemas, rising to eighty-five in 1927. It was the appearance of the Gaumont British Picture Corporation and Associated British Cinemas (ABC) in 1927 and 1928 respectively that really changed the structure of the industry. Gaumont British swallowed up the old Provincial Cinematograph Theatres circuit and established itself with 187 cinemas, rising to 287 by 1933. ABC started more modestly with only twenty-eight cinemas but by 1933 it had 147. It was in this year that another great chain was developed with the establishment of the Odeon circuit, which ran 146 cinemas by 1936, eventually reaching a peak of over 300. These three giant combines began to devour other circuits, for example ABC's takeover of the Union circuit of 136 cinemas in 1937. By 1937, ABC had 431 cinemas, Gaumont British 345. The big three combines controlled between them 1,011 cinemas, about 21 per cent of the total number and nearly all of the larger cinemas. Another 15 per cent were owned by smaller circuits with ten or more cinemas. All of these provided plenty of work for dance bands.

In May 1932, for example, Associated British Cinemas Ltd. took over management of a number of new bands for presentation work in their cinemas, including Edward Ball and His Empire State Orchestra at Lewisham's Hippodrome cinema. Established bands under the ABC Circuit included Chasid and His Band, Alan Parsons and His Band, Smith's Embassy Band, Percival Mackey, and Alan Green in their Manchester house. In the same month, Gaumont British were considering taking over Gaby Robin from the Wimbledon Palais. Stanelli was appearing in West End 'ciné-variety' and Jack Courtnay was engaged at the Mayfair Kinema, Tooting.[43] As well as resident employment, bands also toured the principal halls of the major circuits.

For those musicians who tried to make money out of dance music, both professional and semi-professional, the business was fraught with difficulties. Musicians had to work long and unsociable hours, often

---

[42] See J. Richards, *The Age of the Dream Palace* (1984), 35–8.
[43] *MM*, May 1932, p. 357.

performing without breaks and usually finishing their work well after midnight. Terms of employment were often highly irregular and rarely concrete. The dance musician was only paid for the hours that he was working, rehearsals often went unpaid, and contracts were usually temporary. Employers provided no paid holidays or pensions and musicians usually had to wait several weeks to be paid for an engagement. Indeed, so lax were most dance band leaders on this matter that when, in July 1933, the top West End bandleader Lew Stone paid his musicians for a gig two days after it had been performed, it caused a sensation amongst the dance musicians' fraternity.[44] Often the formation of bands and securing of engagements were agreed by word of mouth, with no written contract at all. The majority of rank and file dance musicians had little experience in business matters and this enabled unscrupulous bandleaders and dance promoters to exploit them. The greatest difficulty, however, was the problem of price cutting whereby local dance bands would compete with each other over engagements by charging progressively lower fees to dance promoters.

Price cutting had always been prevalent amongst dance musicians, because of the large number of semi-professionals willing to offer their services for less than professional rates. Despite this, wages for professionals had remained high throughout the 1920s and there was sufficient demand for dance bands to be able to absorb the different levels of musicianship. With the onset of the depression in 1929, the situation changed rapidly. Dance promoters found it convenient to reduce costs by offering less for their musicians. It was found that first-class, and consequently expensive, professional or semi-professional bands could be replaced by cheaper performers, without noticeable effects on attendance figures. This price cutting, together with rising unemployment and poor working conditions, threatened the livelihood of dance band musicians.

As musicians, all dance band players were theoretically free to join the Musicians' Union; few did, however. There were several reasons for this. First, the music industry was very labour intensive; technological advances had little effect on 'productivity'. This could be best increased by attracting larger audiences and performing in larger theatres, and in this respect first-rate musicianship was an asset. In general, however, employers had few means of reducing costs other than keeping down wages and employing as few people as they could get away with. Secondly, there were large numbers of amateur and part-time musicians

---

[44] *MM*, 8 July 1933, p. 10.

within the industry. These non-professionals provided a large pool of cheaper alternative labour and allowed employers another option for increasing profits. This made the music industry highly competitive. Musicians, especially popular music players, performed in relatively small independent groups and were thus less likely to develop a sense of camaraderie with their fellow workers than in those industries with large workforces, in particular factories. There were also some musicians who considered music and trade unionism to be incompatible. The London Orchestral Association (LOA) and the Incorporated Society of Musicians styled themselves as professional associations and artistic movements, rejecting the 'militancy' of trade unionism and considering themselves different from non-artistic workers. On the other side, there was a great deal of suspicion of musicians in the labour movement as they were not regarded as 'real workers'. The large number of 'two jobbers' working long hours also did little to endear musicians to the labour movement. This was a fundamental structural problem and it elicited two responses from those who wished to protect musicians' interests. The LOA developed along the lines of a 'craft union' representing the 'qualified' full-time professional musician and trying to protect its members by restricting access to the industry. In contrast, the Amalgamated Musicians' Union (AMU—the Musicians' Union from 1921) modelled itself on one of the 'new' unions which had developed at the end of the nineteenth century representing the unskilled or semi-skilled musician as well as the professional. The AMU aimed for 100 per cent unionization so as to exert control over the whole labour force and to create closed shops. The AMU, under the leadership of Joseph Williams, had more success in recruiting 'straight' musicians of all levels and it was Williams who headed the newly formed Musicians' Union and continued these policies after 1921. Recruitment of dance band musicians was, however, even more complex.

Despite the presence of large numbers of amateur and part-time musicians among the orthodox music industry, access was to some extent limited by the requirements of musical training. The Royal Academy of Music, the Royal College of Music, the Guildhall School of Music, and so on provided rigorous training. Lower down, a whole host of private music teachers established themselves, and there were also a number of dubious examinations schools such as the National Academy, the National College, and the National Conservatory which issued diplomas. The straight musician, even one who played popular music, required a degree of professional musical training, fake or not, before he could be

considered for employment. However, the dance band musician's training was much less formal, as befitted the more spontaneous style of the
music he was playing. There were no formal qualifications required of
dance band musicians before they could play. Access to the dance band
scene was, therefore, impossible to control. Huge numbers of part-timers
presented great difficulties for the professional dance band musician.

As early as 1924 the Musicians' Union had made an attempt to bring
together various aspects of the entertainment world—musicians, electricians, artistes—into a single federation but the scheme had failed.[45]
Several other attempts to unionize the industry were made, however. In
August 1930, some 500 dance musicians met at the Union's Victory
House to discuss the idea and Jack Hylton and Jack Payne were present.[46]
This led in September 1930 to the establishment of a 'Dance Section'
of the London branch of the Musicians' Union. Despite some success,
notably on the issue of the employment of alien musicians, after a year the
campaign collapsed. Other attempts to unionize followed. In May 1934
the General Musicians' Association, representing 260 dance musicians,
was formed in Manchester and this movement spread to Leeds, Liverpool, Nottingham, Bristol, Glasgow, and elsewhere before petering out
the next year.[47] There was even a second attempt to launch a Dance
Section of the Musicians' Union, in February 1935, which this time set
about drawing up detailed rates of pay for London. Despite limited success, by April 1936 this campaign had also collapsed. After the establishment of a Dance Band Leaders' Association in 1936, which survived but
to little effect, there were no further major attempts to unionize dance
band musicians before the Second World War.

Given the structural problems inherent in the dance music industry,
the failure to unionize was not surprising. The campaigns which were
launched did little to address these structural problems, nor were they
representative of most dance musicians' concerns. Rather than focusing on the issues of low wages, poor working conditions, and rising
unemployment, for example, the Musicians' Union Dance Section had
concentrated on a strategy for dealing with the employment of foreign
musicians. In the 1920s, the number of Americans working in British
dance bands was significant. American dance musicians were seen to offer
an 'authentic' interpretation of the new idiom and were highly sought
after. The presence of one or two leading American instrumentalists in

---

[45] *MM*, Jan. 1931, p. 21.
[46] *MM*, Sept. 1930, pp. 739–40.   [47] *MM*, 9 June 1934, p. 7.

a band could make a considerable difference to its appeal amongst the general public. As well as star instrumentalists in leading dance bands, many bands were led by Americans. Roy Fox, Charlie Kunz, and Carroll Gibbons, for example, were all Americans. Many British musicians resented this influence and were concerned that the best-paid jobs seemed almost exclusively cornered by American dance band musicians. The press did little to help by drawing unfavourable comparisons between British exponents of dance music and their American counterparts. Tensions were heightened when Jack Hylton, on tour of the USA, was refused a work permit on the insistence of the American Musicians' Union. This led to a tit-for-tat retaliation which resulted in the tightening of restrictions in December 1930 on American musicians entering Britain. The Musicians' Union, together with leading hotels and restaurants, negotiated with the Ministry of Labour to establish procedures for preliminary consultation before the award of labour permits for visiting musicians. The effect was a virtual ban on American musicians entering the country, either to work or visit. Although soloists did creep through the net, the ban was largely effective and was not repealed until after the Second World War. However, although this issue was viewed as a major threat by full-time professionals, it concerned others less. Also, insufficient attention was paid to the recruitment of semi-professionals who were, in turn, regarded with suspicion, even contempt, by most professional dance musicians. Without their inclusion any proposal to standardize wages and prevent undercutting was doomed to failure. This was the crux of the problem: any scheme designed to solve the problem of undercutting required a closed shop. Given the nature of the music and musicians involved, with the lack of formal training and qualifications, this was virtually impossible.

Conclusion

Dance bands were a powerful force in the dissemination of popular music in the period 1919 to 1939. The radio broadcasts, gramophone recordings, and stage appearances of the leading dance bands were accompanied by a large number of amateurs, semi-professionals, and professionals, taking live music to every corner of Britain. Despite the economic difficulties and instability of the dance musicians' world, the enthusiasm of these large numbers of 'do-it-yourself' musicians enabled a substantial number to survive throughout the period. The less rigid

1 The gramophone in the home. HMV radiogram advertisement, 1935. *EMI Records Ltd.*

2 The gramophone in public. Gramophones were ideal for a variety of outdoor locations. *National Museums of Scotland (Scottish Life Archive).*

3 The gramophone in public. A group outing, Scotland 1920s. *National Museums of Scotland (Scottish Life Archive).*

4 (*right*)
Selections from
shows were
popular.
EMI Records Ltd.

5 (*far right*)
Dance music,
the biggest seller
on records.
EMI Records Ltd.

6 (*right*)
Americanisation. 1924 blues catalogue. *EMI Records Ltd.*

7 (*far right*)
Further Americanisation. Columbia Hot Record Supplement, 1931. *EMI Records Ltd.*

8 (*above*) Gracie Fields: enormously popular on film, radio and records. Here at the HMV factory, 1933. *EMI Records Ltd.*

9 (*left*) George Formby: Britain's most popular film star, *c.*1937. *EMI Records Ltd.*

11 The talkies were a major source of new hit songs. *Private Collection.*

10 The cinema, even before sound, had an influence on music publishers output. *Private Collection.*

12 Lawrence Wright showcased his latest songs in his Blackpool production, 'On With the Show.' *Private Collection.*

13 One of Jimmy Kennedy's numerous hits, 'The Isle of Capri' from 1935. *Private Collection.*

14 Scotland meets New Orleans: Small semi-professional dance band, Edinburgh, 1923. *National Museums of Scotland (Scottish Life Archive).*

15 Scotland meets New Orleans: Small semi-professional dance band, Leven, 1920s. *National Museums of Scotland (Scottish Life Archive).*

16 'Town'—dance music's classless appeal: Local semi-professional dance band, Oxford, 1937. *Oxfordshire County Council Photographic Archive.*

17 'Gown'—dance music's classless appeal: University semi-professional dance band, Oxford, 1935. *Oxfordshire County Council Photographic Archive.*

18 Jack Hylton and His Band at an EMI recording studio, *c.*1931. *EMI Records Ltd.*

19 Dancing and 'Society': Roy Fox and Orchestra at the Monseigneur Restaurant, London, 1931. *Getty Images.*

20 The palais-
de-danse. An
English dance
hall, c.1937.
Getty Images.

performance and musical training that the new dance music required were a major part in its popularity amongst enthusiasts. This easy access to the musician's world was resented by large numbers of full-time professionals. Despite a growing tendency toward employment by large circuits of employers, there was no effective corresponding move by musicians to organize themselves into a union. In spite of such difficulties the supply of dance bands remained high throughout the period, and the large numbers of amateurs involved guaranteed that virtually all regions of Britain had access to some form of live dance music.

6

THE EXPANSION AND
DEVELOPMENT OF THE
DANCE HALL INDUSTRY

Introduction

It was at dance halls that the most popular music and the most preferred popular musicians, the dance bands, were heard throughout the country. Dancing was an essential element in this 'musical culture' and in the interwar period became a focus of big business interest as large national dance chains provided a palais-de-danse in virtually every town. As Mass-Observation noted in its essay 'Doing the Lambeth Walk', the directors of these institutions were some of the most influential forces in Britain's culture. This chapter will follow the development of dancing as an industry and endeavour to show how it directly shaped this culture.

6.1 The growth of dancing and the dance hall industry

The period after the First World War brought a mass market for dancing, in which all classes, but particularly the working and lower-middle classes, participated more regularly and in greater numbers than in any previous period. The widespread participation of the working and lower-middle classes makes the period from 1918 to 1939 distinctive, for, before this time, public dancing was primarily a leisure pursuit of the wealthy. The most important factor in this development was the creation of purpose-built dance halls or 'palais-de-danse' throughout Britain. However, before coming to their evolution it is necessary to look briefly at the provision and development of dancing as a pastime in Britain in the two decades before the end of the First World War.

Before the First World War, the public dancing facilities available to the working class were restricted. Such as there were were either poorly managed or expensive. Moreover, dancing lessons were required to learn the complicated steps and this was not only expensive but often socially unacceptable for working-class males. Holding dances also involved the hiring of musicians and a public hall and the provision of refreshments— all of which served to confine it, for the most part, to special occasions organized by large groups of people. As Llewellyn Smith noted in 1935, not only was public dancing not widespread among the working class, when it did occur it was fairly disorganized:

Dancing was not a very popular amusement forty years ago. There were no 'palais-de-danse' . . . and the dance club was unknown. Privately organised dances, or the occasional public dances at places like the Albert Hall, the Crystal Palace or Covent Garden, did not of course touch the lives of the working class. Dances in which workers took part were run by the various settlements and clubs at Christmas time and on special occasions, but the dancing was often very rough. The men had little idea of steps, the girls were not much better, and the dance sometimes turned into a 'rough house.'[1]

The majority of public dances open to the working class between 1900 and 1919 were held in assembly halls, which could be found in most towns or cities.[2] There were very few purpose-built public dance halls run exclusively for dancing. Dancing schools also provided dancing facilities, holding cheap weekly dances in addition to their normal lessons and larger monthly dances in town halls. The best opportunities for dancing were found outside London and other major towns and cities, in seaside resorts such as Blackpool, Morecombe, New Brighton, Great Yarmouth, Margate, and Douglas. Here dances were held more frequently than elsewhere in the country, often every night of the week in the holiday season. However, before the widespread adoption of 'holidays with pay' opportunities to visit such resorts were limited for the working class. By 1914, therefore, what little public dancing there was in working-class communities was centred around dance schools and dancing instructors. Except for special occasions and maybe at Christmas, public dancing had a limited role in the lives of the majority of the working-class population.

[1] H. Llewellyn Smith, *The New Survey of London Life and Labour* (1930–5), ix. 42.
[2] For a history of dancing before 1919 see P. Richardson, *A History of English Ballroom Dancing (1910–45): The Story of the Development of the Modern English Style* (1945), 1–35, from which information in this section is taken.

In the period before the First World War, the most enthusiastic dancers in Britain were the upper and middle class. Styles in dancing, music, and dress were focused on this group and the facilities available to them far outnumbered those for the working class.[3] At the higher levels of society private dances were regularly held by the nobility, together with County Balls held by property-owning families in the shires. In London, the Grafton Galleries, the Wharncliffe Rooms, the Portman Rooms, the Savoy Hotel, and the Princess Galleries were popular locations for society dances. London was the centre for the balls of the 'Season' and its large hotels, particularly the Ritz, greatly influenced the nature and popularity of dancing in Britain at this time.

The provision of 'public' facilities catering for the middle and upper class was particularly good and the Edwardian period saw a marked shift away from private to public dances. Between 1900 and 1914 numerous 'dance clubs' were formed in the West End of London but they were not fixed features, owned no permanent premises, and hired hotels and other ballrooms for their meetings. These clubs held a series of dances, up to twice a week, for which payment was made in advance. One of the more important of these clubs, the Boston Club, had evolved from the famous KDS or Keen Dancers' Society established in 1903. The Boston Club was one of the first to organize 'dinner dances'. With the development of dinner dances, London's top restaurants also began to run dances. The dance clubs also catered predominantly for the upper and upper-middle class. Two of the most important were the Royalist Club founded in 1910, which held dances in the Connaught Rooms, and the Public Schools' and Universities' Dance Club established at the Savoy Hotel in 1911.

The increasing popularity of dancing among the upper and upper-middle classes by 1913 resulted in the appearance of the first permanent dance clubs which owned their own premises and provided regular dancing. Again they were exclusively for the rich. The most popular were located at prestigious addresses: the Lotus Club, Garrick Street; Murray's Club, Beak Street; the 400 Club in Old Bond Street; and Ciro's Club in Orange Street—all established themselves as fashionable spots. At about the same time, tea dances began to be held at the Prince's, Carlton, and Waldorf Hotels.

Several factors allowed dancing to break away from its exclusively upper-class following. Of these developments, the most important was a rise in real wages and increased leisure time for the working population.

---

[3] See ibid. 10–21.

More specifically and of direct consequence to the popularity of dancing were the changes in musical and dancing styles imported from the United States just prior to, and during, the First World War, the development of purpose-built dance halls, and the subsequent creation of large chains of dance halls by big business concerns. Each of these developments will be considered.

Parallel with the arrival of the new dance music in Britain before the First World War, there was a revolution in dancing styles to match the irregular syncopated music. The earlier dances, the Turkey Trot, Bunny Hug, and Grizzly Bear became popular in the United States in 1912 and arrived in Britain shortly after. These dances were a move away from the complex reels and quadrilles of the past and towards simpler steps for couples. They also gave dancing more overt sexual expression. The most important development in dancing, however, was the arrival of the fox-trot in the summer of 1914. Foxtrot music was first played at the 400 Club in July 1914 and the first real attempts to dance the foxtrot steps occurred shortly after at the fashionable 'tea-dances' at Harewood Place. After some modifications, it became a big success in Britain, beginning in the fashionable West End hotels and assembly rooms, proceeding through dancing schools and the emerging dance halls to the rest of the population. The new sociable 'couple dancing' and the new music fed on each other. The more popular dances became, the more musicians were needed to play for them. Cabarets and dance halls promoted the spread of 'jazz' and interest in 'jazz' promoted the popularity of dancing.

The immediate post-war period saw tremendous growth in the popularity of dancing. It is estimated that nearly 11,000 dance halls and night clubs opened up between 1919 and 1926 and contemporaries spoke of a 'dance craze'.[4] Certainly, the national press was fascinated by the enormous popularity of dancing and newspapers such as *The Times* in 1919 were inclined to withhold approval:

To one freshly returned from the devastated areas of France and the gutted workshops of Belgium, London presents a wild atmosphere of amusement, recalling some of the worst of the bad old days . . . the present Jazz-madness makes us inclined to sympathize with the rather snobbish Plutarch, who held that dancing . . . held sway in senseless, uncritical theatres, spurned by the intellectual and lofty-minded . . . As for the Jazz, judging from the seriousness of the faces of some of its celebrants it may be religious.[5]

[4] J. McMillan, *The Way it Was 1914–1934* (Kimber, 1979), 76.
[5] *The Times*, 29 Apr. 1919, p. 15.

The end of hostilities was sufficient to lead to a demand for new forms of amusement and enjoyment. This was given further impetus by the economic boom, but even that boom burst in 1920–1. Dancing was given a further boost with the removal of some of the restrictions imposed on civilian life by the provisions of the Defence of the Realm Act (DORA). In 1922 a campaign led by the Brighter London Society, whose members included Lord Curzon, joined the press campaign for the removal of all of the restrictions of DORA. The new Licensing Act of 1921 allowed the further development of restaurant dances and the night club and by 1925 DORA was gone completely. Commentators at the time speculated whether the dance craze was a transient or lasting phenomenon. *The Times*, reporting on 'The Dancing Craze' in March 1922, observed:

All last year dances grew in popularity, and at the present time the craze seems to have reached its zenith. The number of private and public dances has grown enormously, and the official seal of approval was set on the public dancing hall when, a little while ago, the duke of York visited Hammersmith Palais-de-danse . . .[6]

The popularity of dancing had been such that, for a while, it seemed likely to eclipse the cinema as the most popular entertainment. The annual report of the Cinematograph Exhibitors' Association for 1922 voiced this concern:

The public with depleted pockets after a mad orgy of spending, have largely deserted their annual forms of entertainment and have been to a considerable extent devoting such spare cash as they possess to dancing. The head has given way to the feet. Drama (legitimate and otherwise), the music-hall, and the concert room are all suffering from an unprecedented slump. The cinema is sharing the same fate.[7]

Such was the popularity of informal dancing that members of the British Association of Teachers of Dancing, meeting at their annual conference in Aberdeen in 1922, had complained of 'the evil effects arising from the unrestricted granting of dancing licences to hotels, clubs, dancing palaces, and adventurous persons'.[8]

In 1925–6, the Charleston swept Britain. The Charleston arrived in Britain in spring 1925 when it was introduced at the Hotel Metropole in London by cabaret dancers. By the autumn it had spread throughout Britain through the dance halls and a growing number of professional

---

[6] *The Times*, 15 Mar. 1922, p. 9.   [7] Ibid. 9.
[8] Quoted in *The Times*, 29 June 1922, p. 10.

dance instructors appeared keen to profit from dancing's new-found popularity. The press had started a campaign against the Charleston as most people danced it violently and without lessons. A more sedate version, 'the flat progressive charleston' was devised by dance instructors in order to tame the wild exhibitionism it seemed to encourage. On 15 December 1926, the theatre impresario C. B. Cochran organized a 'Charleston Ball' at the Royal Albert Hall attended by nearly 10,000 people and with competitions judged by, among others, Fred Astaire. This was the zenith of the Charleston's popularity and although it remained in vogue for only six months longer, it provided a vivid image for contemporary commentators who were focusing their attention on a minority of 'bright young things' and their supposedly Bohemian lifestyles. It was the growth of palais-de-danse, however, which ensured a genuinely popular market for dancing.

Palais-de-danse were first established in continental Europe. They were permanent, purpose-built public dance halls that evolved specifically to cater for a large working and lower-middle-class audience. Being purpose built they were able to offer first-class dance floors, orchestras of musicians, and other facilities, such as cafés or restaurants, which no Assembly Hall or Dancing School could provide. Furthermore, whereas the Dancing Schools had clung steadfastly to the older dance steps and dance music, the palais offered programmes of modern music and dance steps performed by modern 'dance bands', the very thing their audiences wanted.

The first palais-de-danse to be built in Britain was the Hammersmith Palais, opened on 28 October 1919. A crowd of 7,000 dancers queued to enter, eager to listen to its music, provided for the first nine months by the Original Dixieland Jazz Band on tour from America. Many were turned away as the hall's capacity of 2,000 was reached. It was luxurious, with an expensive 'sprung' floor, brilliant decorations, a café, restaurant, and, of course, the most modern style in music playing every night. Even when the Original Dixieland Jazz Band left, the Hammersmith Palais was able to attract many of the best dance bands in Britain and was often the venue for visiting American bands. The Hammersmith Palais attracted actors, sportsmen, filmstars, and even royalty, with a list of patrons that included the Prince of Wales (a keen dancer), the Duke of York, Mary Pickford, Douglas Fairbanks, Lady Diana Duff Cooper, and Georges Carpentier. It was estimated that 3 million dancers had danced there by 1928 and it became a national attraction, known throughout Britain. Its manager, M. E. Dowdall estimated that less than 5 per cent of its patrons were drawn locally, the rest coming from all over London and farther afield.[9]

The success of the Hammersmith venture was so great that its owners opened a second palais in Birmingham shortly after. There is no doubt that the Hammersmith Palais provided inspiration for hundreds of other palais-de-danse. In 1921, Leon Meredith opened Cricklewood Dance Hall and popular dances were inaugurated shortly after in 1925 at the Royal Opera House, Covent Garden, under the management of Bertram Mills, the circus owner. During this time hundreds of palais-de-danse had sprung up throughout Britain, often opened by businessmen who had no previous experience of dancing and the dance business but who could recognize a good opportunity when it presented itself. This opportunity was the provision of first-rate facilities and an ability to move with the times.

The growth of purpose-built dance halls providing first-rate facilities at affordable prices, with proper organization and orderly conduct, shifted the focus of dancing from its former upper-class strongholds in the West End of London towards an urban lower-middle and working-class patronage. The palais-de-danse were providing the facilities that would, by the mid-1930s, make dancing a truly mass leisure pursuit. Regular, cheap, and modern, dances at a palais-de-danse were ideal for those with low incomes who were interested in the new dance steps and dance music that was causing such a sensation in the West End. In this respect the palais were copying the dances of their social superiors but soon they were to take the lead in shaping fashions

The growth in the popularity of dancing during the 1920s was impressive but it was not continuous. Dancing had become a mass pastime in the immediate post-war boom but it was hit by the economic cycles of the interwar period as much as any other business. It was not until the mid-1930s that it could claim once more to be a mass leisure pursuit and the development of the Mecca circuit of dance halls played a leading part in this revival.

For a number of reasons, the immediate post-war boom in dancing was not sustained and the numbers of people dancing began to stabilize after about 1922–3. First, the cinema was not dislodged from its dominant position in entertainment. The acceleration in the rate of construction of cinemas was testimony to the growing popularity of the film as entertainment. By 1926 there were 3,000 cinemas in operation, a rate of growth given a further fillip with the advent of sound films in 1925. Secondly, the dancing profession attempted to raise the status of dancing by

[9] *Dancing Times*, Mar. 1928, pp. 843–5.

incorporating complicated dance steps, difficult to execute and requiring expensive lessons—factors which combined to deter some from entering dance halls. Thirdly, radio was emerging and although not yet the mass medium it was later to become, it already had a large following, with over half a million licensed listeners by 1923, rising rapidly to 5 million by 1932. Radio began to consume money and occupy leisure time. Fourthly, the appearance on the market of increasingly cheap portable gramophones was moving the focus of some leisure activities back into the home. More importantly, all of these developments were taking place in the context of regionally based economic decline after the post-war boom, especially in those areas affected by high unemployment.

In 1927, an editorial in the *Dancing Times* raised doubts about the validity of claims concerning the popularity of dancing:

We refer glibly to the present 'dancing craze' and a year or two ago wrote about the 'boom' in dancing. There is no such thing to-day as a dancing craze, neither has there been a boom in dancing during the present generation. Listen to this. A director of a company which owns more important Dance Halls than any other in the country estimates that on a Saturday night in London not more than twenty thousand people are at dances whereas on the same day of the week upwards of half a million people visit the cinema in the Metropolitan area. The dancing craze has not yet come . . . we have scarcely reached the fringe of it.[10]

There is no doubt that throughout the 1920s, the facilities for dancing had improved. However, with the exception of the immediate post-war period, talk of a dancing craze and a dancing boom was premature. Nevertheless, in the late 1920s a number of important developments occurred in the organization of the dancing industry that were to allow full expansion only in the 1930s. In the late 1920s and early 1930s a number of dance hall chains were established that were to remove control of dancing away from professional dancers into the hands of businessmen. It took the development of these highly organized business concerns to make dancing a genuinely mass pastime. The rapid commercialization of the dance business is nowhere more typified than in the development of the largest of these dance hall chains, the Mecca chain.

The Mecca dance chain was founded by Carl L. Heimann.[11] Heimann, a Dane, moved to England in 1912, aged 16, possessing only a few shillings and unable to speak English. In London, he gained employment

[10] *Dancing Times*, Oct. 1927, p. 2.

[11] Much of the following information is taken from interviews of C. L. Heimann and B. Davies carried out by Tom Harrisson and Alec Hurley. M-O A: MDJ 3/A: 'C. L. Heimann' (1938) and MDJ 3/E: 'Facts about C. L. Heimann' (1938) and 'Byron Davies' (1939). See also R. Fairley, *Come Dancing Miss World* (1966).

in the catering business, working his way up from waiter. In 1924 he was made catering manager for the People's Palace, East London, employed by a firm called 'Ye Mecca Cafés'. Through his work for Mecca, Heimann soon became interested in the opportunities offered by dancing. In 1925 the firm, taking advantage of the boom for dancing, started to provide catering facilities for the popular dances held at the Royal Opera House, Covent Garden, then a dance hall. Catering for the top nightclub, the Café de Paris, in 1928, was a further source of inspiration. He was quick to recognize the potential mass market open to dance halls if they were properly organized and targeted the mass market decisively enough, believing that top-class facilities should be available to everyone. In 1928, whilst working as catering manager there, he persuaded 'Mecca Cafés' to purchase Sherry's Dance Hall in Brighton with himself as general manager. He put his ideas to the test. Heimann was so successful that Sherry's was followed by the Ritz, Manchester, in 1930, the Locarno, Streatham, in 1931, and the Lido, Croydon, in 1932. In 1933 he also persuaded Mecca to purchase a small band and cabaret booking agency run by Byron Davies, an entrepreneur he had first met at the Hammersmith Palais. Davies had previously been involved in numerous forms of business and had a keen sense of what was needed to succeed in the increasingly sophisticated consumer and service industry of the interwar period. Such direct experience was to prove vital to the success of Mecca.

By 1934, Heimann was general manager of Mecca Dancing, an offshoot of the original company. He had also begun to buy shares in the company, but was not yet in a controlling position. Stung by his only failure to date (a £50,000 loss at the Lido, Croydon) the Mecca board halted the dance hall expansion. Heimann managed a compromise, however, persuading Mecca to allow him to branch out on his own. He was still general manager of the Mecca dance halls, but was free to develop his own halls, utilizing the Mecca name.

In 1935, therefore, Heimann started a joint venture with Alan Fairley, an important operator in the amusement and leisure industry in Scotland. This association was to prove his most fruitful. In 1936 they became joint managing directors of the Locarno, Glasgow. Their new circuit of dance halls then grew rapidly and by 1938 they had become associate directors of dance halls throughout the country, with halls in Edinburgh, Leeds, Sheffield, Nottingham, Bradford, and Birmingham. In London they ran the Tottenham and Wimbledon Palais and the Paramount Dance Hall, Tottenham Court Rd. By 1940 they even controlled the Royal Opera House, Covent Garden, from where Heimann had first derived inspiration. In addition to the halls, by 1938 the Mecca Agency controlled 300 dance bands playing in some 2,000 establishments throughout the country, more than any other organization in Britain.[12] This agency dealt with virtually all aspects of the dance hall business from management to laying dance floors, building bandstands, supplying bands, cabarets, professional dancers, accounting services, publicity, and so on. There was also a subsidiary, 'Dance Hall Equipment Ltd.', that specialized in supplying everything dance halls needed according to the Mecca principle, 'from carpets to cups, from tea urns to tea spoons; from bandstands to balloons; from shades to streamers. We're decorators, electricians, constructors . . .'[13]

The original catering firm, 'Mecca Cafés' was still trading but business grew such that the Mecca Head Offices, located in Dean Street, Soho, expanded from a single floor in 1930 to the occupation of the whole building—six floors—and a staff of nearly 1,000 by 1939. On the back of his independent success, Heimann was invited to join the Board at Mecca in 1942, where he still managed their dance halls. He was followed in 1945 by Fairley. In 1946 the two interests merged and Heimann and Fairley became joint chairmen of the new Mecca Ltd., taking 600,000 of the 700, 000 shares issued. It was to become one of the largest companies in post-war British entertainment. Even by the late 1930s, however, Mecca dance halls, together with Carl Heimann and Alan Fairley, was the most influential dance hall and dance music concern in the country.

Yet Mecca was not alone. In May 1928 one of the largest dance hall and theatre chains was formed when General Theatres Ltd. took over the interests of the Szarvasy-Gibbons Syndicate which controlled 100 dance halls, including the New Casino Palais and Rialto dance hall in Liverpool and the Astoria, Charing Cross Road, London.[14] In addition to these dance halls, General Theatres Ltd. also took over numerous variety halls and leading dance band leader Billy Cotton was given the post of musical director to the company. As musical director, Billy Cotton directed the dance band arrangements at the group's dance halls as well as the newly acquired variety theatres. Management of the chain's ballrooms was left to E. W. Bourne, who had opened Southport Palais and managed the Regent, Brighton. They were, therefore, a major force in dance hall provision. Many other theatres and cinema groups, such as Gaumont British and Odeon, also diversified into dance hall ownership.

[12] See Chapter 5 above.   [13] Anon., *Stepping Out* (1940), backpiece.
[14] *MM*, May 1928, p. 519.

The presence of Mecca and other chains catalysed the development of a mass market and raised the profile of public dance halls among the working and middle classes. By 1938 it was estimated that 2 million people went dancing throughout Britain each week, of which about three-quarters of a million patronized public dance halls whilst the remainder went to private dances, restaurants, and clubs.[15] There were, of course, seasonal fluctuations but these figures suggest that annual admissions to dances were near to 100 million in 1938. After the outbreak of war, the popularity of dancing, if anything, increased. It was estimated that by 1947, nearly 3 million people in Britain were admitted each week to dance halls, of which 450 were used exclusively for ballroom dancing. A further 2,000 'other locations' such as town, village, and assembly halls, were also available.[16]

Certainly the number of dance halls had grown steadily throughout the 1920s but their full capacity was not reached until the 1930s. A 1934 survey of dance halls throughout Britain illustrated this.[17] In 1934 Liverpool and Merseyside had 'well over' ten public dance halls, a number larger than most, in a city where dancing was one of the most popular pastimes. The important dance halls in central Liverpool were the Grafton Rooms (capacity 1,000), the Locarno, and the Rialto. In 1939 the manager of the Grafton Rooms estimated his average weekly attendance as 4,000 in season, compared with 10,000 per week for the Locarno. Dancing was an essential part of Liverpool nightlife, as J. B. Priestley observed in 1933:

two trams brought me back to the centre of the city, whose essential darkness made a good background for quite a metropolitan display of Neon lighting and flashing signs. Cinemas, theatres . . . dance-halls, grill-rooms, boxing matches, cocktail bars, all in full glittering swing. The Adelphi Hotel had dressed for the evening, was playing waltzes, and for the time being did not care a fig about the lost atlantic traffic.[18]

Glasgow, a city that some people estimated had more dance halls per head of population than anywhere else in the country, had, in addition to five large public dance halls, 'many other smaller halls'. The largest, the Plaza, held 900 dancers with a regular attendance of 400–500 per night, many coming from the large suburban districts of Iffnock, Whitecross,

[15] P. Holt, *Daily Express*, 16 Nov. 1938, p. 16.

[16] B. Seebohm Rowntree and G. R. Lavers, *English Life and Leisure* (1951), 279–85.

[17] Horace Richards, 'Dancing throughout Britain', a series of six reports printed in *PMDW*, 22 Nov. to 29 Dec. 1934.

[18] J. B. Priestley, *An English Journey* (1934), 249–50.

and Newlands. The city also had a large ballroom above the new Playhouse super-cinema, one of the largest cinemas in Europe, and a Dance Club, with dancing until 2 a.m. and accommodation for 400 dancers. In Edinburgh in 1934, there were four main dance halls; the Palais-de-Danse (average attendance 500–600 by 1939, rising to *c.*1,700 on special occasions), the Havana Dance Club, Maximes, and the Cockburn Palais. Each catered for its own particular clientele and between them they provided dancing until midnight in the public halls and 4 a.m. in the clubs. The Havana Dance Club was one of the centres of the popular music and dance scene in Scotland.

In Manchester, the centrally located Ritz dance hall and the Plaza were supplemented by numerous other halls located throughout the city and its suburbs. In the working-class district of Hulme, for example, there were as many as twelve public dance halls. In central Manchester, however, the prestigious Ritz dance hall catered for those throughout the city and its suburbs and was described by a contemporary commentator as 'a swagger Palais that does not belie its name. Non-stop dancing reigns here.'[19] Manchester, like many other major cities, was 'enjoying the dancing boom that has swept the country, and night after night the Ritz is packed'.[20] Birmingham, too, had major attractions, possessing one of the two original palais-de-danse, the Birmingham Palais-de-danse, which was also one of the largest, with seating accommodation for 1,500. There were also two other major dance halls, Tony's Ballroom (which had two separate 'themed' dance floors) and the West End Dance Hall. This was joined by the Grand Casino in 1936. In Birmingham, as with other large cities, numerous smaller halls spread into suburbia throughout the 1930s.

In Portsmouth there were nine locations for public dancing by 1939, including five ballrooms and dance halls and four other halls licensed for dancing. Demand was large because of the major dockyards and military presence. In the Lancashire cotton town of Bolton, six dance halls (the four biggest being the Astoria, Aspen Hall, Palais-de-Danse, and Empress Hall) had capacities ranging from 500 to 1,000 each (out of a total population of 180,000 in 1938), providing dances six nights a week (not Sundays), throughout the year. Nottingham could boast two major public dance halls with a capacity of 500 and 800 dancers each.

Yet, to focus purely on the development of palais-de-danse and circuits of dance halls would be to ignore the numerous other locations for dancing which existed in even the smallest of communities.

[19] *PMDW*, 22 Dec. 1934, p. 20.   [20] Ibid. 20.

In 1933 H. Llewellyn Smith counted twenty-three palais-de-danse in the county of London.[21] However, he reckoned that this was only about one-tenth of the total number of locations for dancing as there were numerous halls and rooms where dancing regularly took place and to which the public were admitted. Moreover, in addition to the specially constructed public dance halls, every town had many more public and private locations for dancing. Local and County Councils would grant licences for dancing and music in locations as diverse as church and mission halls, club rooms, municipal halls, assembly halls, swimming baths, hotels, and restaurants.

Typical of the variety of locations that each town or city would offer is the description of a 'seaport' town (probably Portsmouth or Southampton) given by Renée Radford in 1927:

In this particular seaport there are estimated to be some four hundred works, big and small. Few are without their annual whist drive and dance, many have Welfare Institutions that hold weekly 'hops' in the works hall . . . Church social clubs, private dancing clubs, professional dancing halls, the bakers, confectioners, grocers, drapers, dairymen, butchers, police—almost every occupation runs its dances. The Territorials' Drill hall is pressed in to service on an average once a week. Each detachment of territorials gives its dance, with officers and non coms' dances thrown in besides. About sixty to seventy times a year one local café alone holds dances, at which from a hundred and fifty to two hundred people attend each time. At another restaurant there would be about fifty a year and at many more anything from four to forty functions during the 'busy' season. At the larger halls the attendances may run up to a thousand, and four or five hundred at a time are commonplace. At one of these such halls over two hundred functions, most of them dances or whist drives and dances, take place—one every night of the week.[22]

Llewellyn Smith calculated, using London County Council statistics, that there were 499 licences granted for music and dancing in the county of London in 1933. By 1937 there were 554. The majority of these licences, 33 per cent, were granted to hotels, pubs, and restaurants; followed by cinemas (24%); church and mission halls (11%), and assembly rooms and exhibitions (9%).[23] In the borough of Wandsworth, London, in 1939 there were 25 locations for public dancing, including 6 church and mission halls, 4 private halls and assembly rooms, and 4 purpose-built dance halls. In York in the same year there were a similar number of dance locations, 26.

---

[21] Llewellyn Smith, *New Survey*, ix. 64.   [22] *Dancing Times*, Apr. 1927, pp. 84–5.
[23] M-O A: MDJ: 1/A 'LCC Statistics' (1939).

The 1930s also saw the development of 'road-houses', institutions that took advantage of the growing ownership of cars and which also provided nightlife in suburbia and the countryside. Imported from America, these were entertainment complexes situated outside major towns and cities, usually involving dance band, entertainers, restaurant, and cocktail bars. Swimming pools were also available in the summer and some even provided landing grounds for private aircraft. Purpose built, often from concrete and some with modernist exteriors, they nevertheless joined the growing trend of mock Tudorism found in suburbia, with panelling and oak beamed interiors. They offered a bizarre contrast between nightlife and countryside:

. . . a way of having a night in town in the country; because, however Arcadian the situation of the place might be, once you entered the doors you were back in Shaftesbury Avenue or Coventry Street. It gave you the feeling of one of those dreams in which you are in two places at once. You could sit in a Jermyn Street snack-bar, and through the window, fifty yards away, you saw the moonlit countryside.[24]

Such roadhouses were very popular and it was only the outbreak of the war in 1939 that prevented their further development.

6.2 Mecca and the commercialization of dancing

The dance industry had by the mid-1930s become concentrated in the hands of a few large dance chains. Decisions in the dancing world began to be taken increasingly on the basis of business judgements. Before this, the dancing profession had exerted considerable control over dancing and dancing styles. Control was shifting away from the dancers and from the dancing profession towards large businesses, of which Mecca was the largest.

The growth of the dance business after 1919 was accompanied by rapid growth in the number of professional dancing instructors and associations. Throughout the 1920s, these associations made numerous attempts to raise the standard of dancing in dance halls and ballrooms and tried to regulate the atmosphere in which dancers danced. Although dancing was popular, the dance music and dance steps that accompanied it were often complex and intricate. The demand for lessons was large. Not only were dancing instructors eager to capitalize on the new-found

[24] T. Burke, *English Night-Life* (1941), 141.

popularity of dancing, they were also keen to make their profession 'respectable'. In order to gain respectability they organized themselves into professional associations and began a process of regulating and stand-ardizing dancing and its environment. The first 'Informal Conference' of the Teachers of Ballroom Dancing, for example, held in May 1920, expressed outrage at the 'artistic bolshevism' displayed by the new dances flooding in from the United States. It decided that the basic steps of the foxtrot, one-step, and waltz should be standardized. The conference was given surprisingly widespread press coverage and this, together with further informal conferences that year and in 1921, led to a national campaign against 'objectionable dancing'. These decisions manifested themselves at a local level through the numerous dancing schools which opened in many towns and cities. Dance instructors had to pass a series of rigorous examinations before they were able to hold the qualifications necessary to be authorized instructors. They also launched competitions throughout the country in order to raise the status of dancing. In 1924, a ballroom branch of the Imperial Society of Teachers of Dancing was formed, setting exact standards for competition dancing. As the 1920s progressed they began to develop a distinct style of dancing, known as 'The English Style' which eventually became associated exclusively with 'ballroom dancing'. Little by little dance instructors were regulating and standardizing a pastime that many had found initially attractive because it allowed a means of expression and freedom of movement. Dancing was becoming a serious business.

The consequence of these developments, together with the better behaviour and more ordered dancing found in the new palais-de-danse, was to raise standards. Byron Davies of the Mecca group estimated that dancing standards were higher in the '2/6 hall' than in the fashionable hotels of the West End where 'society' danced. The standardizing of steps also tended to regulate the wilder atmosphere of the dance halls which had caused so much criticism in the immediate post-war period.

Among those who did not learn, there was resentment at the new-found seriousness of some dancers and some dance halls. As a result it became possible to distinguish between two quite separate and opposed groups of dancers, as the *Oxford Magazine* noted in 1929: 'Ballroom dancing appeals to thousands upon thousands . . . its followers form two great camps, those who learn to dance, and that quite appreciable number who dance without learning.'[25] The dancing business suffered as

[25] 'S. G. R.', 'Rhythmic Dancing', *Oxford Magazine* (Oxford), 28 Feb. 1929, p. 453.

a result, because this attention to the detail of dance steps, standardization, tempo, style, and so on, helped to deter thousands from entering dance halls. Heimann and Davies argued that elaborate and intricate dances made people embarrassed and awkward in dance halls and hence felt the need to introduce easier dances that required less skill to execute, in order to expand business.[26]

By the 1930s, the growing power of business interests in the provision of dancing facilities brought about radical changes to these formalizing processes. The objective for businesses such as Mecca was clear—to attract as many people as possible using the lowest common denominator. Facilities were improved, prices lowered, and every attempt was made to get people dancing. Heimann, speaking in 1938, said his philosophy was, 'you must give the public a show'. Where previously one band had been employed, two, sometimes three, were taken on. Elaborate cabarets with professional dancers and acts of all kinds were provided for the same admission charge. Dancing competitions were also encouraged.

Certainly, the Mecca group was not alone in its pursuit of business in this way. Many dance hall businesses used similar tactics. The manager of the Nottingham Palais-de-Danse, Mr J. Fallon, embarked on a similar drive to get the people of Nottingham dancing when he arrived there in 1929. Like Heimann, he was an entrepreneur. As was noted in 1934,

He is a man who, besides being an accomplished dancer, is an astute business man, and one who realises that the first move in making a town 'dancing-conscious' is to get people into the ball-rooms . . . He organised a Terpsichore Club, dancing lessons, pole-squatting competitions, miniature cycle-races. Anything, in reason, to get Palais talked about, and to lure people into it. His optimism and hard work has had its effect . . . 'If She's Beautiful—She Dances!' is the subtle slogan with which he lured both men and girls into his Palais.[27]

Uniquely, however, the Mecca circuit of dance halls introduced changes to the way in which people danced that improved the level of business in the dance industry as a whole. Mecca and Heimann helped develop a series of simple, easy-to-dance group dances such as the Palais Glide and the St Bernard's Waltz in 1935, followed by novelty dances like the Lambeth Walk and the Chestnut Tree in 1938—a series of dances that lifted the fortunes of the dance business by countering the hesitation of potential dancers concerned about their ability to dance. Such dances

---

[26] See M-O A: MDJ 3/A: 'C. L. Heimann' (1938) and 'Byron Davies' (1939).
[27] H. Richards, 'Dancing through Britain 3: Nottingham', in *PMDW*, 8 Dec. 1934, p. 20.

changed the way in which dancers interacted in the dance hall, as Tom Harrisson writing for the *Picture Post* in 1938 observed:

. . . [they] marked an important breakaway from the post-war norm, of couple dancing to highly conventionalised movements. The Palais Glide stimulated freer open dancing, everyone in the ballroom joining in together.[28]

This development is particularly interesting as it illustrates the immense influence that Mecca exerted by the late 1930s. Tom Harrisson also noted:

This ['The Lambeth Walk'] is the song that half the world started singing in 1938. To the song a dance was added, a dance that was half a walk, and it caught on as no new dance has done for years. You could, and can, find them doing the Lambeth Walk in Mayfair ball-rooms, suburban dance-halls, cockney parties and village hops. Scotland and the industrial north took it up as keenly as the south. From all sorts of out-of-the-way places came news of its penetration. An observer who visited the far-away isle of Arran reported that the 'natives' were doing it there. It spread to New York and thence right across America; to Paris and thence to Prague . . .[29]

Its popularity was the direct result of its promotion by the Mecca group. Heimann had heard the song whilst watching the show *Me and My Girl*, then playing at the Victoria Palace and starring cockney comedian Lupino Lane. Realizing the potential for a mass dance, he instructed his senior dancing instructor, Adele England, to 'elaborate the walk into a dance' and a routine was established, simple enough for all dancers to join in. As Adele England stated:

Everyone can do it, they don't have to learn it. There's never been an English dance success like it before. We have so many dance halls we can push it. I started in the Locarno, then I went round to the Ritz, Manchester; the Grand Casino, Birmingham; Sherrys, Brighton; the Locarno, Glasgow and the Piccadilly Club, Glasgow; the Palais, Edinburgh; and the Royal, Tottenham. I did it all in a month. By the end it had really caught on.

Mr. Heimann hopes every so often we shall present a new dance to the public. We want to keep them all English now and they'll be simple.[30]

The Lambeth Walk became extraordinarily popular. With massive exposure on the radio, successful gramophone recordings, large sheet

[28] Draft version of T. Harrisson, 'A Dance is Born' for *Picture Post*, 12 Dec. 1938, p. 6.

[29] T. Harrisson, 'Doing the Lambeth Walk', in C. Madge and T. Harrisson, *Britain by Mass-Observation* (Harmondsworth, 1939), 139.

[30] Ibid. 161.

music sales, and an enormous dancing public, it distinguished itself as no dance since the Charleston had done. Indeed, the success of the Lambeth Walk had increased the popularity of dancing so much that Heimann and Davies planned to release new dances at least twice a year, every few months if possible. In 1938–9 they promoted the dances the Park Parade and the Chestnut Tree.

For the Chestnut Tree, Heimann commissioned Jimmy Kennedy of the Peter Maurice Music Company to write a new dance song. It was to have been the start of a ten-year contract to supply new songs specifically for dancing, such was the confidence of Mecca in this system but the war subsequently changed this arrangement. In collaboration with Jimmy Phillips, also of Peter Maurice, the song was completed a few weeks after commissioning. Adele England then began to devise the steps for the dance. Within two weeks the song was available on sale as sheet music, selling 893 copies on the day after publication and reaching 12,084 a day within a month, making it the second-best selling sheet music song at that time. Special arrangements were sent out to the dance bands which were employed by the Mecca Agency to 'plug' the tune in the halls and on the radio. Mecca even went so far as to give free musical arrangements to independent dance halls and offered to give free demonstrations of the dance steps, something they continued to do with each new dance they brought out. Their motives were regarded with suspicion by others in the industry, many of whom believed Mecca would start charging them for demonstrations once a certain dance had become so popular no dance hall could refuse to play it or teach its steps.

The radio was also used to promote the new song and the popular dance band led by Joe Loss was one of the first to broadcast it on the radio. Although officially the radio promotion of certain songs and arrangements by dance bands was outlawed by the BBC, the practice was widespread and numerous other 'plugs' followed this one, most arranged by the music publishers.[31] Shortly afterwards, another mass medium was enrolled in the promotional campaign, the gramophone. HMV recorded 'The Chestnut Tree' on gramophone record and it was soon followed up by recordings by the major dance bands.

Two weeks after it was premièred as a dance, on 15 November 1938, Mass-Observation discovered that 45 per cent of Londoners had heard of it and knew what it was, though less than 1 per cent had danced it. On the same day, observers reported that it was being danced in Edinburgh,

---

[31] See Chapter 8 below.

Oldham, Southport, Manchester, Luton, Blackpool, Bristol, Glasgow, and Derby.[32] Through continual playing in halls and repetition on the radio its popularity increased, and it remained popular until Heimann commissioned a successor. Although these 'novelty dances' never replaced the standard foxtrot and waltzes, they were included in most dance programmes in dance halls throughout Britain. They did much to bring reluctant dancers into public dance halls and they served to re-socialize an atmosphere that had begun to grow too formalized.

This elaborate system used to promote dances and the criteria used to shape them illustrate how C. L. Heimann and his circuit of dance halls and dance bands had, by the end of the period, gained an unprecedented influence over the dancing public. The change in dancing habits which is discernible in the late 1930s, away from dancing in couples and towards social and community dances, not only reflects the desire of dancers to feel part of a larger community in the face of increasingly grim political events but also shows how Mecca could utilize the machinery at its disposal to encourage certain dances.

Conclusion

Within the space of a little over forty years the facilities provided for dancing had improved immensely and by 1939 purpose-built dance halls provided cheap, regular, and well-run dances in virtually every town and city in Britain. It was an entertainment form inextricably linked to popular music and its popularity reflects the growing importance of dance music culture to interwar British society. These new facilities, combined with less permanent provision, as in church halls and assembly halls, meant that the opportunities for dancing in working-class communities were greater than they had ever been. Even allowing for the fluctuations in attendance by periods of 'dance booms', going to dance halls was a leisure time activity engaged in by a large proportion of the population. The growth of the popular music industry and the spread of dance music had much to do with the expansion in dancing. As the period progressed attempts were made to regulate and standardize the atmosphere of these dance halls by the businesses which owned the large chains of dance halls. These chains undermined the professional dancing instructors and

[32] Draft version of T. Harrisson, 'A Dance is Born' for *Picture Post*, 12 Dec. 1938, pp. 11–12.

although they initially set out to gain respectability in order to maximize profits, when respectability did not necessarily produce profits, they introduced a philosophy of the lowest common denominator, whereby the maximization of profits came first. The impact on individuals and on interwar society will be considered in the next chapter.

7

THE EXPERIENCE OF DANCING, DANCE HALLS, AND THE 'DANCE CULTURE', 1918–1939

Introduction

Aside from the obvious pleasure dancing gave people, it served a variety of important social functions, not least of which were the opportunities that it afforded for meeting friends and members of the opposite sex. Dancing was also an essential feature in the emergence of a youth-oriented culture.

Although there were a large number of different locations where dancing took place on a regular basis, the purpose-built public dance halls provide the most interesting manifestation of the dance culture and were the most influential. This chapter, although noting the variety of differences in provision, will focus chiefly on these public, commercial dance halls. Not only were they more popular, but they provide the best example of a distinctive leisure form.

The chapter is divided into three sections. The first will describe the atmosphere and surroundings of the dance hall, what it meant to 'go to the Palais'. The second deals with the dancers themselves and the significance of the dance hall and the dance culture to the lives of its patrons and its importance in interwar society. The last considers the relationship between dance halls and sex.

7.1 'Going to the palais'

Made my way up to the second floor of building. Met man at head of stair. He came forward, looked at me. Near him were roll of tickets labelled 9d. I said 'how much?' He said 'Sixpunce'. Paid. Walked into darkened dance room. Turned left to deposit coat in cloakroom, where attendant was sitting in wicker chair, both feet on counter, reading American magazine. He got up, gave me ticket number 56. Pegs nearly full, coats, hats, waistcoats. On floor brown parcels of outdoor shoes. Went on to dancefloor . . . Orchestra, nine men in dinner jackets (no one else wore these), on raised dais in one corner, start a tune. Large groups of each sex, segregated and concentrated round door, break up and mingle into couples. Common mode of approach is simply to touch girl on elbow; she moves out, dance. Within a minute only dozen of the hundred or so in the room (all under 30) are not dancing. A girl has just come up to me. SHE wants me to dance with her. I say this is a new one on me, 'Doesn't the man generally ask the girl for a dance?' She says she is on the staff, one of eight, job is to dance with anyone. Paid by owner of the hall. Three minutes, dance stops. All couples stay on floor, slight applause. Band do encore. Three minutes, same again; encore. It's hard work steering on small floor among crowd; couples constantly bump; no apologies, just grins. At end of second encore (there are three automatically all evening) men walk straight away from their partners, not escorting them off the floor. Sexes accumulate into their original separate groups around door.[1]

This impression was recorded by a London observer visiting a dance hall in Bolton in 1938. The voluntary segregation of the dance hall into single-sex groups coming together almost magically when the band began to play and then returning to their separate spheres was not, however, exclusive to Bolton. Neither were the crowded dance floors, stage-managed encores, the professional dancing partners, or smartly dressed band. Many of the public dance halls in interwar Britain shared these characteristics and they provided a ritualized leisure pursuit of great social importance.

An essential part of the experience of 'going to the Palais' was the comfortable and elaborate surroundings provided by the dance hall itself. Most dance halls were similarly designed with a main dance floor, usually sprung and constructed of maple or oak, around which were placed clothed tables and chairs together with a band on a raised dais. The larger halls also had balconies where people could watch the dancing, together with cafés and restaurants, lounges, bars, and revolving bandstands. Such decoration was designed to create an atmosphere of glamour, echoing that of the cinemas. Unlike the cinemas, however, not all dance halls were purpose built. Many of the earlier palais-de-danse had been converted from ice and roller skating rinks, following a craze popular before the First World War. The first, the Hammersmith Palais, was a converted ice rink. Externally, therefore, dance hall buildings had little of the modernist architecture developed, for example, by Harry Weedon

[1] T. Harrisson, 'Whistle While You Work', in *New Writing* (Winter 1938), 47.

and Cecil Clavering for Oscar Deutsch's Odeon cinema chain. However, the modernist and neo-gothic designs of the great cinema chains were imitated in individual design detail and those dance halls with road frontages were often decorated with modernist pretensions, using smooth lines, curves, and so on. There were also other similarities with the cinemas. Uniformed attendants, smart waiters and waitresses, and all manner of advertising paraphernalia greeted the patron on entry.

The interiors of dance halls were often opulent and decorated extravagantly, and halls aimed to distinguish themselves from others by using particular decorative features. At the Plaza dance hall, Glasgow, for example, a hall with 'deluxe interior with modernist design', the dance floor was sunk below the level of the surrounding table space and coloured footlights illuminated it. A fountain in the centre of the dance floor was decorated with flowers, with goldfish inside. This water theme was taken further at the Palais-de-Danse, Nottingham, where the fountain could rise to 20 feet and was illuminated by a series of coloured lights that was constantly changing. The exterior of this Nottingham dance hall was also designed to catch the attention, with a huge flashing globe that lit up Parliament Street in the heart of the city centre. In the West End Dance Hall in Birmingham, a distinctive ceiling with huge caricatures of 'Old King Sol' and 'The Man in the Moon' painted in bright, white electric bulbs, showered light onto the dancers below. Murals, lighting effects, geometric backdrops, and revolving bandstands were common features of the dance hall and all part of an entertainment package designed to emphasize glamour.

Some dance halls were 'themed'. Their whole decoration was aimed at recreating a specific atmosphere. This was an attempt to copy the 'atmospherics' which were developed for cinemas in America by John Eberson in the 1920s and came to Britain in 1929 when Edward A. Stone and T. R. Somerfield designed the decoration for three Astoria cinemas in Brixton, Streatham, and Finsbury Park. 'Atmospherics' attempted to bring the 'outside' inside, with interiors made to resemble Spanish patios or Italian villa gardens. In dance halls throughout Britain elements of this technique were widespread. The other great cinema influence on dance hall interiors was the grand 'theatrical' style that was employed by Sidney Bernstein's cinema chain, making cinemas into 'cathedrals for the masses' apart from the modernist style of Deutsch's Odeons.[2]

---

[2] See J. Richards, *The Age of the Dream Palace* (1984), 18–21 for details of cinema architecture.

At Tony's Ballroom, Birmingham, there were two halls with sumptuous interiors. The larger of the two, 'The Majestic', was decorated in an 'Eastern' theme, the hall representing a mosque with prayer mats hanging from the walls and a ceiling painted with stars. The lounges were given equally exotic names—the 'Alcazar Lounge' and the 'Baghdad Lounge'. Names are important when considering the atmosphere and appeal of dance halls. Common names such as the 'Plaza', 'Locarno' (after the Treaty of Locarno), 'Majestic', 'Ritz', 'Lido', and 'Rialto' suggest an air of sophistication and foreignness. The Ritz dance hall in Manchester advertised itself as 'The Dance Hall of 1,000 Delights'.[3] Other dance halls tried to be 'ultra-modern', using vivid, clashing colours, bold geometric shapes, 'up-to-date' neon lighting, chrome, stylized murals, and other interior design features imitating the modernist designs in vogue throughout the 1920s and 1930s.

Dressing up was an essential part of 'going to the Palais' and added much to the atmosphere of glamour. The women would wear a variety of outfits but their 'best' clothes were saved for the weekend dances. The working- and lower-middle-class women in the dance halls were skilled in the deployment of devices designed to achieve maximum glamour from restricted resources. The way women dressed and behaved in the dance hall challenged familiar notions of class. A miner from Durham described the impression that they made on him:

It hits me between the eyes when I go to the Palais. The girls—how smart they look—how well they use colour; and then—think of them coming out of the mill with the cotton waste in their hair—and the lot of them after they have been married. To me, the way they dance is far superior to that of Birmingham or London, and streets ahead of undergraduettes at Oxford—they're in another world.[4]

The majority of women in the Bolton survey got their clothing through 'clothing club cheques', which they would pay off at a shilling per week. Most large shops and department stores provided such a service. Elsewhere, at home or at sewing classes, other women made their own clothes or mended and adapted older styles. Home-made clothing was still common despite the appearance of cheap off-the-peg clothing. To protect their best dresses, many women would wear another dress over the top when going to and leaving the dance halls. In the dance hall, the toilets

---

[3] However, as with pubs, dance halls were often given pseudonyms. The Plaza was also known as 'The Dance Hall of 1,000 kicks'. In Bolton these nicknames included the 'Bughutch' and 'The Bum Needle'.

[4] T. Harrisson, 'Whistle While You Work', 48.

and make-up rooms provided the amenities for last-minute clothing and make-up alterations as well as gossip and advice. Magazines and the cinema were important influences too. It was common for younger women to be stylistically influenced by Hollywood. The hairstyles and clothing of film stars, more often American than British, were followed closely. The results were impressive:

People from other areas can sometimes scarcely believe that the resulting beauties, divided into some ten main types based on film stars, are girls working, as these are, from 7.45 till 5.30 each day in tropical temperature and humidity and tremendous noises of the cotton mills, for an average wage of thirty shillings a week.[5]

With the advent of mass produced clothing in the interwar period it became harder to distinguish class on the basis of clothing. The success of high street chain stores like Burtons and Marks and Spencer, together with hire purchase credit meant that most working people could afford at least one set of well-designed and well-made 'best' clothing; such things were eroding obvious class distinctions.

However, some obvious differences between classes did remain. The Carnegie Trust noted that some unemployed males in Glasgow and Cardiff were deterred from dancing by the absence of proper clothing.[6] The possession of only one suit which had to serve for 'best' and everyday use was a greater obstacle to regular dancing than the cost of entrance. Most young men in employment possessed several lounge suits, which was the normal dress for the dance hall. Attention to appearance among males was widespread and there were few who were dirty or scruffy. As with the women, mass produced clothing had made it possible for youths to be well turned out and fashionable.

With glamorous surroundings and well-dressed patrons, the dance hall provided a first-rate venue for entertainment. The dance band, nonetheless, was central. The better dance halls would employ several bands, raised above the dancers on a dais or stage, to provide a non-stop programme of live music, often with considerable panache. The dance programme would usually last for four hours, during which about 48 to 50 dances would be played. Each dance would be accompanied by a lowering of different coloured lights, blue for a waltz, red for a foxtrot, or full light for the quickstep. At the end of each dance, if there was sufficient

---

[5] Ibid. 48.

[6] C. Cameron, A. J. Lush, and G. Meara (eds.), *Disinherited Youth* (Edinburgh, 1943), 103.

applause, encores would be played. The showmanship of the dance bands is described by an observer at the Streatham Locarno:

The band goes on playing all the time with hardly any intervals, and those short, just time for the floor to begin to empty and then to fill up again. In the middle of a number the stage revolves and a fresh band comes into view, playing the same tune, but hotted up more. These are 'The Sophomores', with blue jackets, white trousers. Red-coated female crooner, a red hot blonde, sits in front of them tapping her feet furiously. This band plays fast . . .[7]

Most of the bands were 'house bands' made up of local musicians, some professional, most semi-professional, but usually tied to one or two of the dance halls in a town or city. The size of the band or orchestra depended very much on the location. In smaller dance halls there were bands of about five or six, usually comprising a saxophone, cornet, bass, piano, and drums. Sometimes only a trio would be provided. Bigger orchestras played in the larger halls. Those dance halls with a good band attracted a dedicated following. Famous name dance bands made regular tours of the dance halls and the appearance of Jack Hylton, Henry Hall, or Jack Payne's orchestras was likely to attract a large audience. The BBC made occasional broadcasts of the larger bands from regional dance halls. In addition there were 'guest' band and 'talent nights' where local singers or musicians could demonstrate their abilities. The programme of dances played by the house bands was influenced by the various radio broadcasts and gramophone recordings of their larger, more famous counterparts. Songs from current films and popular shows were also very much in demand.

So what of the actual dancing? Most people danced with their own friends, either in pairs or groups and there was occasional inter-group dancing too. For those without dance partners a nod or glance from across the room would be sufficient. In some dance halls male and female semi-professional dancing partners were available, usually free of charge, although they were less common in the later part of the period. These dancers were employed by the dance hall and could be 'hired out' for one dance or the whole evening. Although their popularity varied from hall to hall, they were regarded with suspicion by many and had a reputation for being of dubious moral character.[8] Most commentators noted a 'serious-ness of intent' on the faces of those dancing with few people smiling.

[7] M-O A: MDJ: 1/A, 'Streatham Locarno', 17 Nov. 1938, p. 2.
[8] For views on professional dance partners see M-O A: Directive Reply: 'Jazz 2, July 1939'.

Occasionally dancers would sing along to the music if a popular tune was played but there was usually little conversation or laughter. Crowded floors were a common feature and with several hundred dancers moving around in the same direction at once, treading on feet was widespread, as was bumping. The proportion of people in the hall who danced varied with location, but hesitation on the part of many was commonly observed. If a dance was unfamiliar or the dance hall not yet full, there was often reluctance on the part of couples to get up on the floor and dance. The dance floor seemed to be subject to sudden waves of activity, taking no time at all to fill or empty.

The atmosphere on the floor depended largely upon what was being danced. For most of the programme, the dancers were executing a series of prescribed steps, for the foxtrot, waltz, or quickstep, with little room for individual expression. The emphasis was on the steps and the enjoyment of getting them right. As Tom Harrisson noted, 'The movements are highly formalised, efficiently executed, variations on a theme of walking, slipping, turning, pausing, hurrying. The emphasis is on the dance itself.'[9]

The quality of dancing appears to have been high throughout the country and there were no appreciable regional differences observed in the standards attained among amateurs. Some provincial dance hall managers who had worked in both the south and north of Britain considered that the dancers of cities such as Leeds, Manchester, Sheffield, and Glasgow were superior to those of London. Others thought the opposite. What is clear, is that there was enthusiasm for dancing the steps correctly. Horace Richards noted the improvement in dancing standards since the 1920s:

Remember how it used to be? Hundreds of young men and girls content to shuffle gracelessly round the floor and pretend that they were dancing. But now the shuffle is dying an overdue death. Mr and Miss 1934 are keen on the new steps, and they want to do them well. The standard of dancing all over Britain can now be rated high.[10]

There were exceptions to the formalized ballroom atmosphere, however. Towards the end of the 1930s the arrival of swing music brought with it a more expressive, less formalized dancing. In general this dancing, or 'trucking' as it was known, marked a move towards greater solo

    [9] Harrisson, 'Whistle While You Work', 51.
    [10] H. Richards, 'Dancing throughout Britain, No 1: What Britain is Dancing', *PMDW*, 17 Nov. 1934, p. 12.

dancing and a more creative, individual dancing that changed the atmosphere of the dance hall whenever it was introduced. The slightly wilder, freer movement of trucking is described by a London observer:

. . . many 'truck', walk arm in arm, strut, wag fore-fingers restlessly, shake hips; sometimes groups of couples doing this come together, form a little procession . . . Others, trucking, leave go, walk away from each other, turn backs, come together again smiling . . . The idea of swing music is that you make it up as you go along; these people are doing swing with their feet, freelance shufflings and jigging; it's all a long way from the formalised foxtrotting steps . . .[11]

Group dances also became increasingly popular in the late 1930s, providing an alternative to the formal partner dancing. In London suburban dance halls, such as in Streatham, observers noting the popularity of group dances like the Palais Glide and the Lambeth Walk, sensed a changed atmosphere after their playing, with a sense of 'release' and greater mixing of groups.

In the larger halls the patrons were provided with additional forms of entertainment. Exhibition dancers would complement the programme with occasional demonstrations of the latest dance steps, followed by audience participation. To break up the programme, many halls provided a cabaret, with acrobats, jugglers, comedians, and so on. Dancing was not the only occasion for interaction. In all dance halls a proportion of those present, on some evenings a majority, would sit on the periphery of the floor at one of the clothed tables where food and drink were provided by waiter service. This was a place for smoking and conversation. Many of those who came to the hall with groups of friends would start the evening here, singing to the music or demonstrating dance steps to each other, before moving on to the dance floor. The cafés also provided a range of cheap snacks and meals served in pleasant surroundings with potted palms and table lights, where couples could go to buy an orange squash or a New York Sundae and get acquainted. Comfortable sofas were provided in many of the lounges of larger halls. The mood was described by an observer in Blackpool: 'In the Palm Lounge a quite different atmosphere. It is pretty crowded with people all silent. Love birds twittering, water trickling, subdued lighting . . . spooning in corners . . . listening to the music.'[12]

The balcony was another venue where some would spend the entire evening. It was possible to pay a reduced entrance rate to sit in the

[11] M-O A: MDJ: 1/A, 'Streatham Locarno', 17 Nov. 1938, p. 2.
[12] M-O A: Worktown: 60/D, 'Dancing', 1938, p. 24.

balcony and not use the dance floor at all. This was a popular choice. Here groups would observe the dancing below and exchange gossip concerning personalities in the hall. The balcony was also where those who followed certain dance bands were to be found and this was a major attraction for keen dance music enthusiasts. A manager in a Bolton dance hall remarked that it was not uncommon to find people from as far away as Huddersfield and Liverpool coming to hear his bands.[13] The cabaret was also visible, but most were content to listen to the music and watch the evenings proceedings.

Not all halls were licensed to sell alcohol and when they were not, as in all of Bolton's public dance halls, the men were given 'passes' which allowed them to leave the hall, go to pubs, and then return without having to pay again. Women were not given this opportunity. In some of the less well-managed halls alcohol was often smuggled in through windows but, on the whole, behaviour was sober. Where a licensed bar was available rowdy drunkenness was not widespread and indeed not tolerated by dance hall managements who could lose business and their licences if their halls gained a bad reputation. The staff at dance halls was made up of at least one of each of the following; doormen, cloakroom assistants, waiters, the manager, and occasionally dancing professionals and an MC. Where an MC was present, his job was to keep order on the dance floor. They were usually fair and effective, as an observer in Blackpool's Tower Ballroom noted:

Unusual behaviour among the dancers, which would be censured at a private dance, often passes unchecked and only occasionally does the MC stop a couple to warn them to keep away from the centre of the floor. Every large ballroom has its MC in evening dress who rules the dance floor, and no observer records any occasion on which he was challenged.[14]

Fights did occur but were largely confined to the smaller, seedier halls.[15] Dance promoters and dance hall managers circulated details of trouble makers to each other in an attempt to maintain a safe environment for their clients. The keen dancer intent on learning and executing the new dance steps, and the keen interest of many in the dance music and the bands, had apparently pushed these elements to the margins. A manager from London noted the transformation:

---

[13] M-O A: Worktown: 48/D, 'Astoria Palais de Danse', 18 Dec. 1939, p. 5.
[14] M-O A: Worktown: 60/D, 'Dancing', 1938, p. 12.
[15] See A. Davies, *Leisure, Gender and Poverty: Working-class Culture in Salford and Manchester, 1900–1939* (Buckingham, 1992), 92–4.

It pays to keep such elements out. When they see one in the hall they will go up to him and ask him if he would mind leaving . . . This may mean bother at some times but it is worth it to keep the decent people together—and most of them are well behaved. . . . The dances used to be very vicious. It didn't used to be a dance unless there was a fight. They used to enjoy them. Now they seem to be more intelligent and are enjoying the dances.[16]

7.2 Dancers, dance culture, and interwar society

So what effects did the dance halls have on the lives of their patrons? The impact of this ritualized form of entertainment on interwar society was profound. Dance halls and dancing were important additions to the social fabric of working and lower-middle-class communities, providing a venue for social interaction, a means of expression, and, perhaps most importantly, an arena for meeting the opposite sex.

Although most people in Britain during the interwar period could claim to have attended a dance at least once, there was a large section of society that went dancing on a regular basis. Representing its transition from an upper-middle-class pastime to one with a mass market, this regular dancing public was found to be young, predominantly female, and largely working class.

Dancing had cross-class appeal and yet by the mid-1920s it was predominantly a working- and lower-middle-class activity (see Plates 19 and 20). This verdict is supported by virtually all surveys of the period. *The New Survey of London Life and Labour*, conducted in 1928, illustrates that point:

To-day dancing as an active recreation appeals to many people of all classes . . . The dance-halls are within the range of nearly everybody's purse, and typists, shop assistants and factory girls rub shoulders in them . . . People drop into a palais after the day's work or on Saturday evenings as casually as they go to a cinema.[17]

A national survey conducted in 1939 by Mass-Observation found that this continued to be the case into the 1930s.[18] Although the Mass-Observation sample may not be wholly reliable, it is one of the best

[16] M-O A: MDJ: 2/A, 'Lenny Haynes', 13 Apr. 1939, p. 1.
[17] H. Llewellyn Smith, *The New Survey of London Life and Labour* (1930–5), ix. 64–5.
[18] Calculated from a sample of 100 respondents (50 male, 50 female) in M-O A: Directive Reply: 'Jazz (Jan. 1939)' (1939).

available on the subject. That survey shows that 69 per cent of people went to dances, with 22 per cent claiming to go 'regularly'. When looked at from a class basis, 76 per cent of working class said that they had been dancing, 21 per cent regularly, and 67 per cent of middle class said they had been dancing, 24 per cent regularly. From this it can seen that a large proportion of the population went dancing at least occasionally, with a hard core being regular attendees, but that the working class had to constitute a large majority of dancers.

The low cost of dancing, from 6d. up to 2/6, indicates that dance organizers and commercial dance halls were aiming at a predominantly working-class audience. The manager of a dance hall in Bolton suggests that this was the case: 'We get steel workers, lots of mill girls and men, textile workers, machinists, cloths, rayon people, plumbers, joiners, de Havilland workers . . . , building traders, office workers.'[19] Robert Roberts, writing about dance halls in Salford in the 1920s, observes that they were frequented by a largely working-class audience:

The great 'barn' we patronised as apprentices held at least a thousand . . . at 6d per head (1s on Saturdays) youth at every level of the manual working class, from the bound apprentice to the 'scum of the slum', fox-trotted through the new bliss in each other's arms.[20]

It should be noted, however, that dancing was becoming an increasingly respectable activity. As the period progressed, it was the palais-de-danse that began to make dancing both affordable and respectable. As J. B. Priestley noted on a visit to a Leicester dance hall in 1933:

Most of the patrons were young and there were nearly as many boys there as girls. They seemed to me to dance very well—fox-trots, quick-steps, rumbas, waltzes—and in a much more reserved and dignified fashion than their social superiors in the West End. They were, I imagine, mostly factory hands, and apart from an occasional guffawing from a group of lads, they were quiet and serious, as sedately intent on their steps as a conference of dancing teachers.[21]

A result of this growing respectability was that as the period progressed, dancing found a large audience among the middle class. Part of the reason for this growth was the spread of suburban housing estates

[19] M-O A: Worktown Collection: 48/D: A. H., 'Manager. Aspin Hall. Bolton', 8 Jan. 1940, p. 11.
[20] R. Roberts, *The Classic Slum* (Harmondsworth, 1973), 188.
[21] J. B. Priestley, *An English Journey* (1934), 121.

and, often, their occupation by a newly emerging lower-middle class. The palais-de-danse became part of the fabric of suburban housing estates, along with cinemas, public houses, modern churches, and terraces of shops.

Despite the predominance of the working class in the majority of halls, some of the 'better' palais-de-danse were favoured by this audience. Speaking of the clientele of his dance hall, the manager of the Grafton Rooms in Liverpool stated: 'It is hard to say what class people are in today. The girls work in Littlewoods, Vernons, and Ogdens Pools. The boys are mainly in shops. They are not labouring workers. They are what you may call the sedentary occupations—clerks, shop boys etc. There are not many labourers. They are too tired after a hard day's work.'[22] This trend was confirmed by a dance hall manager in suburban Wimbledon: 'I should call them lower middle class. There is a large residential area here and the place is a hot-bed of dancing.'[23] For some suburban housewives the 'thé dansant' was a respectable way to spend the afternoon.

However, although the dance hall appealed to all classes, it was not necessarily classless. In the eyes of Carl Heimann, co-director of the Mecca chain, dance halls were a place where class distinctions disappeared: 'In the dance hall there is no differentiation between the patrons—they are all on the same "floor level", all pay the same price of admission; there is no class distinction whatsoever; complete freedom of speech for all and sundry.'[24] In reality, there was not a great deal of social mixing within the halls and each catered for its own section of society. Of the four main dance halls in Edinburgh at this time, for example, the Edinburgh Palais-de-Danse was the dancing centre for Scottish 'society', with royal patronage and a number of 'high-class private functions' held every week. The Havanna Dance Club also provided for a varied but predominantly upper-middle-class clientele. The remaining dance halls provided for the working and lower-middle class.

The most habitual dancers were young people of both sexes. This was the group that made visits to the dance hall up to three, four, or even six times a week. The only limit to their attendance was the amount of money and leisure time they had. Attendance for some working-class youths was habitual, as one Bolton dance hall manager pointed out:

[22] M-O A: MDJ: 5/F, A. H., 'Manager Grafton Rooms Liverpool', 18 May 1939, p. 2.
[23] M-O A: MDJ: 5/F, A. H., 'Manager Wimbledon Glider Rink', 13 Feb. 1939, p. 1.
[24] C. L. Heimann, 'Dancing after the War', in Anon., *Stepping Out* (1940), 54.

We rely on a class here that comes 4 or 5 nights a week. They have about 5/—
spending money a week and they don't want to spend it all on one night. So for
their 3-4/—they can get 3 or 4 nights dancing out of it.[25]

One reason that the surveys found so many young people attending
dances was that although their leisure time was limited, it was relatively
greater than the time available to adults. In 1939, it was found that those
young people of working age (14–21) in Hulme, Manchester, had
between four and five hours' leisure time each weekday evening, with half
a day on Saturday and all of Sunday free. Harrisson's survey of Bolton
dance halls identified and analysed the impact on the community of these
young dancing enthusiasts:

In a typical room in a cotton mill, fifteen of the forty two female workers were
dance-hall regulars, all the ones under twenty-five. In churches, pubs, political
organizations and all other groups with social and co-operative interests, young
people are to-day conspicuously absent in Worktown; the elder folk continuously
complain about it. In six main dance-halls on Saturday evening there are nearly
as many young men as on Sunday evening in all the town's 170 churches.[26]

Harrisson concluded that although the dance halls played a vital part in
the life of all of Bolton's 180,000 inhabitants, their greatest significance
was confined to unmarried youths of both sexes. Indeed all the evidence
of the numerous surveys of dancing indicates that the most prolific
dancers were those aged 16–21: 'Many young men pass through a phase
which has often been described by their parents and friends, and sometimes even by themselves, as "dancing mad." The only limitation to the
number of dances they attend is the amount of pocket-money available.'[27]
    Importantly, economic factors meant that many youths were in a bet-
ter position than many other sections of society. David Fowler highlights
how demographic and economic developments in interwar Britain gave
some young wage earners an unprecedented degree of independence
and influence. In 1921 there were 2,092,545 boys aged 14 to 19 in
England and Wales, and 2,138,384 girls. By 1931, this had risen to
2,355,355 and 2,378,508 respectively. The proportion of those in employment or seeking it rose from 83.7 per cent for boys and 63.8 per cent for
girls in 1921, to 85.1 per cent and 70.8 per cent in 1931.[28] Although youth

    [25] M-O A: Worktown Collection: 48/D, A. H., 'Manager. Aspin Hall. Bolton', 8 Jan.
1940, p. 14.
    [26] Harrisson, 'Whistle While You Work', 50.
    [27] Cameron, Lush, and Meara (eds.), *Disinherited Youth*, 105.
    [28] D. Fowler, *The First Teenagers* (1995), Table 1.1, 172.

unemployment, averaging 10 per cent for the period, was a serious problem, those in employment had considerable bargaining power due to a shortage of juvenile labour and its relative cheapness compared with adult labour. The teenage wage earner was thus in an advantageous economic position, being less likely to experience poverty than at any other stage in his or her life. Rowntree highlighted the fact that economic hardship struck working-class families in early childhood, old age, and in mid-life (age 25–44) and was least common in the period between starting work and marriage. Rowntree also showed that whilst 76.3 per cent of the 15–25-year-olds in his survey were above the poverty line, only 60.9 per cent of 5–14-year-olds, 50.3 per cent of 1–4-year-olds, and 47.5 per cent of those less than twelve months old were in a similar position.[29]

Several contemporary social surveys indicate that the level of disposable income available to young wage earners was high. Although it was common for the majority of younger wage earners to hand their whole wage packet over to the family and receive a set amount of pocket money each week, Rowntree found that this practice stopped after the age of 16. At 16 the young workers would pay sufficient to cover 'board and lodgings' and retain an average of 50 per cent of their own wage packet, sometimes a higher proportion, the amount increasing with age. This gave them a degree of economic freedom that few young people previously, or their elders at that time, could enjoy.

Their increased leisure time and spending power were transforming the way in which youths chose to relax and find entertainment. Rowntree's York Survey pointed to a marked move away from the public house and 'hanging about on street corners' towards more 'ready-made' commercialized leisure forms, such as the cinema and dance hall. Teenagers were now willing and for the most part able, to pay to be entertained. Indeed they were developing sophisticated tastes and making distinctive choices in the way in which they spent their leisure time. The *Dancing Times* drew attention to this transformation:

The cloth-capped and mufflered works' boy of the older generations has passed. The winged collar and butterfly tie and dancing pumps are now more familiar, just as the modern works' youngster in this district, whether he be a collier or steel worker or tinplate worker or what not, knows that Italian-run café better than the public-house—much better, too.[30]

There is evidence, too, of the dance halls deliberately targeting this group. Heimann, the co-director of the Mecca chain of dance halls, was

---

[29] Ibid. 94–5.   [30] *Dancing Times*, Apr. 1927, pp. 83–4.

shrewd enough to see the potential of the youth market and the changes he brought to dancing, including the introduction of 'group' dances such as the Lambeth Walk, were made to appeal directly to their sense of fun. He advised others in the dance hall business to 'Encourage the patronage of young people, and particularly children, but always under strict supervision, as we all know how careful one has to be when handling young people.'[31]

Several important qualifications must be made, however. There *was* a mixing of ages within the dance hall, as Horace Richards observed in his 1934 study of dancing throughout Britain.[32] 'Old-Time Dancing' gained vogue in the mid-1930s and many dance halls provided a programme of old-style music at least once a week. Some dance halls even began to cater exclusively for this sort of dancing At these evenings, older patrons, from middle age to old age, would rub shoulders with the young. It provided a 'family atmosphere' and was very popular. The manager of the Grafton Rooms, Liverpool, had charabanc parties from all over Lancashire visiting his twice weekly old-time dances. There were similar successes recorded in the Oxford Galleries, Newcastle, at Leeds Palais-de Danse, Nottingham Palais-de-Danse, and Tony's Ballroom, Birmingham, to name but a few.

Nevertheless, many dance halls were 'made their own' by the younger crowd. Dance music and jazz were the music of the younger generation. This is not to say that these types of music did not enjoy popularity across the age range; they did. However, the newer forms of music, such as swing and hotter jazz music, found their most enthusiastic followers among the young. Mass-Observation observed a noticeable drop in enthusiasm for jazz after the age of about 20–5, with 'jazz fanaticism' a distinctive adolescent 'stage' that many went through. As Tom Harrisson noted, 'Jazz has become or is becoming the religious ritual of post-war youth, and these songs of hope and happiness . . . are the hymns of young England.'[33]

There were other ways in which young unmarried workers were able to make the dance culture their own. Dressing in the latest styles, with hairstyles and mannerisms copied from popular films of the day, marked out the younger dancers from the older ones. This was not just confined

---

[31] Heimann, 'Dancing after the War', 54.
[32] Richards, 'Dancing throughout Britain', a series of six reports in *PMDW*, Nov. to Dec. 1934.
[33] Harrisson, 'Whistle While You Work', 66.

to girls. In Manchester, the Napoo gang frequented dance halls in Belle Vue wearing outfits of navy blue suits, trilbies, and pink neckerchiefs.[34] They had modelled themselves on characters from American gangster films and apparently terrorized local residents.

Dancing and going to dance halls were social skills and practices that were a key element in the transition from childhood to adulthood for working-class youths of both sexes. As Tom Harrisson noted:

It is now an essential part of any youth's social equipment, that he or she be able to go through two variations of these movements (waltz and fox-trot) with sufficient grace to avoid treading on a partner's toe. When you leave school you learn to work, to smoke, to bet and to dance.[35]

Altogether the dance hall was young, modern, and exhilarating. It had a particular significance for women, however. The dance hall allowed girls opportunities and a freedom of expression often denied them at work and home, allowing them to mix with the opposite sex and to social-ize with other working-class girls.

Working-class girls took an interest in dancing several years younger than boys. Often boys would find it difficult (or socially unacceptable) to learn to dance and there were numerous other active pursuits competing for their leisure time. Girls, on the other hand, seemed to learn steps more easily and had fewer alternative pursuits to interest them. In the numer-ous social clubs provided by the Church and other organizations it was predominantly the girls who took the dancing classes, not the boys. A. P. Jephcott in her study of young working girls confirms that this continued to be the case through the 1930s and into the war:

Dancing itself is extraordinarily popular among [female] adolescents. They spend an amazing amount of their energy upon it. Schoolgirls of thirteen and fourteen generally first go dancing with an older sister. They may go to a learners' night or to a place where part of the hall is roped off for beginners, rather like the shallow end of a swimming pool. . . . Boys, on the whole, are less enthusiastic about dancing than girls, and are generally rather older, perhaps sixteen or seven-teen, when they begin to take it seriously. With both boys and girls the real craze has probably partly worn off by the time that they are twenty.[36]

Indeed, dancing was an activity that was more popular among women of all ages than men, as the 1934 *Social Survey of Merseyside* pointed out:

[34] Fowler, *The First Teenagers*, 104.   [35] Harrisson, 'Whistle While You Work', 50.
[36] A. P. Jephcott, *Girls Growing up* (1942), 121.

Dancing is one of the very few activities in which women engage more frequently than men. Of the women 20 per cent, but of the men only 7 per cent, made entries under this head. The predominance of women in most dance halls is, indeed, well known. Among men, only Classes A and B seem to dance, while among women the largest—and very similar—proportions are found in B and C. Several of the Reports commented on the regularity with which working-class girls dance; dances are particularly popular in the slums.[37]

Dancing was particularly important in the lives of young women and girls. The alliance of elder and younger sisters, together with groups of friends, provided a controlled means of independence for girls, giving them support while largely unsupervised by adults. Socializing with their own sex was a vital part of a girl's development.

Groups of girls dancing together was a common sight in the dance hall and this was not always because there were too few men to dance with. Women could express themselves better without male company. As A. P. Jephcott noted: 'Girls generally go dancing in twos and are often quite content to dance with each other as well as with a boy partner. Some people prefer a clever girl partner to an unskilful boy.'[38]

Dancing also provided one of the most important means of physical exercise for women. Many working-class and lower-middle-class girls working in factories, shops, or as typists, were required to stand or sit for long periods of time throughout the day. This was as true of millworkers in Lancashire as it was of those assembling wireless sets in the new industries of the south-east of England. For these girls there was an urgent need for active recreation, no longer available to them in the form of school games and physical drill. Not only did it offer exercise, it also allowed expression.

The longing for self-expression which is the characteristic of the age is driving the girls of to-day to seek satisfaction in dancing. In response to this compelling impulse they flock to join the world of rhythm . . . To many it is a channel for emotional outlet, to others . . . it is a relaxation and an inspiration . . . a delivery from the monotony of routine. To others again it comes as a solace and they endeavour to find compensation in it. And among numerous other reasons there remains the aspect of escape from care or trouble.[39]

[37] D. Caradog Jones, *The Social Survey of Merseyside* (Liverpool, 1934), iii. 277–8. Class A = Professional, administerial, technical, and managerial positions. Class B = Ordinary clerks, shopkeepers, and shop assistants. Class C = All manual workers, domestic, hotel, and café workers.

[38] Jephcott, *Girls Growing up*, 121.   [39] *Dancing Times*, Nov. 1927, pp. 162–3.

The dance hall also provided an arena where young women could explore their sexuality and develop an assertiveness seldom found outside. In the dance hall, women not only copied the hairstyles and make-up of Hollywood stars, they imitated their behaviour too:

One girl stands out—very, very short tight-fitting skirt, salmon coloured jumper. Heavily painted face, jet black hair, chewing gum; nice figure and legs but walks with an exaggerated swing of the hips—she is trying so hard to look like the 'loose vamping women', so often seen in American films. She is young . . . '15 or 16'. She is always being asked for a dance . . . posing all the time . . .[40]

How to kiss or how to behave with men might be learned from the films but in the dance hall women could actually try out these techniques.

Obviously, marriage had an important effect on determining whether people went dancing. This was predominantly the pastime of the single person. Once they were married and had children, it was often difficult for women to find the time for any leisure pursuits. Such circumstances prevented married working-class women from dancing in large numbers, for even when leisure time was available it was difficult to find suitable child-minders. In addition, many working-class women came under pressure from their husbands to stop dancing once married, as men tended to regard the dance hall as an arena chiefly for forming sexual relations. Among married middle-class women, however, the restraints were often less numerous, and many couples continued to dance after marriage.

7.3 Dance halls and sex

Amongst dancers themselves, one of the most commonly mentioned social functions of the dance halls was the opportunity that they afforded to meet members of the opposite sex. More men than women were attracted to dance halls for this reason. Among a 1939 survey of Mass-Observation panel volunteers, for example, 'meeting members of the opposite sex' was the joint top reason given by men (29%) together with 'good entertainment and recreation' (29%) for going to the dance halls. However, only 12 per cent of women saw 'meeting members of the opposite sex' as the dance halls' main attraction.[41] In a survey of middle-class adolescent boys, also taken in 1939, the most popular single reason given

[40] M-O A: MDJ: 1/A, 'Streatham Locarno', 7 Jan. 1938, p. 5.
[41] Calculated from a sample of 100 respondents (50 male, 50 female) in M-O A: Directive Reply: 'Jazz 2, July 1939'.

for going to dances was 'on account of female companionship' (24%), the next stated reason being the dance steps (14%) and the rhythm (14%). Some comments from those surveyed: 'I go to dances to enjoy myself and to make friends with as many girls as possible. I seldom leave without at least one kiss'; 'I go to enjoy myself and to have a good time with various girl friends'.[42] Those who approved of the public dance hall were well aware of its function as a place to meet members of the opposite sex. A 32-year-old male civil engineer from Surrey describes where he considered their importance to lie:

The chief social function of dance halls is to get young people of both sexes together. It is very often a young boy or girl's first introduction to the opposite sex . . . many men first met their wives at the dance hall.[43]

Indeed, the dance hall made the preliminary introductions between the sexes easier, offering a set of prescribed conventions on the choosing of dancing partners and permitting interaction between strangers. As Tom Harrisson noted:

The ballroom sanctions the approach without introduction, 'picking-up' and 'getting-off' are accepted as normal behaviour . . . Here, there is none of the preliminary manoeuvring . . . The method of approach is more confident, since prescribed by convention, and the chances of success are greater. Once the introduction is made the course of the acquaintanceship is a matter of mutual preference.[44]

With a touch on the elbow, a nod or glance from across the room, a dancing partner could be procured for the dance. It was conventional for the man to ask the woman to dance and particular dances provided greater opportunities to find partners than others. 'Optional' or 'Excuse-Me' dances were ones where an individual could approach any couple on the dance floor and touch a member of their own sex, who would stop and give up their partner. Such dances allowed strangers to mix easily but despite the conventions, many males remained nervous.

The atmosphere of the dance hall, with its soft lighting, partner dancing, and enticing music, certainly provided an adequate backdrop for romantic and sexual activity. Intimacy was more frequent and more open than in most other public places, for without the watchful eyes of their elders, MCs apart, young people of both sexes were more free to express themselves. Kissing and holding hands were common.

[42] M-O A: Directive Reply: 'Jazz 2, July 1939', 'G. L. Wallace'.
[43] Ibid., 'F. H. Milner'.   [44] M-O A: Worktown: 60/D, 'Dancing', 1938, p. 9.

However, the majority of people remained in groupings of their own sex and once a dance was over dancing couples returned to their separate gender groups in the hall. Only a minority would continue the acquaintance beyond that. For that minority several options were available: to carry on dancing, to retire to the balcony or floorside tables and watch, or to have a drink in the bar or café. The bar was the most popular location, the other locations being the preserve of groups or couples more familiar with each other. There was an air of awkwardness surrounding most of the proceedings when members of the opposite sex met. The following observations made in Bolton illustrate this:

The chaps did not even smile or show any sign at all of recognition—but talked together and laughed. The girls drank the port—neither side recognising the other—but when the girls moved out one of them said 'Thanks' with a smile—I noticed later in the evening the two were paired up—But they did not take them home—much to the young men's disgust.[45]

Even when they plucked up courage to ask a girl for a drink, many men found the situation difficult and 'picking up' was usually conducted with the minimum of conversation or physical contact. Although the dance hall allowed greater oppportunities, the majority still found it hard to manage.

There appears to have been little overtly sexual behaviour. With the attendance of supervisors in the larger dance halls and attendants in cloakrooms and toilets, regulation was often tight. As one Bolton dance hall manager commented, 'There isn't any room for the funny business in the Modern Dance Hall as the people watch too keenly for that.'[46]

The degree of 'picking up' and 'getting off' also depended on the night of the week and, therefore, the sort of clientele that was in attendance. 'Learners' nights', for those beginning to dance, were the most obvious place to go for introductions and they had a reputation for attracting a sociable crowd. 'Dancers' nights', however, were for the enthusiast. The keenest dancers appeared to have no time for other activities and were absorbed in their dancing. The following comments were made about a specialist 'Harlem night' in a Bolton dance hall:

One of these girls said to the obs[erver], 'I'm a man-hater . . . I come here for the dancing, not to meet men' and this represents what observers felt about the whole affair—that all the chaps and girls were here because they enjoyed dancing

[45] M-O A: Worktown: 48/C, 'Co-Op (Comrades Circle) Dance', 31 Mar. 1937, p. 4.
[46] M-O A: MDJ: 5/F, 'Alfred Clarke, Empress Hall, Bolton', 1938, p. 8.

for its own sake, and did not use the dance as an avenue to the process of getting-off with one another.[47]

Despite the generally repectable atmosphere, there was plenty of rumour at the halls. A male dancing professional working in the Streatham Locarno suggested that the number of people who were looking for sex was large:

AH mentioned a girl he had seen trying to get off with two of the professionals. Cyril replied: 'Oh yes, one of the fast kind—that pokes with all and everyone. About 5 per cent of the women in Locarno don't poke, and about 2 per cent are virgin—if that.' . . . some of the women are so easy, you only have to say: 'Would you like to come and have a coffee?' . . . Some of them even ask us.[48]

In Blackpool the situation was similar; perhaps behaviour here was even more uninhibited due to the holiday spirit:

. . . two chaps were dancing and then came up and said, 'There's plenty of tash here' (tash—meaning girls who fuck). They also told me that if you get a 'set-home' it's all right here.[49]

Little of this overt sexual activity actually took place within the dance hall. Once a partner had been found it would depend on whether they were willing to be escorted home (a 'set-home'). Most sexual activity occurred outside the hall, on the way home. Most would probably engage in petting and kissing. Sexual intercourse before marriage was still notionally taboo, although common. It is likely, however, that many people acquired initial sexual experience with those they met at the dance halls.

The dance hall, therefore, provided an arena for varying degrees of sexual activity. Some attended the halls in order to find sexual partners and were prepared to go at least some way to satisfy these demands. On the whole, however, sexual activity and behaviour within the dance hall was restrained and respectable and often awkward. A middle-class woman working on Mass-Observation's 1937 survey of dancing in Blackpool concluded: 'My impression is that dancers are mostly adolescents, going to meet [the] opposite sex, but quite innocently. Young men wanting to get confidence by dancing with a lot of girls, perhaps wanting love, but very vaguely.'[50]

[47] M-O A: Worktown: 48/C, 'Harlem Night at the Aspen Hall', 13 July 1938, p. 6.
[48] M-O A: MDJ: 3/G, 'Interview: Cyril Amersham', 25 June 1939, p. 1.
[49] M-O A: Worktown: 48/C, 'An Evening with a Friend Drinking and Dancing', 2 Apr. 1938, p. 6.
[50] M-O A: Worktown: 60/D, 'Dancing', 1938, p. 8.

As respectable as most dance halls were, no survey of the 'dance culture' would be complete without reference to nightclubs. It must be remembered, however, that they were rare in most towns and cities outside London and they catered for a 'specialist' audience. The night-club provided a completely different atmosphere from the average public dance hall. This was one cloaked in secrecy, as an observer visiting a Soho nightclub described:

We go in behind three girls—obviously prostitutes . . . we have all arrived at a door in the passage, set aslant. There is a little glass paned peephole about 3″ square. One of the girls knocks. The wooden screen behind the glass opens and an eye appears. Back goes the wood and the door is opened by a Negro . . . The girls go in and Johnny leads us two in. There are five negroes inside and an intelligent looking prostitute who is seated at a table.[51]

The majority of such clubs found in London were situated in Soho. They worked under the pretence of being private members' clubs but in prac-tice it was easy to join at the door. Nightclubs opened until 3 or 4 o'clock in the morning and served food in order to get around the licensing laws. Most clubs were small and badly decorated and combined live music with music from radiograms. We do not know much about the audiences but we can assume close connections with underworld. The autobiography of Kate Meyrick, a London nightclub hostess, highlighted members of the IRA and several gangsters as regular guests.[52]

Fights in nightclubs were probably more frequent than in the pub-lic dance halls. Several observers witnessed the throwing of bricks and bottles. When asked about fighting, a member of the 'Hi-Ho Club' in Soho replied:

When they start fighting they use razors, chairs, bottles and they break off the tops of tumblers and dash them under your chin, you can hear the row all over the street . . . at one affair . . . two negroes had been having a gun fight and one was shot in the mouth and the other in the head.[53]

Although the *raison d'être* of the nightclubs was to offer drinking, music, and dancing, there were clearly other motives for attendance. Male and female prostitutes were to be found in the majority of night-clubs. The link between jazz music and drugs was also obvious at these venues, with 'dope' and cocaine on sale in several of those studied. The

[51] M-O A: MDJ: 4/H, 'Night in Soho', 14 Apr. 1939, p. 2.
[52] K. Meyrick, *Secrets of the 43* (1933), 52–62.
[53] M-O A: MDJ: 4/H, 'Night in Soho', 14 Apr. 1939, p. 1.

entire atmosphere of the clubs was a lot more sexually suggestive than in most dance halls:

One coquette in heels at least 2″ high dances with Johnny. He swings rather well, aided by drink, and after two minutes of this he pauses in front of the gramophone and starts swaying about. He presses his body close to hers and they sway about sensually, his hips swinging in rotary rhythm as do hers. They look intently at each other and smile slightly. It all looks like the act of sexual intercourse, although nothing actually takes place . . . other couples do the same thing, hips pressed together, heads thrown slightly back, and eyes glinting.[54]

Such places serviced a need but they were usually small, with accommodation for less than fifty people and only a marginal part of the dancing world.

Conclusion

Dancing, dance halls, and the dance culture were extremely important in interwar Britain. By 1939, dancing played an increasingly important part in the leisure time of nearly all in Britain, but especially working and lower-middle class people. Providing a glamorous rival to the cinema, dance halls were the venue for a highly ritualized form of entertainment. The opulent decoration and exciting programmes of many of the dance halls provided amusement and escape. They served a vital social function, especially for the young. As a focus for the working and lower-middle classes to socialize and meet members of the opposite sex, the dance hall provided an arena where sexuality could be explored. For women, in particular, dancing provided a significant means of independence and physical expression, the equivalent of sport for men. Despite the concerns of many, behaviour in the dance halls was, for the most part, orderly and respectable with little rowdiness and even less promiscuity observed.

[54] M-O A: MDJ: 4/H, 'Night in Soho', 14 Apr. 1939, pp. 5–6.

Part Three

POPULAR MUSIC AND POPULAR MUSIC ARTISTS

8

TASTES IN POPULAR MUSIC, 1918–1939

Introduction

The variety of different styles of music available during the interwar period was substantial. Several musical traditions, such as music hall, operetta, and Victorian and Edwardian ballads and 'light' orchestral pieces, existed alongside new forms of dance music and jazz. Increasingly, native British popular music was exposed to foreign influences, chiefly from the United States of America, but also from the gypsy rhythms of central Europe, the rumba of Latin America, and the 'chanson' of France and the Mediterranean. Popular music thus became increasingly 'cosmopolitan' and British audiences chose their music from many sources. It is important to stress, however, that, despite the impact of foreign styles, native 'British' popular music forms remained extremely popular.

The chapter is divided into three main sections. The first deals with the sorts of music that were popular, drawing particular attention to the catholicity of tastes and also looking at individual genres and particular artists. The second looks at the music itself, detailing a 'hit parade' of the most popular songs and analysing popular music genres in terms of their lyrics and song content. Lastly, some factors involved in the shaping of popular tastes are examined. This looks at how certain songs were promoted by the popular music industry and how others were withheld by censorship or other restrictions.

8.1 Popular genres and artists

Although dance band music of all genres grew fastest in popularity, British tastes in popular music remained surprisingly catholic in the period 1918 to 1939. There were two main 'markets' for popular music. The first was the minority groups who preferred distinct categories of music, such as jazz fans, dance music fans, and fans of music hall. This market was specialized. It had clearly defined tastes. The second and larger market was the great mass of the public who liked popular music of many kinds and drew little distinction between genres and artists. As the music critic Walter Whitman said in 1935:

the great mass of people . . . like to listen to music occasionally but are not particularly interested in what that music is . . . the great mass of listeners have no particular tastes of their own. It is only individual groups of enthusiasts who say what they want and moan if they do not get it. The great public, the 'popular entertainment' public, like popular music, and with them popular music is music that they all know. Popular music is familiar music.[1]

The tendency to buy popular music indiscriminately was at its strongest during the 1920s, fuelled by the dance craze which precipitated a rapid increase in demand for popular and light music of all varieties. As the period progressed, a clear majority remained indiscriminate when purchasing popular music, but an increasing number began to discriminate between particular genres and artists. The popularity of individual stars and bands became more pronounced during the 1930s, perhaps because the depression forced people to choose more carefully than before what they wished to buy and in doing so they clarified their tastes. People increasingly began to categorise their tastes, helped by record catalogues and music shops, and buying according to names and styles. One manifestation of this was that 'fan clubs' for individual artists and bands grew rapidly in number from the mid-1930s.

The extent to which people categorized their own tastes in popular music by the end of the period is indicated in the results of a Mass-Observation survey on the subject. It suggests that people were able to make clear choices as to which kinds of music they preferred and yet remained accessible to popular music of all varieties. As with other Mass-Observation material, however, its reliability must be treated with caution. The following figures, though useful, may not be representative of society as a whole.

The majority of those interviewed (95 per cent middle class and 89 per cent working class)[2] liked some sort of music. Asked what sort of music

---

[1] *BB*, Feb. 1935, p. 22.
[2] M-O A: MDJ: 8/B: Wandsworth Jazz Survey, July 1939; 6/E 'MO looks at Jazz', 22 Nov. 1939, p. 2.

TABLE 6. *Musical preferences by class (per cent)*

	Middle class		Working class	
	Men	Women	Men	Women
Classical	21	34	8	14
Light	27	14	37	26
Jazz	12	14	42	32
All types	40	24	9	15
None	—	3	1	3
Unclassed	—	11	3	10

TABLE 7. *Musical preferences by age (per cent)*

Age:	15–35	35–50	50+
Jazz	44	18	12
Light	18	37	40
Classical	17	15	23
Others	21	30	25

they liked best they gave the answers shown in Table 6.[3] Middle-class tastes were more eclectic than those of the working class, with nearly a third (31 per cent) of those questioned claiming to like 'all types of music'. After this, classical music was the preferred taste for the middle class, with 'light music' following closely, and 'jazz' trailing a poor third. For the working class, tastes were less diverse. Preferences were concentrated in the categories of light music and jazz: 37 per cent of male respondents named jazz as their favourite sort of music.

There are clear gender differences. For women, of all classes, the three most favoured categories are classical first then jazz and finally light. For men, however it is light then jazz followed by 'all types'. Age also made a difference to the appeal of certain types of music. Jazz had the largest proportion of fans among the young. Asked what their favourite kind of music was, responses according to age were: as shown in Table 7. Light music found most favour among those over 35 and particularly over 50. More people in both age groups named light music as their favourite

[3] Ibid.

TABLE 8. *A liking for dance music*

	Middle class		Working class	
	Men	Women	Men	Women
Yes	76	76	84	88
No	6	19	13	3
Unsure	18	5	3	9

than any other type of music. Finally, 'classical' music was surprisingly popular among all ages. However, more people aged 50+ named it their preferred music type than any other age group.

The figures, however, give a false impression of the appeal of 'dance music'. In questioning, the word 'jazz' was used deliberately by Mass-Observation enquirers in order to stimulate the maximum emotional response. It had different meanings for different people and was variously referred to as 'noisy', 'like a lot of old pans', or 'something bright and lively'. It must be noted that many people had an unclear notion of 'jazz' and included any sort of dance music and many Tin Pan Alley songs in their definition.[4] When asked if they liked 'dance music' those interviewed responded far differently (Table 8).[5] Like jazz, dance music was more popular among the young, but it had high approval ratings among all ages. Of those aged 15 to 35, 88 per cent liked dance music, 81 per cent of those aged 36 to 49, and 78 per cent of those aged 50+. Dance music had its highest approval rating among young working-class males aged between 15 and 35, at 91 per cent.

The questions have a tendency to obscure evidence of the catholicity of tastes by focusing on 'favourite' types of music. Many people did not choose one type of music to the exclusion of other types. Although tastes were fairly well defined by the end of the period the majority of people were content to listen to a variety of styles. A liking for dance music, for example, was to be noted among lovers of all types of music.

Dance music dominated the interwar popular music scene. A variety of different playing styles were adopted by dance bands, from 'sweet' to

[4] For discussions of the differences between 'jazz' and dance music' see M-O A: Directive Reply: 'Jazz 2, July 1939'.

[5] M-O A: MDJ: 8/B: Wandsworth Jazz Survey, July 1939; 6/E: 'MO looks at Jazz', 22 Nov. 1939, p. 3.

'hot' and individual bands developed distinctive styles to mark them out from their competitors. Several bands established themselves as clear favourites with the British public.

Perhaps the most popular was Jack Hylton and His Orchestra, whose success was phenomenal. In 1929, for example, they played over 700 performances in 365 days, travelled over 63,000 miles on tour, and their records—calculated on a 24-hour a day, seven days a week basis—sold at the rate of over seven a minute.[6] The Hylton Orchestras recorded nearly 1,700 sides between 1921 and 1939 for a variety of gramophone companies including HMV and Decca.[7] From 1923 to 1933 nearly 7 million copies of Hylton's records were sold.[8] They were particularly busy in the years 1929 to 1933. In 1931, for example, they recorded 217 titles. That year they recorded and released an average of 18 new titles every month.[9]

Yet Hylton wasn't the only big name in the dance band world. Particularly successful in the 1920s were the Savoy Orpheans and the Savoy Havana Band. These two bands had prolific recording careers. Between 1923 and 1939, the Savoy Orpheans recorded nearly 1,000 titles. Their biggest record hit, 'Valencia' (1926), sold over 275,000 copies. The Savoy Havana Band sold more than 3 million records in the years 1923–32; a huge total. Equally popular during the 1920s and early 1930s was Jack Payne and His Orchestra. Payne recorded 750 sides from 1925 to 1939. His biggest hits came in 1929 when 'The Stein Song' sold almost 100,000 copies and 'When it's Springtime in the Rockies' backed by 'I'm Falling in Love Again' sold over 70,000.[10] In the early 1930s, Ray Noble and the New Mayfair Orchestra were also household favourites. Between 1929 and 1933, they sold 1.5 million records in Britain.[11] Among Noble's most popular recordings were 'Goodnight Sweetheart' (1931), 'Love is the Sweetest Thing' (1932), 'By the Fireside' (1932), and 'The Very Thought of You' (1934), all of which he composed himself and all of which were recorded by dozens of other artists. By the mid-1930s other names had come to dominate the dance bands: Ambrose recorded nearly 1,000 sides between 1927 and 1939. Billy Cotton recorded over 850 sides from 1928

---

[6] *MM*, Apr. 1930, p. 327.

[7] Calculated from B. Rust and S. Forbes, *British Dance Bands on Record, 1911–1945* (Harrow, 1989).

[8] P. Martland, *Since Records Began: EMI the First 100 years* (1997), 85.

[9] Thus, although this year was at the bottom of the depression, some parts of the country, especially London and the south-east, were still doing well enough for people to buy records.

[10] Martland, *EMI*, 212.   [11] Ibid.

to 1939, Harry Roy 662 from 1931 to 1939, Roy Fox 569 sides from 1930 to 1938, Henry Hall 551, Lew Stone 377 titles from 1929 to 1939, and Geraldo recorded 320 sides from 1930 to 1939.

It was not only tastes in particular dance bands that changed over the period. The style of playing and the nature of dance music itself also changed dramatically from 1918 to 1939. This change was typified by the opposing camps of 'hot' and 'commercial' players. Broadly speaking it can be said that 'hot' music was more popular in the 1920s than the 1930s, when 'sweet' music was favoured. Soon after the arrival of jazz in Britain in 1919, a debate started among musicians and critics as to the different merits of playing 'hot' and 'commercial' styles. The whole debate was confused by the fact that in the 1920s everything played by dance bands was considered to be 'jazz' when in fact very few British performances could have been described as such. By the mid-1930s critics and observers were beginning to distinguish between 'hot' music (jazz and swing) and commercial dance music.[12]

'Hot' jazz was the reserve of a minority of largely middle-class enthusiasts whose search for 'authenticity' was marked by the establishment of the Rhythm Clubs. The Rhythm Clubs were the creation of devoted dance music enthusiasts. They were a spontaneous reaction against mass tastes in dance music. These clubs rejected highly commercialized 'pop' tunes in favour of 'hot' dance music and jazz. A minority interest catering for specialist tastes, they were linked with the professional and semi-professional dance bands and an important element in dance music culture.

Rhythm clubs originated on the Continent where André Ache, a musician and dance music fan, founded the Sweet and Hot Club of Brussels in February 1932. The Sweet and Hot hoped to foster a better appreciation of the music and improve standards of performance in Europe. Ache established a series of other clubs throughout Belgium organized under a Federation of Hot Clubs and the movement rapidly spread throughout the whole of Europe. Perhaps the most influential club was the Quintette de Hot Club de France with Django Reinhardt and Stephanne Grappelli.[13] The British Rhythm Club movement was less influential but did much to foster enthusiasm for swing music and jazz. The British movement came into existence in June 1933 and was launched by W. Elliot and Eric A. C.

[12] See also M. Hustwitt, 'Caught in a Whirlpool Sound: The Production of Dance Music in Britain in the 1920s', in *Popular Music*, 3 (1983), 7–31.
[13] *MM*, 7 Apr. 1934, p. 11.

Ballard with almost religious zeal. It hoped to educate and inform the average listener on the merits of true hot music. Its object was:

> to bring together those interested in hot music and, by holding regular recitals . . . to add to the enjoyment of the enthusiast while offering some centre where the uninitiated could find out what hot music was all about . . . Record recitals are the main feature, but discussions on questions of interests, visits of prominent musicians, and so on, give variety to the meetings.[14]

By March 1934, supported by the *Melody Maker* and *Rhythm,* there were thirty-eight clubs in Britain. Most large towns had branches including Northampton, Bournemouth, Leicester, Reigate, Hull, Croydon, Sheffield, Ipswich, Bradford, Reading, Seaford, Manchester, Uxbridge, York, and Greenwich.[15] Membership of individual clubs was usually modest (from 30 to 50) but attendance at meetings could swell to several hundred when dances were run or well-known performers visited. The movement established its own national journal, *Swing Music,* in March 1935 under the editorship of Leonard Hibbs, a jazz critic for the *Melody Maker.* Another journal, *Hot News and Rhythm Record Review,* edited by Eric Ballard, followed in April of the same year.

In May 1935, with 90 clubs in existence representing some 4,000 members, a British Federation of Rhythm Clubs was established to coordinate the movement.[16] Although the Federation was slow to start and soon petered out it achieved important work in getting the major record companies to produce specialist albums of swing music for club members. Gramophone record recitals were a major part of the Rhythm Club movement. Since few British dance bands would perform 'hot music' the enthusiast had to rely on American recordings to satisfy their tastes. As most clubs ran their own record libraries the enthusiast could listen to expensive discs without having to buy them for himself and exchanges were often arranged by members. The major record companies sent representatives to tour the various clubs promoting works. The Decca Record Company even launched a Contemporary Rhythm Society under the presidency of Duke Ellington which invited both jazz and modern classical performers to submit works. Ambrose and His Orchestra were retained to make the discs of these compositions.

The members of these Rhythm Clubs were predominantly male, middle class, and suburban and tended to be young. Besides ready-made music, many clubs established their own bands and orchestras to develop

[14] *BB*, Nov. 1934, p. 26.   [15] *MM*, 17 Mar. 1934, p. 5.
[16] *MM*, 4 May 1935, p. 11.

TABLE 9. *Dance music preferences, 1939 (per cent)*

	Middle class		Working class	
	Men	Women	Men	Women
Ballroom (commercial)	49	56	48	60
Swing	24	2	19	9
Old-time	9	11	7	4
All types	—	8	8	12
None	6	2	4	1
Miscellaneous	6	10	5	4
Unsure	6	11	9	10

their own interpretations of swing music. At the Rhythm Clubs, bands developed which were free from the restraints of commercial work.

One British artist who developed a hot style and did do well with the wider public, however, was Nat Gonella. Gonella and his various bands, principally the 'Georgians', played fast and furiously. He was billed as Britain's version of Louis Armstrong and he moulded himself on his hero. Gonella's recording of 'Tiger Rag' was a big success, and he also produced a large number of other best selling 'hot' recordings. However, record sales of this style of music were, on the whole, poor. The 1920s and early 1930s saw moderate sales of jazz records by American artists and there was a small but enthusiastic minority market. Once the Musicians' Union ban on American artists had begun to take effect sales declined. Louis Armstrong, Duke Ellington, Cab Calloway and others' presence in general record catalogues gradually diminished. Although available by import or subscription, by the end of the 1930s this swing and jazz was a truly specialist, minority taste.

The great mass of the British public preferred slower commercial forms of dance music as is suggested by Mass-Observation's survey: when asked which type of dance music they liked best, replies were as shown in Table 9.[17] Commercial dance music was clearly the most favoured type and appealed to the somewhat conservative tastes of the mass of the British public. 'Swing', on the other hand found only limited

[17] M-O A: MDJ: 8/B: Wandsworth Jazz Survey, July 1939; 6/E 'MO looks at Jazz', 22 Nov. 1939, p. 5.

favour, largely among middle-class males.[18] Most importantly, this was 'British' dance music, not American jazz. The international idiom of 'jazz' and dance music underwent a transformation in Britain between 1918 and 1939. It was Anglicized, shaped to local conditions, and assimilated some of the nation's traditional playing techniques. As Jack Hylton said, the British disliked the 'hotter' American music:

It has not appealed to the public. Before it can be played here it must be modified, *given the British touch*, which Americans and other foreigners never understand. Symphonic syncopation, which I feel proud to have developed in this country, is pre-eminently British. In the dance-hall or on the gramophone record alike, it makes a subtle appeal to our British temperament. It is fast becoming a truly national music.[19]

There were several elements in this 'British' style which marked it out from the American dance music and jazz. First, British dance bands tended to be less spontaneous than American ones. There were few 'jam sessions' and a more formal, orchestrated delivery. The tendency of hot music to improvise and therefore distort the original melody made it difficult for most people to follow. In 1933, Lawrence Wright blamed the tendency to 'jazz up' songs for falling sheet music sales. British tastes tended to be simpler. The majority of the public, it was felt by band-leaders, wanted to hear the tune properly. Charlie Kunz wrote:

The Britisher must have a song to sing—something simple and easy to learn. Even the errand boy must have something to whistle. It is characteristic of the race . . . the masses, highbrow and lowbrow, representative of all classes, are not interested in the highly involved patterns of ultra-modern dance music. . . . What they want is a simple, appealing tune.[20]

Secondly, British dance bands developed a gentler style of presentation in the majority of their works, favouring 'sweet' music over 'hot'. The British style of playing was smooth and relaxing, a very domesticated sound that made for comfortable domestic enjoyment. 'Hot' music was played but the most popular numbers were of the sentimental and romantic kind. Carroll Gibbons specialized in this particular style of sweet music with easy flowing melodies and a relaxing delivery. Through his broadcasts on the BBC and commercial radio he provided a relaxing

[18] See S. Frith, 'Playing with Real Feeling: Jazz and Suburbia', in S. Frith, *Music for Pleasure: Essays in the Sociology of Pop* (Cambridge, 1988), 45–63.

[19] J. Hylton, 'The British Touch', *Gramophone*, Sept. 1927, p. 146.

[20] *RP*, 2 Mar. 1934, p. 7.

background to the suburban home. In 1934 he spoke of his late-night broadcasts:

people at this time of night are in a restful mood after a day's work. Dance music in a soothing form is therefore more acceptable to them as a whole. Surely the majority of listeners are comfortably settled by their firesides in a lethargic state of mind at that time of the night. It is reasonable to believe then, that sweet melodious dance music, devoid of all the barbaric influence of the more sophist-icated jazz should be more acceptable to them by reason of its restraint and restful influence.[21]

And, finally, the British style and repertoire owed more to traditional music hall than its American counterpart. Comedy numbers were fea-tured heavily by British dance bands, and in their stage performances they established set comic routines by members of the band.

Indeed, more widely, music-hall, variety, and comedy songs were a mainstay of working-class popular culture before the Second World War. The two most important musical stars of the interwar period, Gracie Fields and George Formby, were artists steeped in a music-hall tradition. Their enormous popularity rivalled that of the dance bands and made Formby and Fields potent symbols of working-class culture.

Gracie Fields became a national symbol. Her career started on the musical stage, moving from music-hall appearances in the provinces to stage productions in London—her first a revue, *Yes I Think So*, in 1915 at the Middlesex Music Hall. She topped the bill in revue, variety, and cabaret in London's West End during the 1920s, appearing at the Alhambra, the Coliseum, and the Café Royal. Her recording career started in 1928 with a popular ballad of the time 'My Blue Heaven'. Sales of her recordings were enormous; after only five years she had sold four million. In February 1933 she went to the HMV factory at Hayes to press this four millionth record. (See Plate 8). The event was captured on news-reel by Pathe for cinema audiences. Indeed, by 1931 she had embarked on the start of a highly successful film career with the film *Sally in Our Alley* which launched her most famous song, 'Sally'. Gracie Field's repertoire of songs was wide and she alternated between comedy numbers and sen-timental ballads with ease. She even made highly popular recordings of 'Land of Hope and Glory' and 'Ave Maria'. Gracie Fields's only serious rival for popularity at this time was George Formby.

[21] *RP*, 23 Mar. 1934, p. 11.

George Formby was one of the first entertainers to master all the new forms of mass media—the cinema, the radio, and the gramophone. His main appeal was as the singer of comic songs and in a repertoire of several hundred songs the majority dealt with sex. Through his stage appearances in revues, concerts, pantomimes, and variety he built up a large provincial following during the 1920s which allowed him to springboard to national fame via the cinema with his first film *Boots, Boots* in 1934. Formby's success in the cinema increased the sale of his gramophone records. Working briefly for the Edison Bell Company (1926) and then Decca (1932–5) and Regal Zonophone (1935–46), Formby sold several million copies of his records. This made him one of the most popular recording artists of the interwar period. 'When I'm Cleaning Windows', for example, was so successful that within two weeks of its release sales had reached over 100,000, for which Formby received a 'silver disk'. His most popular titles before the Second World War included 'Chinese Laundry Blues (Mr Wu)' (1932), 'Swimmin' with the Wimmin' (1934), 'Leaning on a Lamppost' (1937), 'With My Little Stick of Blackpool Rock' (1937), and 'In My Little Snapshot Album' (1938). As popular with audiences in the north as in the south, it is also said that Formby was a favourite star of the Royal Family and in particular Queen Mary. He appeared in the Royal Command Performance of 1937 and was invited to give private performances at Windsor. Even the Princesses Elizabeth and Margaret bought his records and were able to sing his lyrics.[22]

Formby and Fields were not the only variety artists to attain popularity among popular music audiences. Black American variety artists Turner Layton and Clarence Johnstone were also extremely popular. They came to Britain in 1923 and were signed up to record by Columbia, becoming amongst their biggest stars. During their career they recorded prolifically, selling a total of over 8 million records. They also continued to appear in variety and revues.[23] Other successful variety stars who survived the decline of music hall included Max Miller, Tommy Trinder, and Arthur Askey who, together with Richard 'Stinker' Murdoch, gained national popularity through the pioneering situation comedy radio programme *Band Waggon*. Askey made several popular recordings of a whimsical nature, including 'The Bee Song' and 'The Seagull'.

[22] Beryl Formby, private recording of BBC radio interview, late 1930s.
[23] Martland, *EMI*, 124.

Monologues were popular, the most famous exponents being Stanley Holloway and Robb Wilton. Musical comedy double acts were also popular: the most successful artists included Clapham and Dwyer, Gert and Daisy, Flanagan and Allen, Murgatroyd and Winterbottom, and Flotsam and Jetsam. Among the most distinctive of these were George and Kenneth Western, whose act 'The Western Brothers' ridiculed the British upper class. Typical of their genteel yet incisive wit were their 1934 recordings 'The Old School Tie', and 'Ain't it Gorgeous'.

Older music-hall stars also continued to be popular throughout the 1920s and 1930s. Sir Harry Lauder, for example, continued to make records and stage appearances. Indeed, his 1924 song 'Keep Right on to the End of the Road' was one of his most popular. The advent of electrical recording in 1925 meant that many older music-hall stars re-recorded their material, and enjoyed renewed popularity. Charles Penrose re-recorded 'The Laughing Policeman' in 1926 and it remained in the record catalogues for many years. Will Fyffe was also popular, his most successful songs being 'I Belong to Glasgow' and 'I'm 94 Today'. George Robey also made a successful transition to the new media, working with radio, film, and recordings.

In addition to the largely working-class stars of variety and the music hall, British popular music produced a number of performers whose appeal was based on a middle and upper-class style, which was more 'highbrow' than the working-class style, but still resolutely 'popular'. Such performers were linked closely with the theatre. They had a variety of intimate and sophisticated styles which were popular at all levels of society.

Noel Coward's association with revues and musical theatre produced a string of best selling songs. Many of them Coward recorded himself, mostly on the HMV lable, the most successful being 'Mad Dogs and Englishmen', 'The Stately Homes of England' and 'Mrs Worthington'. Even more cover versions of his songs were recorded by other artists. As Philip Hoare has noted, 'sales of sheet music, gramophone recordings and the published work brought a sizeable income; they also promoted Coward as a household name outside the audience catchment area of the West End, and spread his fame and . . . popularity . . . throughout the country.'[24]

Gertrude Lawrence had a prestigious career on both sides of the Atlantic as a singer, dancer, and actress. Her upper-middle-class singing

[24] P. Hoare, *Noel Coward: A Biography* (1995), 205.

voice, best described as 'distinctive', was more than compensated for by her charm, grace, and vivaciousness. Most famous for her work in the musical theatre, Lawrence was the star of a large number of 'smash hits', including works by Noel Coward—*London Calling!* (1923), *Private Lives* (1930), *Tonight at 8:30* (1936)—George Gershwin—*Oh, Kay!* (1926/7)—and Cole Porter—*Nymph Errant* (1933). She was one of the most successful British stars to appear on Broadway and her distinctive British upper-middle-class character was largely responsible for this. Like Coward she reached a larger audience through the medium of gramophone recordings and recorded many of the most popular songs of the time. Some of her most memorable numbers included 'Limehouse Blues' (1924), 'Someone to Watch over Me' (1927), 'Experiment' (1933), and 'The Physician' (1933).

Jack Buchanan was another versatile middlebrow performer, being a singer, dancer, actor, and director. Popular in both Britain and America, he was frequently accompanied by the actress Elsie Randolph in several of his film and stage appearances. Buchanan was a 'gentleman' singer, complete with upper-class accent and dashing attire. He had a sophisticated repertoire of songs from the whimsical, 'You Sweet So and So' (1931), to the romantic, 'Goodnight Vienna' (1932). Predominantly a theatre star, he appeared in a large number of revues and shows. His most memorable appearances were in *Sunny* (1926), *That's a Good Girl* (1928), *Mr Whittington* (1934), and *This'll Make You Whistle* (1936). Buchanan's urbane, sophisticated style marked him out as a truly 'British' performer in a decade dominated by American accents and pseudo-American style.

Although of working-class origins, Jessie Matthews was marketed to the public as a middle-class girl and through her singing and dancing career she became one of Britain's most popular stars in the interwar period. Matthews's career was firmly rooted on the musical stage, but, as we have seen, she was also one of the period's most popular film stars, the only British musical star whose films were successful on both sides of the Atlantic.[25] Her repertoire of popular songs was mostly romantic and she delivered them with a mixture of vitality and charming tenderness. Her most popular numbers included 'My Heart Stood Still' (1927), 'Dancing on the Ceiling' (1930), 'Over My Shoulder' (1934), and 'Everything's in Rhythm with My Heart' (1936).

There were also several middlebrow variety stars who did not follow the more traditional route to the 'legitimate' musical theatre, including

---

[25] See Chapter 3 above.

Jack Hulbert, Gillie Potter, Bobby Howes, Binnie Hale, and Cicely Courtneidge. Perhaps the most distinctive of the middle-class variety stars was Ronald Frankau—'perhaps the only intentional comedian ever turned out by Eton'.[26] Frankau was constantly brushing with the censors since his comic songs had a definite 'adult' content. Although suggestive, however, his material was not obscene.

Another extremely popular genre was 'light music'. Light music was a clear favourite with audiences in interwar Britain, a fact reflected in its domination of both the BBC's and commercial radio broadcasts and its healthy record sales. The wide range of orchestral music, sentimental songs, and popular versions of classical musical pieces gave 'light music' a broad appeal. British audiences enjoyed the nostalgic, pre-jazz sounds and traditions of this genre.

The Australian bass-baritone Peter Dawson was one of the most popular light music artists both before and during the interwar period. Recording for various companies, his longest and most successful association was with HMV and his large number of discs remained a key part of their catalogue throughout the period. He made more than 3,000 recordings from 1904 to 1955 and they sold over 25 million copies. 'The Floral Dance' and 'On the Road to Mandalay' were among his most popular.

Paul Robeson was another popular performer. He was known in Britain first through his records, having started his recording career in 1925 and reaching record sales of over 1 million by the 1930s. His repertoire was also varied, including popular songs such as 'Mood Indigo'; light songs, such as 'Trees' and 'Ma Curly Headed Baby'; and, importantly, he was responsible for a revival of interest in Negro spirituals. He first came to Britain on tour in 1928–9 and won critical acclaim that year starring in *Show Boat* at the Drury Lane Theatre. He appeared in several other leading British stage productions too. Whilst based in Britain he also made and starred in films such as *Sanders of the River* (1935), *King Solomon's Mines* (1937), and *The Song of Freedom* (1938).

Light operetta styles were also popular. British composer and actor Ivor Novello was instrumental in keeping light operetta popular throughout the 1930s. Novello, who composed 'Keep the Home Fires Burning' in 1914, had a successful career as a film star during the 1920s but in the 1930s he began to write for the musical theatre. He was largely responsible for reviving the interest in Viennese operetta and a series of produc-

[26] *Who's Who in Broadcasting* (1935), 7.

tions—*Glamorous Night* (1935), *Careless Rapture* (1936), and the *Dancing Years* (1939)—had long runs, appealing to older audiences who preferred romantic music without any 'jazz' influence. Several artists made their reputations in this genre. Americans Jeanette MacDonald and Nelson Eddy were the stars of eight film musicals made for MGM based on the traditional Viennese operetta. Their films *Rose Marie* and *Maytime*, for example, produced several hit songs. 'Indian Love Call' and 'Farewell to Dreams' were typical of their repertoire and sold well, reflecting a demand for popular ballads sung in an operetta style. Britain's answer to MacDonald and Eddy were Anne Ziegler and Webster Booth. Both had careers before they formed their partnership in 1938, Booth having worked for the D'Oyly Carte Company since 1924. Their duets, on both radio broadcasts and records proved very popular; particularly songs such as 'We'll Gather Lilacs in the Spring Again' and 'If You Were the Only Girl in the World'.

Military bands and brass bands also remained popular, as testified by their inclusion on the schedules of both commercial radio and the BBC into the late 1930s and by their survival on the catalogues of many record companies. The Foden's Brass Band recorded for Regal-Zonophone (the label of George Formby and Gracie Fields) and sales of its records were good. Organ music was also popular through the cinema organ, radio broadcasts, and recordings. The cinema organ had its heyday in the super-cinemas of the 1930s and most cinemas had their own version of the mighty Wurlitzer complete with rising platform and glittering effects. Many cinema organists became well known through recordings and broadcasts. The most famous were Reginald Dixon, who was resident at the Tower Ballroom, Blackpool, from 1938, and the BBC's resident organist Sandy McPherson, 1936–63.

8.2 Popular song titles: origins and content

From each of these genres of popular music, some individual titles became 'hits' enjoying either a brief and intense period of success or gathering wide popularity for a longer duration. This section will examine which were the most popular 'hits', where they came from and what they had to say.

An official 'Hit Parade' did not exist in Britain until 1948. Before this, on 12 October 1936, however, the BBC had started a feature programme called *The Music Shop* presented by Geraldo and His Orchestra.[27] The programme featured the top ten most popular songs based upon the results of a canvass of music publishers, sheet music distributors, recording companies, and dance hall bands. The show was a direct copy of the United States programme *The Hit Parade* started by cigarette manufacturers Lucky Strike in 1935, but on a far smaller scale. The BBC programme ran for several months but was criticized by the *Melody Maker*, which doubted the accuracy of its listings. As a result the *Melody Maker*, briefly, published its own competing hit parades (from November 1936) based on the sheet music sales of two large music distributors.[28] Before this, the *Melody Maker* had listed the American Hit Parade only days after it was published in order to give dance band leaders a clue to trends in America. It also attempted to indicate which songs were most popular in the dance music world. *Tunes which Dominate the Broadcasts*, which started in January 1934, was a weekly guide to 'the numbers favoured by the Band Leaders' and calculated charts on the basis of the frequency with which they were broadcast on the radio. *Tunes to Watch out for* was a similar list started around 1928, with no firm basis for its listings. Other indicators of taste could be found in the monthly record supplements issued by Decca, who from 1932, started listing their top fifteen best-selling records and song titles.

There is, therefore, no authoritative list of which tunes and songs were the most popular for the years from 1918 to 1939. Some indication of the sorts of songs that were popular can be gained, however. The Appendix lists the most popular tunes for each of the years 1919, 1925, 1930, 1935, and 1939 arranged month by month. It is based on the documents of the BBC gramophone library, and would reflect the sort of records broadcast on record request programmes and gramophone recital programmes.[29] Its dates are based on the date of issue of the first records. The list is not comprehensive, however. It is biased towards dance music, and although there are a few comedy numbers, it misses out, for example, hits like 'When I'm Cleaning Windows', which were undoubtedly among the biggest sellers of the time. Despite this, it is still of use and it gives a clear indication of some of the most popular titles of the time and where they came from, and it indicates factors which affected the determination of British popular tastes.

[27] *MM*, 24 Oct. 1936, p. 12.   [28] *MM*, 7 Nov. 1936, p. 13.
[29] B. Rust and L. Lowe, *Top Tunes of 1912–1958 on Commercial Gramophone Records* (1959).

In terms of national origin, between 1919 and 1939 popular music was clearly dominated by American songs. The music of the period certainly seemed to reflect the energy of America, as the music critic R. W. S. Mendl wrote:

Jazz music . . . embodies a spirit which is characteristic of their nation. The energy, industry, the hurry and hustle and efficiency of modern American methods find their counterpart in the swift-moving, bustling, snappy, restless rhythm of syncopated dance music, in the splendid techniques of the . . . jazz orchestra.[30]

In 1919 the impact of the new forms of jazz and dance music meant that nearly three-quarters (74 per cent) of the most popular tunes in Britain were of American origin. Even some of those numbers written by British composers tried to capitalize on this trend, using American sounding titles to imitate American songs. 'I've got the Sweetest girl in Maryland' and 'Missouri Waltz', for example, were written by British authors. Many feared for the survival of British song. Alec Neilson, writing in the *Melody Maker*, asked:

Can we not have songs which are really British? Are there no talented lyric writers in our midst? And if there are any, can they not give us songs of a truly British nature, instead of eternally aping the style of our American brothers? . . . Why are we of Britain not permitted to sing in English? Why must we always use our vocal chords to exploit the American tongue? Is it quite impossible to cure our songs of their 'aint's' and 'gonnas' and 'gals' and 'wanna's' and other such American slang?[31]

This domination continued into 1925 when the same proportion, 75 per cent, of the most popular tunes in Britain were American. Some of the most popular tunes of 1925 are still memorable today, such as 'Charleston', 'Sweet Georgia Brown', 'If You Knew Susie', 'Yes Sir! That's My Baby', and 'Always'. All were written by Americans. By 1930 it appeared that the British popular song was in danger of being washed away in a tide of American songs, most from the new medium of the talking film. In 1930, 84 per cent of the most popular tunes in Britain were of American origin. Conspiracy theories evolved. In March 1927 the *Sunday Chronicle* had reported the existence of a 'song-writing ring' controlled by American and Jewish authors, composers, and publishers, operating to the detriment of British popular music.[32] Although no such ring existed, the article generated considerable debate. There were widespread fears of

[30] R. W. S. Mendl, *The Appeal of Jazz* (1927), 97–8.
[31] A. Neilson in *MM*, Dec. 1928, p. 301.   [32] Quoted in *MM*, May 1927, p. 417.

cultural obsolescence. In June 1928 the *Melody Maker* complained that 'embryo latent native talent throughout the British Isles lies buried as successfully as though it never existed in consequence of this flooding of our markets with foreign emanations'.[33]

American domination of popular music was due to a combination of a successful 'product' and the use of successful exploitation tactics. Talented and innovative composers, such as Irving Berlin, Cole Porter, George and Ira Gershwin, etc. produced highly successful 'products'. Several other factors helped establish and maintain this cultural ascendancy. Of great importance to American domination was clever exploitation of the new mass media. During the 1920s the gramophone record allowed American songs to travel the world rapidly. Through licensing arrangements with foreign gramophone companies and through global subsidiaries of their own companies, the Americans were able to establish dominant position for their popular music. The rapid spread of radio throughout the world also provided an arena for exploitation via broadcasts of American gramophone records and a limited number of relays and broadcasts by American musicians. The success of Hollywood musical films in the early 1930s was also extremely important. Mastery of these global media was America's most powerful cultural weapon. Domination of the British popular music industry was also the result of careful marketing techniques used by American music publishers. American music established a firm foothold in Britain during the first years of the jazz craze, just after the First World War, when there was a large market for American works. American songs were attractive for British music publishers as they had already 'proved' themselves in the United States, which was a good indication that they would succeed in Britain. However, American publishers would not sell individual hits to foreigners, only whole catalogues—it was all or nothing. Under the terms of their contracts with the Americans, British publishers had to guarantee to publish and promote a certain number of tunes each year. Having paid for large amounts of material, British publishers were also likely to promote as many of their other American songs as possible, and the British market became flooded.

The increasingly cosmopolitan nature of popular music in interwar Britain also created a preoccupation with the racial origin of songs. Constant Lambert's 1934 critique of contemporary music, *Music Ho!*, points to the horrified rhetoric of 'crusty old colonels', 'choleric judges', and 'beer-sodden columnists' complaining of jazz as 'swamp stuff', 'jungle rhythms', and 'negro decadence'. Lambert suggested that such complainants were 'hugely enjoying their position of Cassandra prophesying the downfall of the white women'.[34] Early British 'jazz' critics took great pains to connect the new music with primitivism, and were preoccupied with tracing the origins of jazz back to 'the jungle'.[35] Jewish 'threats' to authentic British culture were seen as equally serious.

Despite fears of a black and Jewish 'invasion' of culture, British composed songs nonetheless made a comeback in the mid-1930s. By 1935 American numbers still made up 64 per cent of the most popular tunes in Britain, but this was a significant decline from its 1930 figure. The British song hits of 1935 'Roll along, Covered Wagon', 'South American Joe', 'Red Sails in the Sunset', and 'Who's Been Polishing the Sun' reversed the trend of the preceding years by also being big hits in the United States of America. This year was also the year of remarkable success for the British songwriters Jimmy Kennedy and Michael Carr. This songwriting team were, more than anyone else, responsible for a revival in the fortunes of British popular music during the 1930s, as has been shown.[36] Both specialized in producing pastiches of the American genre—'South of the Border' (1939) being the best example. Carr and Kennedy were also successful at creating English language versions of Continental popular music, especially Italian and French songs.

Of the media through which popular music originated, films were, of course, a major force. Another influence, as we have seen, was the musical theatre. In the first half of the period, the musical theatre still had a significant impact on the origin and popularization of popular songs. About one-quarter of the most popular songs from 1919 to 1930 had their origins in musical theatre. In 1925 *No No Nanette* produced the immortal 'Tea for Two' and 'I Want to be Happy'. *Rose Marie* from the same year produced 'Indian Love Call'. In 1930 despite the domination of the film, the musical theatre was still able to introduce the following long-term 'hits': 'Body and Soul' from *Three's a Crowd* and 'On the Sunny Side of the Street' from *The International Revue*. One of the leitmotifs of the period, the Charleston, was also first introduced and popularized via the musical theatre. In the USA it first appeared in the 1923 touring black revue *Running Wild*, and then in London at a revue at the Hotel

---

[34] C. Lambert, *Music Ho!* (1934), 202.

[35] For example, see Mendl, *Appeal of Jazz* and S. R. Nelson, *All About* Jazz (1934).

[36] See Chapter 4 above.

Metropole in 1925. After 1930, however, the influence of the musical theatre in introducing hit songs declined, and by 1939 only about 10 per cent
of the most popular songs in Britain had originated in musical theatre.

Many songs were written independently of the requirements of films or
musical plays. Songwriters composed a large number of songs for radio
broadcasts and gramophone recordings, but they also continued to write
large numbers of songs merely to fill their publishers catalogues. Unlike
today, most popular songs in interwar Britain were not exclusive to one
person or dance band, and if a song became popular most dance bands
would feature their own versions of it. The music-hall tradition of asso-
ciating certain songs with certain stars was declining, although it did
survive among some entertainers. George Formby, for example, chose
most of his material from a few favoured lyricists and composers, and the
songs he sang became closely associated with his name. Gracie Fields was
more eclectic in her choice of repertoire, and although she had several
hits that she made her own, 'Sally', 'The Biggest Aspidistra in the World',
etc., she also sang popular 'standards'.

The majority of popular songs written during the period 1918 to 1939
dealt with the universal theme of 'love', either as romantic comedy,
sentimental love songs, or ballads. In 1919 this category accounted for
42 per cent of the most popular songs, increasing to 55 per cent by 1935.
This focus on the 'personal' gave love songs a wide appeal and enabled
American songs in particular to become universally popular. There was
a discernible tendency for love songs of the 1930s to be increasingly sentimental and saccharine, with less optimism than those love songs of the
1920s. Many of the most popular tunes of the 1920s were love songs with
a decidedly assertive and optimistic message. 'Ain't She Sweet', 'Sweet
Georgia Brown', 'If You Knew Susie', and 'Yes Sir! That's My Baby',
were upbeat, positive, and showed few traces of sentiment. By 1930, however, the mood had changed. 'Nobody's Using it Now'; 'Body and Soul',
'Falling in Love Again', 'Dancing with Tears in My Eyes', and 'Dancing
on the Ceiling' were all hits in 1930. These love songs were negative,
sentimental, and defeatist. Many music critics lamented the decline of
a hearty and optimistic, native popular culture. Constant Lambert in
his 1934 book *Music Ho!: A Study of Music in Decline* describes the songs
of the interwar period as having a 'curiously sagging quality' and a
'masochistic melancholia'. This he blames on 'New York Jewry'. He is
worth quoting at length on the subject:

A general air of physical attractiveness, sexual bounce and financial independence is naturally assumed by the writers of pre-war hits. The singer's hat is at a

jaunty angle, his gloves are in his hand, he suffers from no inhibitions or self-consciousness as he walks down the pier, receiving the glad eye from presumably attractive girls with whom he ultimately and triumphantly 'clicks'. If he 'can't afford a carriage' he can at least stump up enough for a tandem bicycle, which is considerably more than the hero of 'I can't give you anything but love, baby,' can claim to be able to do.

In modern songs it is taken for granted that one is poor, unsuccessful, and either sex-starved or unable to hold the affections of such a partner as one may have had the luck to pick up. Even when the singer says that he has a woman crazy about him he hastens to point out that her attitude is clearly eccentric and in no way to be expected. For the most part, though, the heroes and heroines of modern songs meet with the rebuffs they deserve and take refuge in the unmute reproach of 'Ain't misbehavin'', and 'Mean to me', or the facile melancholy of 'Dancing with tears in my eyes', 'You've got me cryin' again, you've got me sighin' again,' and 'When you want somebody who don't want you, perhaps you'll think of me.'[37]

This transformation was typified by the development of 'crooners' and the torch song. The 'crooner' sang in an intimate, quiet, romantic manner, and was largely the product of technological advances. The development of the microphone enabled vocalists greater versatility; it was now possible to 'whisper' songs and still remain audible in the majority of venues. Popular crooners such as Al Bowlly and Les Allen developed large female followings, with fan clubs and gossip columns detailing their every move. Female vocalists also developed large followings and based their appeal on the slow 'torch song'. The torch song, a sentimental genre concerned with unrequited love, was a development of the 'cabaret' found in smart restaurants and small clubs, where an intimate entertainment was required. They reached a wider audience via the radio and gramophone. By the late 1930s dance band vocalists had become popular in their own right, and many launched solo careers. This process was accelerated during the war and ultimately led to the end of the dance band era—the singer became more popular than the songs and the band that backed them.

Despite this trend toward sentimentality in love songs, comedy songs were also popular. As may be seen in the Appendix, they constituted nearly one in five of the most popular songs in Britain in 1919, and remained consistently popular, also accounting for 20 per cent of 'hits' in 1935. The comic song was one of the central features of music hall, and despite the decline of the institution, comic songs remained among the

---

[37] Lambert, *Music Ho!*, 151.

most popular of all types of popular music. Dozens of popular music stars specialized in comic songs and one of the most successful was George Formby. With their *doubles entendres* and brazen presentation, the chief attraction and importance of Formby's songs was their comic preoccupation with sex. The repertoire includes continuous reference to old maids, fat ladies, nakedness, underwear, honeymooning couples, flirtatious females, phallicism, illegitimate children, and nagging wives. Often referred to as musical versions of Donald McGill's seaside postcards, they revelled in shocking conventional sensibilities, but they did so in a light-hearted way. What George Orwell wrote about McGill's postcards he could have written about Formby's songs: 'Their existence, the fact that people want them, is symptomatically important. Like the music-halls, they are a sort of saturnalia, a harmless rebellion against virtue.'[38] Despite this continual reference to sex, it is not a world of promiscuity and lapsed morals; on the contrary, the subject matter was always kept firmly within the bounds of decency. In a deeply repressed society, songs like Formby's were an important way of expressing an opinion about sex and relationships between the sexes. The comedy was also essentially upbeat, catchy, and full of laughter; a blithe retort to the vapid romanticism of the dance bands and their music. A whole host of songs with titles such as 'Its Turned out Nice Again', 'Hitting the High Spots', and 'I'm Making Headway Now', were attempts to allay fears about their audience's future, by urging mettlesome good humour and perseverance.

Optimism and comedy were also found in popular 'novelty' and 'dance' songs. This category ranges from the 'crazy words, crazy tunes' numbers such as 'Ogo Pogo' in 1925, to pure dance numbers like the 'Charleston' (1925) and 'Sunrise Serenade' (1939). In 1919, 32 per cent of the most popular songs were of this variety, and 23 per cent in 1935. The 1920s in particular saw a succession of upbeat 'crazy words, crazy tune' numbers reaching hit status. A genre of ever-optimistic songs and films remained popular during the depression and subsequent international crises, however. Defiantly cheerful titles such as 'Happy Days are Here Again' (1930), 'On the Sunny Side of the Street' (1930), and 'Blue Skies are round the Corner' (1939) hoped to provide escape from the contemporary gloom. Such songs championed patience and consensus, optimism and stability; a simple philosophy of 'laugh now, think about it tomorrow'. Perhaps the greatest advocate of this philosophy was

---

[38]   G. Orwell, 'The Art of Donald McGill', in *The Penguin Essays of George Orwell* (1984), 208.

Gracie Fields and the titles of some of her most popular songs reveal this tendency. Songs such as 'Looking on the Bright Side of Life', 'Sing as We Go', and 'Look Up and Laugh' celebrated the supposed working-class virtues of good humour and sanguinity in the face of adversity and championed the idea of self-reliance and individuality.

This 'escapist' tendency was highlighted by Tom Harrisson, who described popular music under the blanket term 'jazz', as 'mass-poetry' and 'a new folk-lore', seeing it as fulfilling an escapist role. Analysing the lyrics of the most popular songs of the period in 'Whistle While You Work', he drew attention to their optimism, their ability to turn 'death into eternity, despair into personal moments and hope'. Harrison observed a fascination with dreaming and imagination, using the symbolism of paradise; focusing on heaven ('When did you leave Heaven?', 'Pennies from Heaven'), blue skies, the moon ('Moonlight on the Highway', 'Silver Sails on Moonlit Waters'), the wind and the rain. He concluded: 'Jazz has become or is becoming the religious ritual of post-war youth, and these songs of hope and happiness in a dreamworld every moon-night are the hymns of young England.'[39] The Federation of British Music Industries, established to further the interests of businesses concerned with music and music making, promoted the idea that popular music served its best use when it was 'light' and 'trivial'. The main thrust of its propaganda was that music deserved to be enjoyed as a recreation, not as a high-minded 'improving' exercise. It commended music as 'entertainment pure and simple. It is recreation. It is diversion. Let us enjoy it like that, and . . . think of it less as a serious interest . . . an improving interest.'[40]

The collective impact of such songs was to focus attention on the personal and individual, and support a philosophy of laughter and calm in the face of crisis. The extent to which the audience for popular music took any notice of such lyrics is open to question, however. A 1939 Mass-Observation survey suggests that many people were not even able to remember the words of songs, let alone adopt their sentiments. Asked whether people were able to remember the words to songs the majority of people, 71 per cent, said no, with only 16 per cent saying yes.[41] The survey also suggest that many people disliked the lyrics of songs. Only 13 per cent

[39] T. Harrison, 'Whistle While You Work' in *New Writing* (Winter 1938), 66.
[40] *FBMI Journal*, Sept. 1925, p. 71.
[41] Calculated from a sample of 100 respondents (50 male, 50 female) in M-O A: Directive Reply: 'Jazz (Jan. 1939).' 13% gave no answer.

approved of the words of popular songs, with 54 per cent disapproving, and 34 per cent unsure.[42] Such evidence is inconclusive, however, as it is clear that many people enjoyed singing and learning the lyrics to popular songs. Tom Harrisson's survey of Bolton dance halls also points to the fact that many girls wrote the words of songs down, from the radio or gramophone recordings, and they kept them in their handbags.[43] It was fashionable to be able to sing along to the latest 'hits'. It does not automatically follow, however, that people accepted the 'message' contained within lyrics blindly—most people, perhaps, liked singing the lyrics but at the same time were aware of their limitations. It is also likely that most people regarded the lyrics, and the music, as little more than entertainment, pure and simple.

8.3 The determination of popular tastes

Although the public for popular music were free to choose the styles and songs that most suited them, they were the subject of intense pressure from all parts of the popular music industry to choose certain styles or artists over others. In addition, the content and nature of popular music was to some extent regulated by official bodies, which hoped to shape the music according to their tastes, rather than those of the general public.

The making of 'hit' songs and the marketing of popular music was taken seriously by the popular music industry. To a large extent, the market for particular songs or artists was deliberately 'created' by the use of large 'plugging' campaigns, which sought to 'push' the products of music publishers, recording companies, singers, dance bands, etc. It is true that certain songs were 'natural hits', requiring little promotion and gaining success on their own merit. Some songs had that certain 'something', seeming to fit the public mood and tastes at any given time. Jack Payne described this phenomenon in 1936:

Some tunes, like some film stars, undoubtedly possess 'it.' Scientists, who are busy in their laboratories analysing the 'it' of film stars, have not yet found a recipe for a 'catch' song. 'When is the birth of its fame?' is as enigmatical to solve as 'Where do flies go?' for one day the tune simply isn't, and the next morning, lo and behold, it is famous . . . The 'hit' is usually a fluke . . . They fill the needs of the popular demand at that moment, in the same way as one's palate suddenly

---

[42] M-O A: MDJ: 8/B: Wandsworth Jazz Survey, July 1939.
[43] Harrison, 'Whistle While You Work', 48–67.

craves for sweet delicacies and must be appeased by cream buns or chocolate eclairs.[44]

The majority of 'hits', however, were at least partly the result of major marketing campaigns. We have already seen how the vast machinery of the popular music industry was used to promote dances like the Lambeth Walk, the Chestnut Tree, and the Park Parade. Such techniques were used habitually by the popular music industry.

To some involved in providing popular music, the audience was a passive and pliable force whose tastes could easily be manipulated. One 'anonymous well-known British band Leader' complained of those who pandered to the public, arguing that

they think that audiences have a very clear idea of what they like and dislike. Actually . . . they have not. The great majority of them like just what they are told to like . . . If an expert, real or self-appointed, tells them that they should like a certain thing—then they do like it. Or think they do; which amounts to very much the same thing . . . Their views can be moulded. They do not know what they want; consequently they can be made to want almost anything.[45]

The massive amount of expenditure put into promoting particular songs illustrates the extent to which others in the popular music industry considered this to be true—rightly or wrongly.

Song plugging was nothing new; it had been around ever since the popular music publishing industry had begun, with representatives from all of the music publishing companies touring theatres, music halls, seaside resorts, etc. trying to sell their products to performers. Seaside resorts like Blackpool and the Isle of Man had numerous 'song booths' where the music publishers would also try to sell their music to the public. Demonstration shops were also established in Blackpool and at various other coastal resorts and by 1924 Lawrence Wright had twenty such shops in Blackpool alone. Blackpool was an important test of popular tastes. As a working-class mecca of entertainment and fun, if a song sold well in Blackpool it would most likely sell well in the rest of the country. Song selling techniques were hard-nosed and even before the First World War music publishers were prepared to spend heavily to promote their catalogues.

It was during the 1920s and 1930s, however, that song plugging reached its apotheosis, with music publishers enlisting the help of the new mass media forms of radio, gramophone, and mass circulation newspapers to

[44] J. Payne, *This is Jack Payne* (1932), 81–2.   [45] *BB*, Nov. 1934, p. 38.

promote their products. The most prolific exploiter of songs was Lawrence Wright, who gained a reputation for lavish promotion campaigns throughout the 1920s and 1930s.[46] Wright's first large promotion campaign was for the 1923 song 'Yes! We Have no Bananas', when he distributed free bananas with song copies for bandleaders and singers to give away to audiences. Elders and Fyffes, the banana importers, were so happy that they contributed £500 towards the campaign. In 1926, for the song 'I've Never Seen a Straight Banana' he offered £1,000 to anybody who could produce a straight banana, and thousands of bananas arrived through the post at his offices in Denmark Street. In the same year Lawrence Wright bought the whole front page of the *Daily Mail*, at a cost of £1,450, to advertise his song 'Among My Souvenirs'. It was the first time the *Daily Mail's* front page had been used in this way by any advertiser. More elaborate stunts were used in 1927. For promotion of the song 'Me and Jane in a Plane' Wright hired an aeroplane from Imperial Airways and put the complete Jack Hylton orchestra on it, flying low over Blackpool while the band played the new song. The plane circled Blackpool Tower whilst hundreds of copies were dropped onto the crowded beaches. In the same year Lawrence Wright engaged on his most elaborate plugging campaign, for the song 'Shepherd of the Hills'. Here he took advantage of the general publics' huge enthusiasm for new technology and its love of all things American. Billed as 'the 3000-miles-a-second-New York-London hit', the song was widely publicized as the first to be composed over the transatlantic telephone. Lawrence Wright composed the song in the United States, telephoning his composition, 'live', to his London Office. It was then orchestrated and printed up, and played the same evening by the Jack Hylton Orchestra at the London Alhambra Theatre. A smash hit song, composed in America and played in London on the same day. It was a huge success. When Lawrence Wright arrived back from the United States of America a shepherd and a flock of sheep were taken from Victoria to Southampton to meet the boat.

In the promotion of a song or dance number there were several key institutions. First were the music publishing companies who were trying to promote or sell certain songs. Next there were the dance bands or other artists who were persuaded to perform the songs and include them in their repertoire. Finally there was the radio, which promoted particular songs by inclusion in broadcasts, and the gramophone companies who recorded the songs and also promoted them.

[46] Information in this paragraph from E. Rogers, *Tin Pan Alley* (1964), 45–50.

Each of the major music publishing companies established large 'professional departments' whose sole concern was the promotion of songs on their catalogue. The most important people involved in the 'plugging' campaign were the professional manager, the arranger, the orchestral manager, and the recording manager. Music publishers were skilled in spotting what they considered would sell. Once a song had been accepted by a publisher, the professional manager had the job of contacting singers, performers, and theatrical agents with the aim of getting as many as possible to work the number onto the stage.

Next in the process, the arranger would transform the basic melody of the song into a form suitable for dance bands or particular artists to perform. The arranger was 'the architect who builds up a musical house from the composer's ground plan'.[47] It was the job of the orchestral manager to get the dance bands to feature the number as soon as possible. Orchestral managers had close contacts with the leading dance bands: most importantly those with broadcasting and recording contracts. Thus the orchestral manager attempted to persuade radio bands to feature the song on their broadcasts, and they were prepared to break the BBC's rules and pay artists to do this. In addition, the recording manager had contacts in the gramophone companies and would persuade recording artists and gramophone company officials to record as many versions of the song being promoted as was possible. This highly orchestrated campaign involved large sums of money. The music publishers were prepared to go a long way to get their numbers promoted, and this led inevitably to abuses.

The use of song plugging on the radio was very contentious. Radio had been used as a medium for promoting particular songs from its beginning in the 1920s, and as it grew in popularity it provided a huge potential audience. Thus it was important for the music publishers to ensure that their numbers were broadcast as often as possible. On average, it was estimated by music publishers that fifty radio plugs would make a tune a 'hit'.[48] Officially the BBC outlawed the use of radio for this purpose, but the practice flourished. Song pluggers from each of the music publishers would offer their products to the leaders of broadcasting dance bands and solo artists. Payments were made, and payment soon became expected as a right by the dance band leaders. By the 1930s, for example, Harry Roy was collecting as much as £750 per week in 'plug money' from record

[47] *PMDW*, 27 Oct. 1934, p. 4.
[48] M-O A: File Report 11A, 'Jazz and Dancing', 21 Nov. 1939, p. 20.

companies and song publishers.[49] Each broadcasting plug would cost about £30, but such an outlay could result in sales of 5,000 copies of sheet music the day after a broadcast. Broadcasting bands were packing in as many tunes as possible per broadcast in order to get the maximum subsidy. Nat Gonella recalled a one-hour programme which contained no fewer than fifty-one paid plugs.

Such abuses were attacked by the popular press. The *Melody Maker* argued that the general public lost out because of monotonous programmes of repeated music with little variety, and laid the blame with the BBC:

The microphone is indisputedly the property of the nation and its custodian is the British Broadcasting Corporation. Whenever the latter calls the tune it does so at the voice of the people. When this power to call is permitted to fall from other lips, it must always be likely that the wrong master will call the wrong tune—and that is how things are at the present.[50]

The BBC did attempt to solve the problem of song plugging, but its efforts amounted to little. In the mid–1920s the BBC stipulated that only twelve numbers should be broadcast in one hour. The BBC met leading members of the Music Publishing Industry and signed a pact to stop the plugging epidemic; any publisher found to be continuing the practice was threatened with expulsion from the BBC. However, after a few months the abuses returned. Subsequent attempts by the BBC to prevent the practice also failed. The BBC, though worried, was not overtly concerned at the abuse, not least because the large sums of money being made by dance band leaders meant that they were less likely to agitate for higher fees from the BBC.

Radio song plugging affected popular tastes in several ways. First, it largely restricted the music heard on the radio to the output of the larger music publishers, since those firms who could not afford to pay for plugs were boycotted by the broadcasting artists. The larger music publishers were also able to exert considerable influence over many non-broadcasting bands. The effect was to narrow the repertoire from which bands could feel safe to choose. In 1936, the editor of *Musical News and Dance Band*, for example, advised bandleaders to play what the music publishers thought was best, arguing:

The publisher is obviously out to make money and it is only logical that he does not want bad or unattractive tunes. It costs a lot of money to buy, publish and publicise a number, and, naturally, from his vast experience of popular music, a

⁴⁹ Rogers, *Tin Pan Alley*, 127.   ⁵⁰ *MM*, Feb. 1929, p. 209.

publisher rarely buys badly. If he is offering you good music, surely you can rely on his judgement as well as put your own stuff over.[51]

Song plugging made it more difficult for new writers to enter the music publishing industry, as publishers were not prepared to take the risk of expensive marketing campaigns for the works of inexperienced writers.

Secondly, those dance bands with the most broadcasting time had the greatest influence over what was played on the air and thus in setting trends. Certain dance band leaders developed considerable control over the dance music output of the radio, and their dictatorial manner led to friction within the industry.[52] Leaders of small, non-broadcasting dance bands complained of the direct control of the 'best' songs by a small coterie of 'favoured bands'. Pre-releasing songs in this way had a detrimental effect on provincial bands, as one leader from Tunbridge Wells explained in a letter to the *Melody Maker*:

My band . . . is continually requested for numbers which patrons have 'heard on the radio' or on records. The numbers are not ready for publication, and it is difficult to make these enquirers believe this . . . This means, in many cases, that the tune is thoroughly stale and worn out before we get it.[53]

The quality of the songs broadcast was not always as high as it could have been either. Many dance band leaders made the publishing of their own compositions, most of which would not otherwise have been good enough for publication, a provision of featuring works from the music publishers' catalogues.[54]

The substantial sums of money involved in the song plugging process would suggest that music publishers considered it worthwhile. Although poorly written material would ultimately fail no matter how much plugging it received, it can be assumed that many songs became successful largely on the basis of the exposure afforded to them by plugging. This process was not new, but the medium of radio guaranteed a potential audience music publishers of previous eras could only have dreamt of.

But there were categories of song which the popular music industry did not want the public to hear and forms of censorship were used to ensure this. It has been pointed out by historians that the cinema did come under close scrutiny by the government via the British Board of Film Censors,

[51] *MNDB*, Nov. 1936, p. 5.
[52] M-O A: File Report 11A, 'Jazz and Dancing', 21 Nov. 1939, p. 20.
[53] *MM*, Mar. 1933, p. 175.
[54] M-O A: MDJ: 5/A, 'Melody Maker', 26 May 1939, p. 3.

which, though not officially a government agency, was effectively under the control of the Home Office.[55] This Board, together with the government's Cinema Advisory Council, censored material thought to be socially or politically sensitive. The BBC also steered clear of most things controversial. The BBC was acutely aware that the entertainment it provided was 'domestic' entertainment, going straight into people's homes, and not that enjoyed collectively in public places. Thus, 'bawdy' entertainment that would have been permissible in music halls was not permissible in BBC broadcasts. The BBC maintained strict rules concerning 'vulgarity' and 'good taste'. Jokes and songs which contained references to politics and politicians, advertisements, drink, clergymen, medical matters and human infirmities, Scotsmen and Welshmen, and, of course, overt references to sex were banned. Sunday broadcasting was particularly sensitive to these bans. Much variety and music-hall material was thus sanitized by its inclusion in BBC schedules.

Examples of songs which were banned reveal the extent of prudery within Reith's BBC. In 1932, among songs banned were 'I've Gone and Lost My Little Yo-Yo' recorded by Billy Cotton and His Band. Although fairly harmless, its *doubles entendres* offended the BBC watch committee. The chorus ran:

> I had it when I left the house at half past ten,
> I had it in me hand alright,
> I showed it to a woman at the corner then
> —it filled her with delight—
> The wife will want to play with it, when I get home,
> but I can't find it—oh! no!—
> She'll take the only course,
> and sue for a divorce,
> when she finds I've gone and lost me little . . . yo-yo!

In the same year a recording of the song 'She Was Only a Postmaster's Daughter' was also banned. It contained the following offensive punch lines:

> . . . She was only a postmaster's daughter
> but she knew how to handle her mail . . .
>
> . . . She was only a scoutmaster's daughter
> but couldn't that little girl guide? . . .
>
> . . . She was only a magistrate's daughter
> but she knew what to do on the bench!

[55] See J. Richards, *The Age of the Dream Palace* (1984), 90–107.

As time progressed the BBC relaxed its control slightly, but only very slightly. In 1936, for example, it was still puritanical enough to ban George Formby's popular 'When I'm Cleaning Windows' with its references to nudity and voyeurism, even though the song had been featured in the film *Keep Your Seats Please* released in March. A BBC announcer compèring a record request programme said that he had been asked to play the song but could not do so 'because the windows aren't quite clean enough yet'.[56] Reith himself declared, 'If the public wants to listen to Formby singing this disgusting little ditty they'll have to be content to hear it in the cinemas, not over the nation's airwaves.'[57] The BBC, furthermore, periodically placed restrictions on the nature and form of dance music. Indeed, the BBC's reorganization of dance music and popular music programmes in 1937 was, to a large extent, driven by the desire to have a firmer control over the content and nature of broadcasts.

The commercial radio stations also regulated their output. The IBC, for example, maintained its own Programme Acceptance Department which monitored the content of programmes. Although nothing obscene was ever broadcast, the commercial stations remained much more liberal than the BBC. Such flexibility, for instance, allowed Max Miller to boast 'You ought to hear me on Luxembourg on Sunday, I'm filthy!' This more flexible attitude was also found in the commercial gramophone companies. The gramophone companies' strategies for marketing and producing gramophone records reveal that there were no direct political or ideological restrictions. Nor does it appear that conscious attempts were made to foster a cultural defence of the status quo. In terms of government control there was no official government body created to deal specifically with the content of gramophone records. The main determinant of what was produced was saleability. Companies such as Columbia, HMV, Decca, and Parlophone were businesses first and foremost; this attitude was extremely important from the point of view of censorship.[58]

The Columbia Graphophone Company, as we have seen, retained close links with its American origins and was run under an American corporate style of management. The managers of this company were Americans and as a result its company culture was very entrepreneurial. Columbia's policy was only commercial: it would release anything that it

[56] A. Randall and R. Seaton, *George Formby: A Biography* (1974), 73.

[57] Quoted in D. Bret, *George Formby: A Troubled Genius* (1999), 54.

[58] For this information I am indebted to Mr Dmitri Coryton and the EMI Music Archives.

thought would sell. The same was true of the Gramophone Company. There were, however, certain limits to this; although there were no formal restraints on the gramophone industry, at least none comparable to those placed on the film industry, there were numerous informal ones. The centralized nature of two of the gramophone industry's most important producers, the Gramophone Company and, to a lesser extent, Columbia, meant that the people at the centre of these large companies had some degree of control over what was recorded. As has been shown, the gramophone companies were anxious in the 1920s to transform the reputation of the gramophone and appeal to 'respectability'. They were inclined to avoid the most avant-garde in popular music, jazz and swing for example, and to produce more sanitized versions of popular idioms. Thus, although jazz was produced it was not in large quantities.

There were several instances, however, of the gramophone companies being directly involved in censorship of popular songs. George Formby's song 'With My Little Ukulele in My Hand' was first recorded on 1 July 1933 but withdrawn before release because the original lyric was considered offensive by the Decca Record Company.[59] Although the several copies of the original version were sent for review, and appeared in the August issue of the *Gramophone* without any outcry, Decca insisted that a slightly modified version be substituted, and a new version, retitled 'My Ukulele' was recorded on 12 November 1933. The changes were slight and indicate oversensitivity on Decca's part. The offending lyrics, 'She said your love just turns me dizzy, come along big boy get busy, but I kept my ukulele in my hand' were changed to 'She said your love just turns me cuckoo, I indeed to goodness luck you [*sic*], but I kept my ukulele in my hand'. 'I could see it was a boy 'cause he had *a* ukulele in his hand' was changed to 'I could see it was a boy' cause he had *my* ukulele in his hand'. Several American recordings were also banned by British gramophone companies. The 1934 song 'Old Man Mose' sung by Patricia Norman with Eddy Duchin and His Orchestra, was originally released in Britain on the Parlophone label. The song soon attracted considerable attention, however, as the recording appeared to feature Patricia Norman substituting the 'b' of 'Oh bucket' with an 'f'. Modern reproducing techniques reveal that she hadn't, although she tried hard to sound ambiguous. The recording was withdrawn from sale immediately. Cole Porter's 'Love for Sale', a song about a prostitute, was also banned. Although several dance bands recorded the tune, the record companies would not allow the lyrics to be recorded. A similar arrangement was made with Noel Coward's

[59] Randall and Seaton, *George Formby*, 59.

'Green Carnations', a song about homosexuality. The policy was not consistent, however, as a 1927 recording 'Masculine Women, Feminine Men', which included the lament 'boys were boys, and girls were girls, when I was a tot, now we don't know who is who and even what's what' passed by without attention.[60]

Thus, although the gramophone companies were more liberal than both the BBC and the film companies in their attitudes to censorship, and despite there not being a central authority to censor their material, they did impose a degree of self-regulation, steering clear of overtly controversial material and upholding contemporary notions of what was 'decent' in popular culture.

Conclusion

One of the most striking features of tastes in popular music from 1918 to 1939 is the variety and catholicity of preferences. This was because the majority did not choose one type of music to the exclusion of other types and a huge variety of different styles were evident—traditional forms coexisted with more modern styles. Importantly though, the popular music of the period was dramatically transformed as it became subject to increasing foreign influences. Popular music in Britain became more cosmopolitan, originating from a host of countries from the Mediterranean to Latin America. The greatest changes in popular music, however, were brought about by growing Americanization. American songs, American tunes, and American firms increasingly dominated British popular music and the popular music industry. This domination caused considerable concern for the survival of British creativity, but despite this British written songs remained popular, especially in the later part of the period. Americanization did bring about changes in the content of the songs. Popular music in Britain began to lose its parochial nature and became increasingly concerned with the universal theme of love and romance. Tastes in popular music were also shaped by a popular music industry which used a variety of different sophisticated marketing techniques. Although people were still free to pick and choose as they wished, tastes were increasingly influenced by the production policies of such companies. Limited forms of censorship and self-regulation meant that such companies were sanitizing popular music whilst also standardizing what people were listening to.

---

[60] Recorded by Savoy Havana Band on HMV B–5027, Feb. 1926.

CONCLUSION

When war was declared in 1914 the popular music industry provided a diversion on both the home and fighting fronts through music-hall artists, marching bands, and brass bands in the music halls, theatres, and public houses of Britain. In the home the piano and sheet music made sure that the 'home fires' kept burning and the music played was overwhelmingly traditional. It was produced predominantly by British authors and performed by British artists, with only limited exposure to the new American rhythms of ragtime. By the outbreak of the Second World War in 1939, popular music was largely provided by the radio, gramophones, newsreels, films, and the music was a British interpretation of a largely American medium. Between 1918 and 1939 popular music and the popular music industry had been transformed and this transformation had important effects.

The central aim of this book has been to examine the changes in popular music and the popular music industry and their impact on interwar British society and culture. Several important themes have emerged. First, by 1939, virtually all aspects of the supply and creation of popular music in Britain had been touched by commercialism. Recreations such as dancing were provided by chains of public dance halls, films were controlled by circuit cinemas, and domestic amusement was usurped by the radio and by the gramophone as supplied by large multinational companies like HMV, Columbia, and Decca. Despite the dominance of the BBC, even broadcasting was transformed by the commercial radio stations. Secondly, mass production and commercialism were helping to bring about an increasingly 'democratic' culture, making products and entertainments available to an ever-increasing number of people, regardless of class or region and appealing directly to the demands of the working and lower middle classes. Thirdly, the influx of American popular music, the introduction of American business methods and the commercially motivated appeal to 'popular tastes' meant that this culture was increasingly 'Americanized'. It was similar to the American-style democracy in which consumerism was of growing importance and rigid notions of class were less evident. In addition, businesses were, in the end, ready to exploit mass markets regardless of conventional notions of cultural 'worth'. Fourthly, these changes were helping to bring about an increasingly standardized and uniform popular music that was influential in redefining 'national culture'.

In an important sense, the application of the profit motive to cultural production was democratic. Reflecting the increasing purchasing power of the working and lower-middle class, businesses involved in the supply of entertainment had to appeal directly to their biggest potential market. Popular music, as provided by the gramophone companies, radio stations, and music publishers had, by necessity, to appeal to, as well as to manipulate, popular tastes. Thus, gramophone companies increasingly abandoned notions of cultural respectability. Popular music sold well and to ignore this market was commercial suicide. The form of the music also changed and the more complex forms of jazz and dance music were simplified to make them more accessible to popular tastes. Similarly, in the dance hall, businesses such as Mecca deliberately targeted a mass market and in doing so transformed the atmosphere of the halls. In the cinema, popular music was an essential element in the selling of films and the promotion of singers and dance bands was an important weapon used by studios to attract audiences. Even the BBC, outside the main thrust of commercialization, had to respond to the developments in the popular music industry and to the style of the commercial radio stations.

This process meant that the voice of popular culture within the nation's culture as a whole was increasingly prominent. The influence of popular music culture, in particular, was striking. Its symbols were everywhere. So were its stars. News of dance band leaders, crooners, and popular heroes such as Formby and Fields filled the newspapers and the gossip columns of magazines. Periodicals such as *Radio Pictorial* and *Popular Music Weekly* featured gossip about every aspect of these stars' lives. The numerous fan clubs that sprang up developed hero worship into a professional business. The popular music industry, in disseminating the tastes of the 'ordinary' man and woman, celebrated the ordinary. This move is reflected in the romanticism, sentimentality, and 'backyardism' of the popular music of the time. The gramophone and radio were also a crucial part of a new culture of domestic enjoyment. Built up around them was an intimate, private enjoyment which served to resocialize relationships at home and to stabilize and make safe a popular culture that was sometimes regarded as dangerous. In so doing the popular music industry was responding to and exploiting the popular demand for entertainment and helping to make popular music increasingly audible.

Such transformations meant that the audience for popular music was one of an unprecedented scale. Virtually everyone, regardless of class, age, or location, had access to some sort of popular music and most had a greater choice than ever before. The gramophone, wireless, dance halls, and cinema provided high-quality entertainment for a relatively low cost and the majority of the population benefited. This expansion of entertainment and recreation improved the quality of the lives of those it touched, in ways comparable to and complementary to the availability of cheap food and better housing, electricity, and cheaper clothing.

In addition to providing excellent entertainment, the widespread commercialization and mechanization of production was widening the cultural horizons of its consumers. Products and experiences became available to a public which had previously been denied them. Music played a larger role in the daily life of the majority of people than at any other time in history and the gramophone and radio did much to improve levels of musical appreciation. Music of all sorts, including classical music, was brought to an ever widening audience. People also became less tolerant of second-rate performance. Radio was a powerful force in the cultural improvement of the nation. The public service ethos of the BBC, outside the commercial thrust of much of mass culture, meant that radio could be used as both entertainer and teacher. Despite huge inadequacies and a tendency to trivialize, even commercial radio, together with newsreels and mass circulation newspapers, were making the interwar generation better informed than virtually all who had preceded it.

Concerned at an increasingly democratic popular culture which seemingly threatened an 'educated' culture, a minority of critics (social commentators, writers, politicians) attacked popular music for its direct appeal to popular tastes, describing it as 'common' or 'vulgar'.[1] The process of commercialization, affecting the production and dissemination of popular songs and dances, was criticized for bringing about a levelling down of cultural standards. The rationale of the market restricted publishers to reliable, attested musical styles which tended to become formulaic and 'predigested' with a lack of innovation.

The appeal to popular and thus universal tastes was equated with the 'trivial' and 'escapist'. The music of the period became, it was argued, increasingly both saccharine and melancholic, concerned with love and

[1] See F. R. Leavis, *Mass Civilisation and Minority Culture* (1930) and id., *Culture and Environment* (1933), H. Durant, *The Problem of Leisure* (1938), and E. S. Woods, *Some Aspects of the Problem of Leisure* (Birmingham, 1937).

romance. The quick turnover in the number of songs led some critics to argue that this was evidence of an inferior product. Music-hall songs often remained popular for several years, whereas the popular music industry in the interwar period was characterized by a string of 'fly by night' hits. However, there is little to suggest that the popular music of the interwar period was worse than that of any other period. On the contrary, it was a very creative time, with a large number of works of merit being produced in both Britain and America. The songs, if anything, were less vulgar than those of the music hall, because of the self-regulating nature of the popular music industry. The increased turnover in hit songs was less an indication of their lack of durability and more a reflection of the quickening pace of the industry. That so many of the songs of the period are still known today is testament to their resilience and quality as entertainment. The focus on 'trivial' and 'domestic' concerns was in part because of the need to appeal to an estimation of 'popular tastes'.

Importantly, the objections of a cultural elite reflected the fact that the growing influence of the gramophone companies, cinemas and film studios, and music publishers in the supply and creation of popular music had caused a shift in the established cultural hierarchy. The increasing primacy of commercial determinants, based on an attempt to reflect popular tastes, was eroding old notions of what was good and bad in cultural terms. Such a process increasingly bypassed traditional forms of cultural criticism and gave greater power to businessmen who had little or no direct musical skills. 'Popular culture' was being shaped and led by these men and its increasing focus on entertainment value rather than any form of political or social criticism (as was sometimes true of the music hall) was seen as evidence of its lowered cultural value. Moreover, to those concerned at the rise of the working class as a political force, as many were in the aftermath of the First World War, the prevalence of a vociferous popular culture was a sign of the increased presence of this class in the life of the nation.

The changes in popular music and the popular music industry between 1918 and 1939 presented a challenge to 'authentic' working-class culture. The growth of music making as an industry was used by critics to suggest that a 'synthetic' culture was being imposed on the people.[2] F. R. Leavis and others complained of loss of this authentic culture. By the 1930s, popular music was produced and disseminated by a highly centralized,

---

[2] See Durant, *Problem of Leisure*, Leavis, *Culture and Environment*, and Woods, *Some Aspects of the Problem of Leisure*.

highly commercialized industry. The profit motive saw businesses deliberately fostering a mass audience by creating and recreating markets for goods that otherwise had no 'natural' demand, it was argued. Millions of pounds were spent developing advanced techniques of exploitation with manufacturers employing advertising with increasing ruthlessness in the face of rising competition. The products of the popular music industry— musical instruments, gramophone records, sheet music, stage shows, and so on—were not 'necessities', in the sense that clothes, houses, and food were. Music was a 'luxury' product and thus had to be sold to the public over and above other non-necessities, of which there was an enormous increase in the period after the First World War. Markets, such as that for the gramophone, were newly created at the end of the nineteenth century and it took sophisticated marketing techniques and considerable research and development to make the gramophone commercially viable. Other sections of the music industry deliberately fostered demand for their products.

The new media based forms of popular music, and those who controlled them, had a significant effect in determining levels of demand and the development of tastes, but the degree to which a culture was imported by such media was easily exaggerated. It was accepted by some contemporaries that demand for new forms of leisure, for example, the palais-de-danse, jazz or dance music, and gramophone records was, to some extent, 'real' and that the general public actually wanted them. Also, even though there *was* an increasing tendency for this culture to be imported, divorcing 'the people' from the centres of cultural production and eroding popular control, it is doubtful whether large numbers of them had ever created their own music. To a very large degree, the popular music industry was appealing to, and reflecting the tastes of, the working-class and lower-middle-class community to an extent not previously seen. Although consumers lost control of music creation, they did have the ultimate economic sanction: which was not to buy it.

One of the most important themes of this book has been the extent to which there was Americanization of the popular music industry. An insistent nationalistic note of anti-Americanism ran through much of the period's harshest objections to popular music, as in so much else. The growing Americanization of popular music in interwar Britain is undeniable. The popular music industry in Britain was closely linked to that in America. The British gramophone industry remained tied commercially to its counterparts in America. The commercial radio stations through links with advertisers and programme production agencies such as J. Walter

Thompson were using American exploitation techniques and presentation styles. The music publishers also used American business methods in order to sell their songs. Moreover, there was direct influence from America and the popular music industry was dominated by American products. A craze for all things American began to take root in Britain shortly after the end of hostilities, as the general public lapped up the accents, mannerisms, songs, styles, and catchphrases of American film stars, crooners, and jazz musicians. Such developments were seen by some as detrimental to the survival of British musical creativity. James Burke described America as 'the cultural centre of the world' and feared its pernicious spread. 'Hollywood wisecracking gets into the brain', Burke argued, 'and the blues rhythm gets into the blood.'[3] Some critics were particularly mindful of the spread of American slang and mannerisms, not only through the cinema but also through popular songs.

Much of the criticism directed against this Americanization of popular music was a reflection of anxiety about Britain's changing position in the post-Great War world. Although outwardly Britain had emerged triumphant from the conflict, economically and politically its position was weakened. The spread of American popular culture was particularly pertinent as it was a visible sign of the new confidence of the United States after the First World War and of its cultural predominance. Moreover, this Americanization was potentially a direct domestic threat to the British social status quo. The triumph of American capitalism and the spread of American democracy threatened the comparatively rigid hierarchical class system prevalent in Britain.

Concern from within musical and intellectual circles about the vitality of 'authentic' British culture amidst this perceived 'American invasion' was also responsible for a sustained racist attack on popular music. The black American origins and associations of jazz music and the Jewish-American origins of many popular songs, were seen by some as another threat to British culture. It is important to note, however, that in general there was no widespread anxiety about the racial origins of popular music among the wider general public. Black American musical artists had been familiar in Britain in the music halls and in minstrel shows before the First World War, but had not attracted much attention. That they were the target of attacks after the First World War is a reflection both of the increased influence of music of black origin and the cultural crisis that followed the conflict. Racist attacks from the press, the Church, the

---

[3] Quoted in V. Cunningham, *British Writers of the 1930s* (Oxford, 1988), 288.

police, and 'serious' musicians against black music were symptomatic of a perceived crisis of authority. The majority of the wider British public did not have strong feelings towards black artists one way or the other, viewing them as just one of a variety of 'entertainers' with as much right to work as any other. In short, they had 'novelty' value. The ethnic communities in Britain at this time were small and blacks thus perceived as no threat. The black American artists Duke Ellington, Fats Waller, Benny Carter, and Louis Armstrong all visited Britain, and were received warmly by the majority of people. Some black Americans, such as Adelaide Hall and Paul Robeson, even chose to settle in Britain, arguing that conditions, as in the rest of Europe, were more liberal than in America.[4]

The extent to which British traditions of popular music became overwhelmed by music of an American, Negro, and Jewish origin is, however, easy to overstate. In response to the growing Americanization, a distinctively British popular music was reasserted. Popular musicians increasingly called for positive action to halt Britain's cultural dependence. For example, the *Melody Maker* in 1935 compared the situation of the British popular song to that of the British film, demanding protection in the form of a Quota Bill similar to that given to the film industry in 1927. The BBC was called on by leading members of the popular music industry to introduce a quota of British songs. Anti-Americanism also manifested itself as the threat of expulsion for American musicians performing in Britain and in the ridiculing of those non-Americans who played the Americanized dance styles. As a bulwark against the Americanization of popular music, there was a growing tendency to develop a distinctive British style of playing, which was largely a result of the survival of traditional musical training by many who were influential in British popular music. The international idiom of jazz and dance music underwent a transformation in Britain between 1918 to 1939, where it was Anglicized—shaped to local conditions by assimilating some of the nation's traditional musical styles and techniques. The leading dance bands hardly ever played what the minority critics and connoisseurs would have called jazz. They had created an almost entirely new musical form. They appropriated elements of jazz and adapted it to the relatively conservative tastes of the British public. Older melodic forms and playing styles survived. The music became more formal, standardized, romantic, sentimental. The development of a British style was also a reflection of the tastes of the wider audience. Dance band leaders had begun to play what their audiences wanted.

[4] See NSA: 'Oral History of Jazz in Britain' interview, Adelaide Hall, Tape C122 54.

Most British interpretations of dance music—strict tempo, muted orchestrations, evenly balanced instrumentalists—were far removed from their American counterparts. 'The Teddy Bears' Picnic' as played by Henry Hall and the BBC Dance Orchestra, for example, was a world away from 'jam sessions' in Harlem basements, the high energy of a Benny Goodman swing session, or even the relatively ordered sound of Glenn Miller. People like Henry Hall and Jack Hylton had invested the international medium of jazz with a specifically British cultural idiom.

In other genres of popular music too, there were peculiarly British idioms. George Formby and Gracie Fields were the embodiment of this 'native' British popular culture. Both entertainers drew on a rich tradition based on the music hall and working-class Lancashire and gradually adapted it for use on a national level. Stars such as Noel Coward, Jack Buchanan, and Jessie Matthews were also quintessentially British in their appeal. There was foreign influence but it did not entirely replace the existing musical forms. In the works of entertainers like George Formby, for example, there was a fusion of genres. There was American dance music in the 'swingy' accompaniments to his ukulele and British music hall in Formby's 'patter' and delivery. Gracie Fields sang many 'standards' of the popular music world that were American in origin but she did so in an inimitable style. Although Formby and Fields were essentially 'national' stars with a peculiarly British appeal, regional stars with an even more limited parochial appeal thrived. This can also be seen in related aspects of the music hall tradition. Although they had appeal throughout the country, the backbone of support for stars such as Frank Randle, Sandy Powell, and Albert Mosely was in the north of England. For Max Miller and Tommy Trinder it was in the south.

Despite such regional variations, however, the interwar popular music industry's predominant effect was its contribution to the emergence of a 'common culture'. The developments in the popular music indutry —mechanization, centralization, mass production—were part of an increasing trend towards uniformity in leisure and cultural activities. In the interwar period, for the first time, nearly all of the regions of the British Isles could share in similar cultural experiences, regardless of class or location. Dance halls, cinemas, gramophone, radios were available to all.

A process of standardization can be clearly elucidated in the popular music industry. The highly centralized music publishing system which evolved after 1918 produced a standardized product. Creation of popular music became increasingly concentrated in the hands of a small number of 'professional' songwriters, employing a handful of stock devices and forms. The sophisticated 'plugging' campaigns orchestrated by the music publishers thrust chosen songs to the forefront of the public's attention and ensured that everyone sang from the same song sheet. The gramophone industry was particularly prone to centralization, becoming dominated by two huge companies by the end of the period. In addition, the gramophone and gramophone records were the first form of technology to allow exactly the same musical performances to be heard at any time throughout the country. Unlike the music making of the amateur, the gramophone record offered a pre-recorded, ready produced interpretation of a song or tune and there was little room for alternative interpretation. Although various versions of popular songs or classical works were available on records, there was a limited choice. This process of cultural duplication was completed by the radio and the cinema. There was, despite the survival of spontaneity, clearly a strong tendency to regulate and a powerful urge to control the popular culture created by such developments. Censorship, direct and indirect, was centred around the desire to appeal to the 'respectable' and to imbue cultural products with an air of decency. All signs of vulgarity and coarseness were increasingly eradicated. The regulating impulses of circuit palais-de-danse, cinemas, song publishers, gramophone companies, and the BBC were testament to this movement. Popular culture was undoubtedly being sanitized. However, the idea that popular music was an instrument for conscious social, cultural, and ideological conditioning is a doubtful one. The large gramophone companies of the interwar period were not subject to government interference and they did not produce records according to a set of political or moral guidelines. Records were produced primarily for commercial reasons, not political ones. If a record sold, it was acceptable. If it did not, it was not acceptable. The tastes of individual company directors were an influence on defining what was acceptable, but in comparison with the profit motive, they were relatively unimportant. The BBC, despite its critics, supplied a well-balanced programme of entertainment, with a heavy leaning to light and popular music notwithstanding its often draconian censorship. In addition, there is evidence to suggest that the main appeal of popular music was not any lyrical construction of certain ideals or beliefs. It is true that many songs focused on the trivial, the escapist, the theme of boy meets girl. Many did not address serious issues, attack institutions and ways of life. Why should they? They were, first and foremost, entertainment. If they did aim to promote the virtues of optimism, patience, independence, patriotism, this was no bad thing.

However, many of the popular songs were also satirical or comical, and the comical often had a subversive purpose.

In any case, it can be argued that by making possible the dance culture of the interwar years, popular music significantly increased the social and expressive possibilities of working-class life. Dancing increased the boundaries of sociability and the range of social freedom. For women it had particular significance: in dancing itself many found the same kind of cultural and physical creativity that men found in sport but which had hitherto been denied women. For working-class women, if not always for middle-class women, dancing and dance music was a wholly liberating force.

The increased availability of popular music arguably played a part in producing and maintaining the political stability of Britain at a time when it was experiencing great upheaval, both economically and socially. The gramophone, together with the wireless and cinema, promoted the evolution of a common culture in Britain. For those in regular employment, and this was always a majority, there was an opportunity to listen to the artists and music to which everyone was listening. The purchasing and playing of gramophone records, attendance at cinemas and dance halls, and listening to the wireless were cultural experiences repeated regularly and by many people, regardless of class or region. 'Hit' songs increasingly came to fix historical moments in the national consciousness, as 'Run, Rabbit, Run' did during the early months of the war: something almost everybody recognized. Such shared cultural experiences probably thereby helped to promote social cohesion. Dance music and dancing had a classless appeal. As Mendl pointed out:

Jazz music has permeated through all strata of society. It shows, so to speak, no respect of persons or classes, but exercises its stimulating or disturbing influence over rich and poor alike. Royalty and labourers, aristocrats and clerks, doctors and shorthand typists obey its call with a unanimity which we shall find amusing or disconcerting according to our outlook. Like the Pied Piper of Hamelin, the modern syncopator bids the children of our cities follow in his wake, and lo! they are prone to foot it to his strains.[5]

[5] R. W. S. Mendl, *The Appeal of Jazz* (1927), 83.

APPENDIX

The Most Popular Songs, 1919–1939

Key

Source

M-T = from musical theatre   F = from film   P-S = written solely as a popular song

Song Type

Cheer-up = Optimistic/Escapist   Dance = Dance only   Novelty = Miscellaneous songs   ROM = Romantic or love song   Jazz = Jazz song/dance

Date	Title	Origin	Source	Song Type
1919				
Jan.	Till the Clouds Roll by	USA	M-T *Oh Boy!*{GB *Oh! Joy!*}	Cheer-up
Feb.	I've Got the Sweetest Girl in Maryland	GB	M-T *Tabs*	ROM
Mar.	Everything is Peaches Down in Georgia	USA	P-S	ROM
	Missouri Waltz	GB	P-S	Dance
May	Indianola	USA	P-S	Dance
July	Smiles	USA	M-T *Passing Show of 1918*	ROM
	Tiger Rag	USA	P-S	Jazz
Sept.	Beautiful Ohio	USA	P-S	ROM
	A Good Man is Hard to Find	USA	P-S	ROM
	By the Camp Fire	USA	P-S	ROM
Oct.	Hindustan	USA	M-T{GB *Joy Bells*}	Dance
	Ja-Da	USA	P-S;{GB *Bran Pie*}	Jazz
Nov.	Till We Meet Again	USA	P-S	ROM
	That Old Fashioned Mother of Mine	GB	P-S	Comedy
	I Know where the Flies Go in the Wintertime	GB	P-S	Comedy
	Memories	USA	P-S	ROM
	Sand Dunes	GB	P-S	Comedy
Dec.	How Ya Gonna Keep 'Em Down on the Farm?	USA	P-S	Comedy
	Mammy O'Mine	USA	P-S	Novelty
1925				
Jan.	Doo Wacka Doo	USA	M-T{GB *Charlot's Revue*}	Jazz
	The Golden West	USA	P-S	Novelty
	Follow the Swallow	USA	P-S	Novelty
	Ogo Pogo	GB	P-S	Novelty
Feb.	Where's My Sweetie Hiding?	GB	P-S	ROM

Date	Title	Origin	Source	Song Type
Mar.	Mandy, Make up Your Mind	USA	M-T Dixie to Broadway	ROM
	I Want to Be Happy	USA	M-T No No Nanette	ROM
	Tea for Two	USA	M-T No No Nanette	ROM
	Alabamy Bound	USA	P-S	Novelty
	Rose Marie	USA	M-T Rose-Marie	ROM
	Indian Love Call	USA	M-T Rose-Marie	ROM
May	I'll See You in My Dreams	USA	P-S	ROM
June	Show Me the Way to Go Home	GB	P-S	Comedy
	Everybody Loves My Baby	USA	P-S	ROM
	Oh! Katharina	GB	P-S	ROM
July	The Toy Drum Major	GB	P-S	Novelty
	Oh! How I Miss You Tonight	USA	P-S	ROM
	Bouquet (I Shall Always Think of You)	GB	P-S	ROM
	Sunny Havana	GB	P-S	Dance
	Charleston	USA	M-T Running Wild	Jazz
	Did Tosti Raise His Bowler Hat when He Said Goodbye?	GB	P-S	Comedy
	Who Takes Care of the Caretaker's Daughter?	GB	P-S	Comedy
Aug.	Sweet Georgia Brown	USA	P-S	Jazz
	If You Knew Susie	USA	M-T Big Boy	ROM
	Ah-Ha!	GB	P-S	Comedy
	Don't Bring Lulu	USA	P-S	Comedy
Sept.	Save Your Sorrow for Tomorrow	USA	P-S	Cheer-up
	Steppin' in Society	USA	P-S	Jazz
	Yes Sir! That's My Baby	USA	P-S	ROM
	Ukulele Lady	USA	P-S	ROM

	Title	Country	Type / Show	Genre
	Pal of My Cradle Days	USA	P-S	Novelty
	Babette	GB	P-S	ROM
Oct.	Honey, I'm in Love with You	USA	M-T *Mercenary Mary*	ROM
Nov.	I Miss My Swiss	USA	P-S	Comedy
	Yearning (Just for You)	USA	P-S	ROM
	You Forgot to Remember	USA	M-T{GB *Co-Optimists*}	ROM
	I'm Gonna Charleston back to Charleston	USA	P-S	Jazz
Dec.	Sometime	USA	P-S	ROM
	Always	USA	M-T{GB *Co-Optimists*}	ROM
	Moonlight and Roses	USA	P-S	ROM
	I'm Knee Deep in Daisies	USA	P-S	ROM
	Paddlin' Madelin' Home	USA	P-S	ROM
	If You Hadn't Gone Away	USA	P-S	ROM
	Manhattan	USA	M-T *Garrick Gaieties*	Dance
1930 **Feb.**	Tip-Toe through the Tulips	USA	F *Gold Diggers of Broadway*	ROM
	Painting the Clouds with Sunshine	USA	F *Gold Diggers of Broadway*	Cheer-up
	Sunny Side up	USA	F *Sunny Side up*	Cheer-up
	I'm a Dreamer	USA	F *Sunny Side up*	ROM
	If I Had a talking Picture of You	USA	F *Sunny Side up*	ROM
	If You're in Love, You'll Waltz	USA	F *Rio Rita*	ROM
	Sweetheart We Need Each Other	USA	F *Rio Rita*	ROM
	Give Yourself a Pat on the Back	GB	P-S	Comedy
	I May Be Wrong	USA	M-T *Murray Anderson's Almanac*	ROM
Mar.	Singing in the Bathtub	USA	F *Show of Shows*	Comedy
	Dream Lover	USA	F *The Love Parade*	ROM
	My Love Parade	USA	F *The Love Parade*	ROM
	Nobody's Using It Now	USA	F *The Love Parade*	ROM
	With a Song in My Heart	USA	M-T{GB *Cochran's Revue of 1930*}	ROM

Date	Title	Origin	Source	Song Type
Apr.	Happy Days are Here Again	USA	F *Chasing Rainbows*	Cheer-up
May	Puttin' on the Ritz	USA	F *Puttin' on the Ritz*	Cheer-up
	Body and Soul	USA	M-T *Three's a Crowd*	ROM
June	Stein Song	USA	P-S	Novelty
	Ro-Ro-Rollin' along	USA	P-S	Cheer-up
	'Leven Thirty Saturday Night	USA	P-S	Dance
July	Singing a Vagabond Song	USA	F *Puttin' on the Ritz*	ROM
	On the Sunny Side of the Street	USA	M-T *The International Revue*	Cheer-up
	Song of the Dawn	USA	F *King of Jazz*	Jazz
	It Happened in Monterey	USA	F *King of Jazz*	ROM
	Molly	USA	P-S	ROM
	Like a Breath of Springtime	USA	P-S	ROM
	Around the Corner and under the Tree	USA	P-S	Novelty
	Should I?	USA	F *Lord Byron of Broadway*	ROM
	I'm in the Market for You	USA	F *High Society Blues*	ROM
Aug.	Amy	GB	P-S	Comedy
Sept.	Falling in Love Again	Other	F *The Blue Angel*	ROM
	When it's Springtime in the Rockies	USA	P-S	Novelty
Oct.	The King's Horses and the King's Men	GB	M-T *Folly to Be Wise*	Novelty
	Sing Something Simple	GB	M-T *Folly to Be Wise*	Cheer-up
	Dancing with Tears in My Eyes	USA	P-S	ROM
	Without a Song	USA	M-T *Great Day*	ROM
	Great Day	USA	M-T *Great Day*	ROM
Nov.	Beyond the Blue Horizon	USA	F *Monte Carlo*	ROM
	Oh Donna Clara!	GB	P-S	ROM

Dec.	Little White Lies	USA	P-S	ROM
	Confessin'	USA	P-S	ROM
	Bye, Bye, Blues	USA	P-S	ROM
	Elizabeth	USA	M-T *Wonder-Bar*	ROM
	Dancing on the Ceiling	GB	M-T *Ever Green*	ROM
1935 Jan.	Who's been Polishing the Sun?	GB	P-S	Cheer-up
	Winter Wonderland	USA	P-S	Novelty
	La Cucharacha	Other	P-S	Dance
	Roll along, Covered Wagon	GB	P-S	Nov/Dance
Feb.	Home James, and Don't Spare the Horses	GB	P-S	Comedy
	Blue Moon	USA	P-S	ROM
	Easter Parade	USA	M-T *As Thousands Cheer*	ROM
	What a Difference a Day made	USA	P-S	ROM
	His Majesty the Baby	USA	P-S	Comedy
Mar.	No! No! A Thousand Times No	USA	P-S	ROM
	Dancing with My Shadow	USA	P-S	ROM
	March Winds and April Showers	USA	P-S	ROM
Apr.	Home Again	USA	P-S	ROM
	Song of the Trees	GB	P-S	Comedy
	Getting around and about	GB	P-S	ROM
	Old Timer	GB	P-S	Novelty
May	Gentlemen! The King!	GB	P-S	Novelty
	The Girl with the Dreamy Eyes	GB	P-S	ROM
	Let's Have a Jubilee	USA	P-S	Novelty
June	Anything Goes	USA	M-T {GB *Anything Goes*}	Comedy
	You're the Top	USA	M-T {GB *Anything Goes*}	ROM
	I Get a Kick out of You	USA	M-T {GB *Anything Goes*}	ROM
	It's Easy to Remember	USA	F *Mississippi*	ROM

Date	Title	Origin	Source	Song Type
	Lullaby of Broadway	USA	F *Gold Diggers of 1935*	Dance/Nov.
	On the Good Ship Lollipop	USA	F *Bright Eyes*	Nov./Comedy
	Zing! Went the Strings of My Heart	USA	M–T *Thumbs up*	ROM
July	There's a Lovley Lake in London	GB	P–S	Comedy
	Me and the Old Folks at home	GB	P–S	Novelty
Aug.	South American Joe	GB	P–S	Comedy
	In a Little Gypsy Tea Room	USA	P–S	Novelty
	The Wheel of the Wagon is Broken	GB	P–S	Dance
	Red Sails in the Sunset	GB	P–S	ROM
Sept.	I Won't Dance	USA	F *Roberta*	ROM
	Lovely to Look at	USA	F *Roberta*	ROM
Oct.	Dinner for One, Please James	GB	P–S	Novelty
	Roll along Prairie Moon	USA	F *Here Comes the Band*	ROM
Nov.	Cheek to Cheek	USA	F *Top Hat*	ROM
	Every Single Little Tingle of My Heart	USA	P–S	Comedy
	The Rose in Her Hair	USA	F *Broadway Gondolier*	ROM
	I'll Never Say 'Never Again' Again	USA	P–S	ROM
Dec.	The General's Fast Asleep	GB	P–S	Novelty
	The Lady in Red	USA	F *In Caliente*	ROM
	I'm in the Mood for Love	USA	F *Every Night at Eight*	ROM
	You are My Lucky Star	USA	F *Big Broadcast of 1936*	ROM
1939 Jan.	Blue Skies are round the Corner	GB	P–S	Cheer-up
	The Umbrella Man	USA	M–T {GB *These Foolish Things*}	Novelty
	You Must Have Been a Beautiful Baby	USA	P–S	Comedy

Month	Title	Country	Type	Category
	Two Sleepy People	USA	F Thanks for the Memory	ROM
	Ferdinand the Bull	USA	P-S	Comedy
Feb.	Penny Serenade	USA	P-S	ROM
Mar.	Deep in a Dream	USA	P-S	ROM
	My Own	USA	F That Certain Age	ROM
May	The Beer Barrel Polka	Other	P-S	Novelty
	South of the Border	GB	P-S	ROM
June	Three Little Fishes	USA	P-S	Novelty
	One Day when We were Young	USA	F The Great Waltz	ROM
	Boomps-A-Daisy	GB	F Band Wagon	Dance/Novelty
	Deep Purple	USA	P-S	Dance
	Little Sir Echo	USA	P-S	Novelty
July	A New Moon and an Old Serenade	USA	P-S	ROM
	The Masquerade is over	USA	P-S	ROM
	I Get along without You Very Well	USA	P-S	ROM
Aug.	Heaven Can Wait	USA	P-S	ROM
Sept.	We're Gonna hang out the Washing on the Siegfried Line	GB	P-S	Cheer-up
	Wish Me Luck as You Wave Me Goodbye	GB	F Shipyard Sally	Cheer-up
	Run, Rabbit, Run	GB	M-T The Little Dog Laughed	Comedy
	Sunrise Serenade	USA	P-S	Dance
	Wishing (Will Make it So)	USA	P-S	ROM
Oct.	FDR Jones	GB	M-T The Little Dog Laughed	Cheer-up
	There'll Always Be an England	GB	P-S	Patriotic
	Lords of the Air	GB	P-S	Patriotic
	Wings over the Navy	GB	P-S	Patriotic
Nov.	A Man and His Dream	USA	F The Star Maker	ROM
	An Apple for the Teacher	USA	F The Star Maker	Dance
Dec.	In an Eighteenth Century Drawing Room	USA	P-S	Novelty

Note

The main source for this appendix was B. Rust and L. Lowe, *Top Tunes of 1912–1958 on Commercial Gramophone Records* (1959) which used data in the BBC Gramophone Library to give a month-by-month list of the most popular records for each year. The origin and source of these records was established using several sources. These were: K. Ganzl, *British Musical Theatre* (Basingstoke, 1986), vol. i: *1865–1914*, vol. ii: *1915–1984*; R. D. Kinkle, *The Complete Encyclopedia of Popular Music and Jazz 1900–1950* (New Rochelle, NY, 1974), vols. i–iv; S. Green, *Encyclopaedia of the Musical Theatre* (1977). In order to establish the 'song type', recordings were used from the National Sound Archive and private collections. Where recordings could not be located sheet music was used. (Bodleian Library, Oxford: Harding Collection and Twentieth Century British Popular Music Collection.) Where sheet music could not be found then estimations of 'song type' were made using Rust and Forbes, *Dance Bands on Record*.

SELECT BIBLIOGRAPHY

(1) Manuscript Sources

Bodleian Library, Oxford

Harding American Popular Music Collection, Music Reading Room
Twentieth Century British Popular Sheet Music Collection, Music Reading Room

BBC Written Archive, Caversham

WAC E2/2/1 and 2: Advertising in England by Foreign Stations (1) 1928–36 (2) 1937–8
WAC E2/365/1 and 2: International Broadcasting Company (1) 1930–3 (2) 1934–46
WAC E18/283/1 to 7: Radio Luxembourg, (1) Sept. 1931 to (7) July 1939
WAC R5/86/1: Radio Luxembourg 1935
WAC R5/87/1: Radio Luxembourg Listening Reports 1937–54
WAC R34/101: Advertising in Programmes, 1935
WAC R34/149: Advertising in Programmes, 1940–56
WAC R34/958: Policy (Commercial Broadcasting) 1935
WAC R34/959: Policy (Commercial Broadcasting) 1930–7
WAC R34/960: Policy (Commercial Broadcasting) 1928, 1937–9
WAC R34/961: History (Commercial Broadcasting), 1945
WAC R43/147: Publications

John Johnson Collection of Printed Ephemera, Bodleian Library, Oxford

Gramophones, File 1–3
Wireless, File 1–9
Dance Programmes, File 1–3

Mass-Observation Archive, University of Sussex

Directive Replies: Jazz (Jan. 1939); Jazz (2)
File Reports: FR 11A Jazz and Dancing; FR 33 Music Halls; FR 49 Gramophone Records; FR 295 Jazz (Bolton)
Topic Collection: Music, Dancing and Jazz 1938–41:
TC: MDJ/1: Observations in Dance Halls 1938–1939, Files A–K
TC: MDJ/2: Dances 1938–40, Files A–E
TC: MDJ/3: Dances, Professional Dancers and the Music Business, Files A–G
TC: MDJ/4: Musicians, Bands, Clubs and Instrument Makers, Files A–H
TC: MDJ/5: Dance Schools, Song Writers, Music Publications and Business, Files A–K

TC: MDJ/6: History and Theory of Jazz; Dance Teachers' Societies, Files A–K
TC: MDJ/7: Songs, Files A–E
TC: MDJ/8: Jazz Surveys 1939–41, Files A–E
TC: MDJ/9: Miscellaneous
Topic Collection: Town and District Surveys 1938–49: 1/E; 2/B; 2/C; 2/D; 2/E; 3/D; 7/C; 7/E; 11/A; 11/L; 17/D; 18/A; 19/C
Topic Collection: Worktown: WT 30/E; WT 48/C; WT 48/D; WT 48/E; WT 57/D; WT 60/D

National Sound Archive, British Library, London

Oral History of Jazz in Britain: tapes C122/19; C122/27–8; C122/41; C122/54–5; C122/144–5; C122/237; C122/262–4; C122/296–7
Catalogues, advertising material etc. for Decca, Edison-Bell, HMV, Parlophone, Regal-Zonophone
Recordings

Oxford City Council, Local History Archives

Register of Music & Dancing Licences granted in the City of Oxford, 1924–39: DO/MISC/15 and PO/MISC/16

Performing Right Society Archive, PRS, London

PRS A: Arbitration with BBC, 1937; Box 1–4
PRS A: Correspondence: Boosey/Campbell Connelly/Cinephonic Music/Lawrence Wright/Music Publishers and the BBC
PRS A: Musical Copyright Bill 1929; Box 1–2
PRS A: Report of Directors and Balance Sheets: 1915–1989; Box 125

(2) Printed Primary Sources

Unless otherwise stated, place of publication is London

Newspapers, journals, magazines, etc.

Ballroom and Band: The Journal of Better Dancing to Better Music
The Broadcaster Radio and Gramophone Trade Annual
Daily Express
Danceland
Dancing Times
FBMI Journal/Convention Journal
Gramophone
Gramophone Review of Records and Inventions
Gramophone and Talking Machine News
His Master's Voice and Gramophone News
Hot News and Rhythm Record Review

Melody Maker and British Metronome
Musical News and Dance Band
Music Dealer
Music Seller
The Music Seller Reference Book
Music Trades International
Music Trades Review
Musical Times
Performing Right Gazette
Phono Trader and Recorder
Phonograph and Gramophone Record
Picture Post
Popular Music and Dancing Weekly
Popular Music and Film Song Weekly
Radio Magazine
Radio Pictorial
Records: Journal of the Gramophone World
Rhythm
Songwriter
Sound Wave
Swing Music: A Monthly Magazine for Rhythm Clubs
Talking Machine News
Theatre Arts Monthly
The Times
Tune Times
Voice

Books, Pamphlets, Official Papers

ARRAM, D. D., and ASH-LYONS, L., *Musicians' Directory: Incorporating the Dance Musicians' Directory* (1932).

ARUNDEL, P., *This Swing Business: A Survey of British Dance Music Today* (1947).

BARNETT, H. T., *Gramophone Tips* (Old Portsmouth, 1927).

Board of Customs and Excise Statistics Office, *Annual Statement of Trade of the U.K. with other Countries* (1938/9).

Board of Trade, *Statistical Abstract for the United Kingdom* (1927/1937); later Central Statistical Office, *Annual Abstract of Statistics*.

CAMERON, C., LUSH, A. J., and MEARA, G., (eds.), *Disinherited Youth: A Report on the 18+ Age Group Enquiry Prepared for the Trustees of the Carnegie United Kingdom Trust* (Edinburgh, 1943).

CHISHOLM, C. (ed.), *Marketing Survey of the United Kingdom, 1937* (1938).

—— (ed.), *Marketing Survey of the United Kingdom, 1938* (1939).

DAVIS, B., *The Saxophone: A Comprehensive Course* (1932).

DURANT, H., *The Problem of Leisure* (1938).

Federation of British Music Industries, *The Directory of the British Music Industries, 1925* (1925).

—— *Annual Reports* (1920–5).

—— *What the Federation is Doing* (1925).

Final Report on the First Census of Production of the United Kingdom 1907 (1912).

Final Report on the Third Census of Production of the United Kingdom 1924, Part IV (1931).

Final Report on the Fourth Census of Production 1930, Part IV (1935).

Final Report on the Fifth Census of Production 1935, Part IV (1940).

Final Report on the Census of Production for 1948, Part 5L (1951).

GOFFIN, R., *Jazz from Congo to Swing* (1946).

Gramophone Companies (1929).

The Gramophone Year-Book and Diary, 1920: A Vade-mecum for Use of Gramophone Dealers, Factors and Manufacturers (1919).

HARRISSON, G., and MITCHELL, F. C., *The Home Market: A Handbook of Statistics* (1936).

HARRISSON, T., 'Whistle While You Work', in *New Writing* (Winter 1938).

—— 'A Dance is Born', for *Picture Post*, 12 Dec. 1938, p. 6.

—— 'Doing the Lambeth Walk', in C. Madge and T. Harrisson, *Britain by Mass-Observation* (Harmondsworth, 1939), 139–84.

HOWES, F., *Folk Music of Britain* (1937).

IBC, *Survey of Radio Advertising Penetration* (1935).

—— *This is the IBC* (1939).

—— *Radio Normandy Programme Book* (1938–9).

International Association for Social Progress, *Report of the British Section on New Aspects of the Problem of Hours of Work: Hours, Leisure and Employment* (1933).

JAMES, H. E. O., and MOORE, F. T., 'Adolescent Leisure in a Working-Class District', in *Occupational Psychology* (1940).

JEPHCOTT, P., *Girls Growing up* (1942).

JOAD, C. E. M., *Diogenes or the Future of Leisure* (1928).

JOHNSON, W. W., *The Gramophone in Education* (1936).

JONES, D. CARADOG, and University of Liverpool, *The Social Survey of Merseyside* (Liverpool, 1934), vols. i–iii.

LAMBERT, C., *Music Ho! A Study of Music in Decline* (1934).

LEAVIS, F. R., *Culture and Environment: The Training of Critical Awareness* (1933).

LEWIS, E. R., *No C. I. C.* (1956).

LEWIS, P. WYNDHAM, *Paleface: The Philosophy of the 'Melting Pot'* (1929).

Liverpool Council of Voluntary Aid, *Report on the Uses of Leisure in Liverpool* (Liverpool, 1923).

LOVEDAY, A., *Britain and World Trade: Quo Vadiums and Other Economic Essays* (1931).

MADGE, C., and HARRISSON, T., *Britain by Mass-Observation* (Harmondsworth, 1939).

MASSEY, P., 'Portrait of a Mining Town', *fact*, 8 (Nov. 1937).

Mass-Observation, *The Pub and the People: A Worktown Study* ([1943] repr. 1987).

MENDL, R. W. S., *The Appeal of Jazz* (1927).

MEYRICK, K., *Secrets of the 43: Reminiscences by Mrs. Meyrick* (1933).

MITCHELL, O., *The Talking Machine Industry* (1922).

MOSELEY, S. A., *Who's Who in Broadcasting: A Biographical Record of the Leading Personalities of the Microphone* (1933–6).

Musicians' Directory Incorporating the Dance Musicians' Directory (1932).

The Music Trade's Diary & Year Book (1920).

The Music Trade's Diary, Directory, and Year Book (1925, 1930, 1935).

The Music Trade's Review Reference Book (1939–40).

MYERS, S., and RAMSAY, E., *London Men and Women: An Account of the London County Councils' Men's and Women's Institutes* (1936).

National Conference on the Leisure of the People, *The Leisure of the People: A Handbook. The Report of the National Conference held at Manchester Nov 17th–20th 1919* (Manchester, 1919).

NELSON, S. R., *All about Jazz* (1934).

ORWELL, G., *The English People* (1947).

—— *The Lion and the Unicorn: Socialism and the English Genius* (1982).

—— 'The Art of Donald McGill', in G. Orwell, *The Penguin Essays of George Orwell* (1984), 199–209.

PAYNE, J., *This is Jack Payne* (1932).

PLANT, A., Incorporated Society of British Advertisers, and Institute of Incorporated Practitioners in Advertising, *Survey of Listening to Sponsored Programmes: Conducted in March 1938* (1938).

—— —— —— *Supplementary Survey of Listening to Sponsored Programmes: Conducted in November 1938* (1938).

PRIESTLEY, J. B., *An English Journey* (1934).

Radio and the Composer: The Economics of Modern Music (1935).

RICE, M. SPRING, and Women's Health Enquiry Committee, *Working-Class Wives: Their Health and Conditions* (Harmondsworth, 1939).

ROWNTREE, B. SEEBOHM, *Poverty and Progress: A Second Social Survey of York* (1941).

—— and Lavers, G. R., *English Life and Leisure* (1951).

SCHLEMAN, H. R., *Rhythm on Record* (1936).

SCHOLES, P. A., *Learning to Listen by Means of the Gramophone* (1921).

SHORT, E., and COMPTON-RICKETT, A., *Ring up the Curtain: Being a Pageant of English Entertainment Covering Half a Century* (1938).

SMITH, H. LLEWELLYN, and London School of Economics and Political Science, *The New Survey of London Life and Labour* (1930–5), ix: *Life and Leisure*.

SPURR, F. C., *The Christian Use of Leisure* (1928).

Stepping Out (1940).

STEWART, M., *Modern Dancing for Young and Old* (n.d.).

STONE, C., *Christopher Stone Speaking* (1933).

STORM JAMESON, M., 'The Soul of Man in the Age of Leisure', in anon., *The Social Credit Pamphleteer* (1935).

TURNBULL, S., *How to Run a Small Dance Band for Profit* (1937).

WILSON, G., *Gramophones, Acoustic and Radio* (1932).

WOODS, E. S., *Some Aspects of the Problem of Leisure: A Paper Read to the Birmingham Branch of the British Social Hygiene Council by The Right Rev. E. S. Woods, Bishop of Croydon* (Birmingham, 1937).

YOUNG, T., *Becontree and Dagenham: A Report Made for The Pilgrim Trust* (1934).

(3) Printed Secondary Works

ABBOTT, J., *The Story of Francis, Day & Hunter* (1952).

AGATE, J., *Immoment Toys: A Survey of Light Entertainment on the London Stage, 1920–1945* (1945).

AMSTELL, B., *Don't Fuss Mr. Ambrose: Memoirs of a Life Spent in Popular Music* (Tunbridge Wells, 1986).

BAILEY, P., *Music Hall: The Business of Pleasure* (Milton Keynes, 1986).

BARR, C. (ed.), *All Our Yesterdays: 90 Years of British Cinema* (1986; repr. 1996).

BATTEN, J., *Joe Batten's Book: The Story of Sound Recording* (1956).

BAXENDALE, J., 'Popular Music and Late Modernity, 1910–1930', in *Popular Music, 14* (1995), 137–54.

BENNETT, T., 'The Politics of "The Popular" and Popular Culture', in T. Bennett, C. Mercer, and J. Woollacott (eds.), *Popular Culture and Social Relations* (Milton Keynes, 1986).

BERGONZI, B., *Old Gramophones and Other Talking Machines* (1991).

BRANSON, N., and HEINEMANN, M., *Britain in the Nineteen Thirties* (1971).

BRET, D., *George Formby: A Troubled Genius* (1999).

BRIGGS, A., *The History of Broadcasting in the United Kingdom*, i: *The Birth of Broadcasting*, ii: *The Golden Age of Wireless* (New Edition, Oxford 1995).

BRIGGS, S., *Those Radio Times* (1981).

British Library, *Revolutions in Sound* (1988).

BROWN, R., and BROWN, C., *Georgia on my Mind: The Nat Gonella Story* (Portsmouth, 1985).

BUCKMAN, P., *Let's Dance: Social, Ballroom and Folk Dancing* (1978).

BURKE, P., 'The Discovery of Popular Culture', in R. Samuels (ed.), *People's History and Socialist Theory* (1981).

BURKE, T., *English Night-Life: From Norman Curfew to Present Black-out* (1941).

CAREY, J., *The Intellectual and the Masses: Pride and Prejudice among the Literary Intelligentsia, 1880–1939* (1992).

CHANAN, M., *Repeated Takes: A Short History of Recording and its Effects on Music* (1995).

COCHRAN, C. B., *Cock-A-Doodle-Do* (1941).

COPELAND, P., *Sound Recordings* (1991).

CUNNINGHAM, V., *British Writers of the 1930s* (Oxford, 1988).

DAVIES, A., *Leisure, Gender and Poverty: Working-Class Culture in Salford and Manchester, 1900–1939* (Buckingham, 1992).

EHRLICH, C., *Harmonious Alliance: A History of the Performing Right Society* (Oxford, 1989).

—— *The Music Profession Since the Eighteenth Century: A Social History* (Oxford, 1988).

FAIRLEY, R., *Come Dancing Miss World* (1966).

FIELDS, G., *Sing as We Go: The Autobiography of Gracie Fields* (1960).

FISHER, J., *George Formby* (1975).

FORD, B. (ed.), *Early Twentieth Century Britain*, vol. viii of *The Cambridge Cultural History* (Cambridge, 1992).

FOWLER, D., *The First Teenagers: The Lifestyle of Young Wage-Earners in Interwar Britain* (1995).

FOX, R., *Hollywood, Mayfair and all that Jazz: The Roy Fox Story* (1975).

FRANKS, A. H., *Social Dance: A Short History* (1963).

FRITH, S., 'Playing with Real Feeling: Jazz and Suburbia' in S. Frith, *Music for Pleasure: Essays in the Sociology of Pop* (Cambridge, 1988), 45–63.

—— 'The Making of the British Record Industry 1920–64' in J. Curran, A. Smith, and P. Wingate (ed.), *Impacts and Influences: Essays on Media and Power in the Twentieth Century* (1987), 278–90.

GAISBERG, F. W., *Music on Record* (1946).

GAMMOND, P., *The Oxford Companion to Popular Music* (Oxford, 1991).

GANZL, K., *British Musical Theatre* (Basingstoke,1986), i: *1865–1914*, ii: *1915–1984*.

GELATT, R., *The Fabulous Phonograph: The Story of the Gramophone from Tin Foil to High Fidelity* (1956).

GIFFORD, D., *The British Film Catalogue 1895–1985* (2nd edn., Newton Abbot, 1986).

—— *The Golden Age of Radio: An Illustrated Companion* (1985).

GLYNN, S., and OXBORROW, J., *Interwar Britain: A Social and Economic History* (1976).

GODBOLT, J., *A History of Jazz in Britain 1919–50* (1984).

—— *All this and 10%* (1976).

GRAVES, R., and HODGE, A., *The Long Week-end: A Social History of Great Britain 1918–1939* (1940; repr. 1990).

GREEN, S., *Encyclopaedia of the Musical Theatre* (1977).

GRONOW, P., 'The Record Industry: The Growth of a Mass Medium', in *Popular Music*, 3 (1983), 53–76.

GUY, S., 'Calling All Stars: Musical Films in a Musical Decade', in Richards, J. (ed.), *The Unknown 1930s: An Alternative History of the British Cinema 1929–39* (1998), 99–118.

HALSEY, A. H. (ed.), *Trends in British Society Since 1900: A Guide to the Changing Social Structure of Britain* (1972).

HOARE, P., *Noel Coward: A Biography* (1995).

HUSTWITT, M., 'Caught in a Whirlpool Sound: The Production of Dance Music in Britain in the 1920s', *Popular Music*, 3 (1983), 7–31.

JAMES, R. RHODES, *The British Revolution: British Politics 1880–1939* (1978).

JENKINS, T., *Let's Go Dancing: Dance Band Memories of 1930s Liverpool* (Liverpool, 1994).

JEWELL, B., *Veteran Talking Machines: History and Collector's Guide* (1977).

JOHNSON, R., 'Culture and the Historians', in J. Clark, C. Critcher, and R. Johnson (eds.), *Working Class Culture: Studies in History and Theory* (1979).

JONES, S. G., *Workers at Play: A Social and Economic History of Leisure 1918–1939* (1986).

KERNFELD, B., *The New Grove Dictionary of Jazz* (repr., 1996).

KINKLE, R. D., *The Complete Encyclopedia of Popular Music and Jazz 1900–1950* (New Rochelle, NY, 1974), vols. i–iv.

KOBAL, JOHN, *Gotta Sing, Gotta Dance: A History of Movie Musicals* (rev. edn., 1983).

LEE, E., *Music of the People: A Study of Popular Music in Great Britain* (1970).

—— *Folk Song and Music Hall* (1982).

LE MAHIEU, D., *A Culture for Democracy: Mass Communications and the Cultivated Mind in Britain between the Wars* (Oxford, 1988).

LESLEY, C., *The Life of Noel Coward* (Harmondsworth, 1976).

LOW, R., *The History of the British Film* (repr. 1997), iv: *1918–29*, v: *1929–39*.

LUDTKE, A., 'The Historiography of Everyday Life: The Personal and the Political', in R. Samuel and G. Stedman Jones (eds.), *Culture, Ideology and Politics* (1982).

MCCARTHY, A., *The Dance Band Era* (Radnor, Pa., 1982).

MCMILLAN, J., *The Way It Was 1914–1934: Based on the Files of Express Newspapers* (Kimber, 1979).

MARR, C., *The Chappell Story 1811–1961* (1961).

MARTLAND, P., *Since Records Began: EMI the First 100 Years* (1997).

MEDHURST, A., 'Music Hall and British Cinema', in C. Barr (ed.), *All Our Yesterdays: 90 Years of British Cinema* (1986 repr. 1996), 168–88.

MIDDLETON, R., *Studying Popular Music* (Milton Keynes, 1990).

MONTAGUE, R., *When the Ovaltineys Sang: A Salute to Some Intrepid Foreign Broadcasters of the 1930s* (rev. edn., Southend-on-Sea, 1993).

MOWAT, C. L., *Britain between the Wars 1918–1940* (1955).

NETTEL, R., *Seven Centuries of Popular Song: A Social History of Urban Ditty* (1956).

PALLETT, R., *Goodnight Sweetheart: Life and Times of Al Bowlly* (Tunbridge Wells, 1986).

PARKER, D., and PARKER, J., *The Story and the Song: A Survey of English Musical Plays, 1926–78* (1979).

PEARSALL, R., *Edwardian Popular Music* (Newton Abbot, 1975).

—— *Popular Music of the Twenties* (Newton Abbot, 1976).

PLEASANTS, H., *Death of a Music? The Decline of the European Tradition and the Rise of Jazz* (1961).

POPE, W. J. MACQUEEN, *The Melodies Linger on: The Story of Music Hall* (1950).
—— *Nights of Gladness* (1956).
RANDALL, A., and SEATON, R., *George Formby: A Biography* (1974).
READ, O., and WELCH, W. T., *From Tin Foil to Stereo: Evolution of the Phonograph* (New York, 1976).
RICHARDS, J., *The Age of the Dream Palace: Cinema and Society in Britain 1930–1939* (1984).
—— (ed.), *The Unknown 1930s: An Alternative History of the British Cinema 1929–39* (1998).
—— and Sheridan, D. (eds.), *Mass-Observation at the Movies* (1987).
RICHARDSON, P. J. S., *A History of English Ballroom Dancing 1910–1945: The Story of the Development of the Modern English Style* (1945).
ROBERTS, R., *The Classic Slum: Salford Life in the First Quarter of the Century* (Harmondsworth, 1973).
ROGERS, E., *Tin Pan Alley* (1964).
RUST, B., *British Music Hall on Record* (Harrow, 1979).
—— *British Musical Shows on Record 1897–1976* (Harrow, 1977).
—— *The Dance Bands* (1972).
—— and FORBES, S., *British Dance Bands on Record 1911 to 1945 and Supplement* (Harrow, 1989).
—— and LOWE, L., *Top Tunes of 1912–1958 on Commercial Gramophone Records* (1959).
RYAN, B., *George Formby: A Catalogue of His Work* (Dublin, 1986).
SCANNELL, P., and CARDIFF, D., *A Social History of Broadcasting* (Oxford, 1991).
SHAFER, S. C., *British Popular Films 1929–1939: The Cinema of Reassurance* (1997).
SEDGWICK, J., 'Cinema-Going Preferences in Britain in the 1930s', in J. Richards (ed.), *The Unknown 1930s: An Alternative History of the British Cinema 1929–39* (1998), 1–35.
SEELEY, R., and BUNNETT, R., *London Musical Shows on Record 1889–1980: A Hundred Years of London's Musical Theatre* (Harrow, 1989).
Songwriters' Guild of Great Britain, *60 Years of British Hits, 1907–1966* (1968).
STEVENSON, J., *British Society 1914–1945* (1984).
—— and Cook, C., *The Slump: Society and Politics during the Depression* (1977).
STONE, R. and ROWE, D. A., *The Measurement of Consumers' Expenditure and Behaviour in the United Kingdom, 1920–1938*, vol. ii (Cambridge, 1966).
TAYLOR, A. J. P., *English History 1914–1945* (Oxford, 1965).
THORNTON, M., *Jessie Matthews: A Biography* (St Albans, 1975).
WIMBUSH, R., (ed.), *The Gramophone Jubilee Book 1923–1973* (1973).

(4) Unpublished Theses

PEGG, M., *British Radio Broadcasting and its audience 1918–1939* (1979), D.Phil, Modern History, Oxford.

INDEX OF SONG TITLES

GENERAL INDEX

Note: Individual songs discussed in detail are included in both this index and the *Index of Song Titles*, which lists all songs.

ABC (Associated British Cinemas) 95
  chain of cinemas 141
  employment of dance bands 142
Ache, Andre 198
Adler, Larry 102
Advertiser's Weekly 79
Alfredo 141
Alhambra Theatre, London 120, 202, 218
All British Dance Band Championship 139
All Star Concerts 79
Allen, Les 213
Allen, Sir Hugh 50
Amalgamated Musician's Union, *see* Musicians Union
Ambrose, Bert:
  appearance in dance halls 133
  and commercial radio 79
  and the Contemporary Rhythm Society 199
  large salary of 137
  and the Mecca Agency 141
  recording career of 197–8
America Calling 131
American Graphophone Company 22
American Record Corporation 25
Americanization:
  attacks against 209–10
  British response to 201–2, 211, 230–3
  and cinema 209, 210
  exaggeration of 230–3
  and the gramophone 53–5
  and hit songs 209–11
  and music publishing 210
'Among My Souvenirs' 105
anti-Semitism, *see* racism
Armstrong, Louis:
  recordings available in Britain 53, 203

Around the World 79
Askey, Arthur:
  and *Band Waggon* 203
  recording career of 203
Associated British Cinemas 95
Astaire, Fred 87, 88, 153

Balcon, Michael 92
Baldwin, Mrs Stanley 42
Ballard, E. 199
Ballroom and Band 132
  survey of dance band activity 135
Band Waggon 63, 65, 203
Barnett-Samuels 23
  see also Decca
Batten, Joe 44, 46–7
BBC (British Broadcasting Corporation):
  attitudes to commercial radio 68, 80, 82–4
  bans its own stars appearing on commercial radio 79–80
  and censorship 222–3
  complaints against 63–6
  and the employment of musicians 81, 85, 126
  formation of 59
  and listener preferences 64–5
  musical output of 59–60
  programmes of dance music on 61–2, 65–6
  programmes of light music on 60–1
  programmes of Variety on 62–3, 85
  John Reith: on 'When I'm cleaning Windows' 223; on 'entertainment' 64
  Religious Advisory Council 84–5
  responds to commercial radio 83–5
  and song plugging 219–21
  and Sunday broadcasting 66, 84–5